Forensic Psychologica Assessment in Immigration Court

Forensic Psychological Assessment in Immigration Court is an essential specialized guide for psychologists and clinicians who work with immigrants. Immigration evaluations differ in many ways from other types of forensic assessments because of the psycholegal issues that extend beyond the individual, including family dynamics, social context, and cross-cultural concerns. Immigrants are often victims of trauma and require specialized expertise to elicit the information needed for assessment. Having spent much of their professional careers as practicing forensic psychologists, authors Evans and Hass have compiled a comprehensive text that draws on forensic psychology, psychological assessment, traumatology, family processes, and national and international political forces to present an approach for the effective and ethical practice of forensic psychological assessment in Immigration Court.

F. Barton Evans, Ph.D. is a clinical and forensic psychologist in private practice in Asheville, NC and a Clinical Professor of Psychiatry and Behavioral Sciences at the James H. Quillen College of Medicine at East Tennessee State University. He is a Fellow of the Society for Personality Assessment and a Fellow of the American Psychological Association (Division 12). He is a forensic psychological consultant and expert for courts in immigration law, family law, personal injury, and criminal matters.

Giselle A. Hass, Psy.D., ABAP is a licensed psychologist in Virginia and the District of Columbia and is a Diplomate by the American Board of Assessment Psychology. For the past 25 years, she has worked as a forensic expert and consultant in family and immigration law for local and national attorneys, nonprofit, and government agencies. Since 2009, she has been an Adjunct Professor of Law at Georgetown University Law Center, Center for Applied Legal Studies.

Forensic Psychological Assessment in Immigration Court

A Guidebook for Evidence-Based and Ethical Practice

F. Barton Evans, III and
Giselle A. Hass

Routledge
Taylor & Francis Group

NEW YORK AND LONDON

First published 2018
by Routledge
711 Third Avenue, New York, NY 10017

and by Routledge
2 Park Square, Milton Park, Abingdon, Oxon, OX14 4RN

Routledge is an imprint of the Taylor & Francis Group, an informa business

© 2018 Taylor & Francis

Library of Congress Cataloging-in-Publication Data
A catalog record for this title has been requested

ISBN: 978-1-138-65772-4 (hbk)
ISBN: 978-1-138-65773-1 (pbk)
ISBN: 978-1-315-62119-7 (ebk)

Typeset in Times New Roman
by Wearset Ltd, Boldon, Tyne and Wear

F.B.E. dedicates this book to David, Lory, Jan, Bruce, Tom, Fabienne, Karen, and the other dedicated attorneys who seek justice in protecting those pursuing safety on our shores, and Uwe and Jeffrey my compadres in the work.

I dedicate this book to the immigrants and refugees who trusted me with their stories. My work with them has enriched me as a professional and as a person.

G.A.H.

Contents

Illustrations

Figures

Tables

About the Authors

F. Barton Evans, Ph.D. is a clinical and forensic psychologist in private practice in Asheville, NC and Clinical Professor of Psychiatry and Behavioral Sciences, James H. Quillen College of Medicine, Eastern Tennessee State University, Johnson City, TN. He is a Fellow of the Society for Personality Assessment and a Fellow of the American Psychological Association (Division 12). He received a B.S. *magna cum laude* in psychology from Tufts University and a Ph.D. in clinical psychology from The American University, and was an NIMH Post-Doctoral Fellowship in clinical psychology at the Yale University School of Medicine. He is a graduate of the Advanced Psychotherapy Program of the Washington School of Psychiatry and the Clinical Training Program at the National Center for PTSD. He is on the Editorial Board and Head of the Assessment Section for *Psychological Injury and Law.* He has held faculty appointments in the schools of medicine at George Washington University, University of Washington, and Georgetown University, as well as faculty positions at The American University, University of North Carolina-Greensboro, and Montana State University. Dr. Evans has presented over 150 workshops and papers nationally and internationally on a wide variety of topics, including forensic psychological evaluation in Immigration Court, psychological trauma, psychological assessment, and personality disorder. Dr. Evans has three published books: *Harry Stack Sullivan: Interpersonal Theory and Psychotherapy* (1996); *Handbook of Forensic Rorschach Assessment* (with Carl Gacono, 2008); and *The Rorschach in Multimethod Forensic Assessment* (with Robert Erard, 2016). He has published over 40 book chapters and articles on topics including forensic assessment in Immigration Court, the Rorschach, interpersonal theory and psychotherapy, psychological trauma, and forensic and psychological assessment. He has performed many independent forensic evaluations for Immigration Court in private practice, which includes assessment of survivors of torture seeking asylum, extreme hardship, VAWA, and criminal issues, recently including Adam Walsh Act waivers. He was a regular guest lecturer on forensic psychological assessment in Immigration Court at the Washington College of Law. He is an expert in forensic psychological assessment in Immigration Court and was an Invited Speaker on forensic psychological evaluation at the Annual Meeting of the American Immigration Lawyers Association. He is a forensic psychological consultant and expert for courts in immigration law, family law, personal injury, and criminal matters.

Giselle A. Hass, Psy.D., ABAP is a native of Costa Rica who was a forensic psychologist in her own country when she migrated to the U.S. in 1983. She earned a Doctorate in Clinical Psychology from Nova Southeastern University (NSU) in 1992. She is licensed to practice as a psychologist in Virginia and the District of Columbia, and is a Diplomate by the American Board of Assessment Psychology. For the past 25 years, she has worked as a forensic expert and consultant in family and immigration law for local and national attorneys, non-profits, and government agencies. She was an Associate Professor in the Clinical Psychology Program of Argosy University, Washington, DC campus from 1995 to 2010, where she taught courses in personality and forensic psychological assessment to doctoral students in the Psy.D. program. Since 2009, she has been an Adjunct Professor of Law at Georgetown University Law Center, Center for Applied Legal Studies. She is a Fellow of the Society for Personality Assessment. She is a Board member of ASISTA Immigration Assistance, a non-governmental organization that advocates for immigrant women who suffered domestic violence and sexual assault. Since 2000, she has worked on federally funded research projects regarding culturally competent interventions for women in abusive relationships and the legal and policy aspects of domestic violence. Her findings from a large-scale research project generated several of her articles and were utilized by Congress in the decision to include immigration relief in the Violence Against Women Act of 1994. She is co-author of the book *Using the MMPI-2 in Forensic Assessment* (2015) with James Butcher, Roger Greene, and Linda Nelson. She has authored five book chapters, including: 'Understanding psychopathology in immigrant populations' (in print), in the *APA Handbook of Psychopathology* (J. N. Butcher, J. M. Hooley, and P. C. Kendall) and 'The intersection of gender and immigration in the personality assessment of women' (2016), in the *Handbook of Gender and Sexuality in Psychological Assessment* (V. M. Brabender and J. L. Mihura). She has co-authored numerous journal articles, most recently: 'A new understanding of substantial abuse: Evaluating harm in U visa petitions for immigrant victims of workplace crime,' (2015) with E. H. Cho, L. Saucedo, and M. Trujillo, published in the *Georgetown Immigration Law Journal*; and 'Barriers and successes in U Visas for immigrant victims: The experiences of legal assistance for victims grantees' (2014), with E. Yang, K. Monahan, L. Orloff, and B. Anver, published in the *Arts and Social Sciences Journal*. She has presented over 100 lectures on immigration and trauma, including training workshops and webinars, and has been featured in a *Vox* interview and two immigration documentaries.

Foreword

Lory D. Rosenberg

Fear or suspicion of people who appear 'foreign' or unfamiliar is not uncommon. At its extreme it may amount to xenophobia, but even in less dramatic expressions it is undeniable that we regularly draw distinctions between 'us' and 'them.' At the root of it all is the existential concept of the 'other,' the stranger.[1]

Although open-minded curiosity might be more of a positive approach, defensive or offensive reactions to new or unfamiliar situations seem to be hard-wired into our human brains as part of our survival instinct, known as the fight, flight, or freeze response. This inherently self-protective reaction can have dire consequences for those with whom we interact.

Nowhere is the distinction of the 'other' as pervasive as in the context of immigration, where the statutory labeling of people who are not citizens as 'aliens' is only the beginning of the separation.[2] The polarization between 'us' and 'them' in this context is reflected not only in nationality, but in religious, gender-based, linguistic, and cultural differences that cannot be avoided or ignored. Too often, because of this divide, immigrants and refugees in the U.S. are misunderstood, mistrusted, misjudged, and mistreated, especially in the context of government adjudication of their eligibility to come to, live in, or remain in the U.S.

This book delves into the phenomenal contribution that forensic psychologists can make to the process of immigrant and refugee status adjudications by using objective instruments and forensic psychological evaluation to clarify cultural differences and dispel miscommunication flowing from the 'otherness,' which has the potential to produce tragic outcomes for misunderstood immigrants and refugees.

Border patrol agents, immigration enforcement officials, adjudicators, attorneys, and immigration judges are not immune from the 'us' and 'them' polarization that infects our perception of 'aliens.' Although assumptions sometimes are made inappropriately, more often the problem is due to an adjudicator or immigration judge's misperception, lack of understanding, or attempt to comprehend the immigrant or refugee's conduct or presentation in terms of his or her own experience, which differs vastly from that of the immigrant or refugee. The customs, traditions, and life circumstances that make up an immigrant or refugee's experience typically reflect significant cultural differences that are literally 'foreign' to adjudicators.

This 'disconnect' is prevalent even among those who should be expected to know better because their work entails interacting with, assessing, and judging foreign nationals from vastly different cultural, religious, linguistic, educational backgrounds, and life experiences. Nevertheless, unconscious mistrust of someone who looks, speaks, and acts differently, misinterpretation of an individual's intent or motives, and miscommunication due to different usage of idioms and linguistic expressions, disparate experiences, and cultural differences are surprisingly commonplace in the context of immigration law practice and immigration status adjudication.

Comments by adjudicators and immigration judges such as, 'if I had to attend the most important hearing of my life, I would leave four hours early in order to be certain I would arrive on time,' are frequently heard, without regard to the trauma and overwhelming anxiety experienced by a refugee at the prospect of having to testify about rape and torture, which may have caused a slight delay. Findings that it is simply not plausible that a young woman in a strange city would ask a stranger for help (because the adjudicator would not have done so) lead directly to an adverse credibility determination that can doom an application. And, a 19-year-old young man's completely consensual sexual relations with a girl of 14 (whom he later married) is deemed statutory rape or child abuse, without regard to the fact that the man's own mother was married at 14 in their home country.

Ignorance or misunderstanding about an immigrant's age of maturity, marital practices, family traditions, religious background, gender identity, or other cultural expectations easily skew both factual and legal conclusions and distort discretionary determinations. In the context of immigration enforcement, detention, and removal proceedings in Immigration Court, where the stakes are extraordinarily high and the consequences of misapprehension or miscommunication are grave, this cannot be tolerated.

Forensic psychological assessment offers a much-needed and impressive tool to rectify what might otherwise result in an inappropriate or unjust outcome. The forensic psychologist's development of an interpretive report that addresses past or current trauma, memory, recidivism, and rehabilitation relevant to an immigrant or refugee's background and cultural tradition, bridges the gap that might exist between the immigrant or refugee's 'other' reality and the expectations of the adjudicator or judge. Such an evaluation has the potential to lend credence to the immigrant or refugee's story, highlight his or her eligibility despite the distinctions that may exist, provide a more accurate picture, and favorably influence the determinations made in the adjudicatory process.

The scope of proceedings and applications in which a forensic psychological evaluation can have an impact is quite broad. An evaluation can be developed for an applicant presenting an asylum claim involving past persecution and trauma, as well as one involving a subjective fear and an objective basis for fearing persecution in the future. Applicants for asylum also are considered for withholding of removal and protection under the Convention Against Torture.

Other recourse from severe harm may be sought by an immigrant victim of a crime who cooperates with the police, including a victim of domestic violence, or a victim of human trafficking. Understanding the impact of such trauma and abuse on memory, the ability to trust, willingness to reveal shameful experiences, and ability to report details, is crucial to the success of an applicant's claim.

When apprehended and placed in a removal proceeding, an immigrant or refugee's first concern is obtaining release from custody. When detention is not mandatory, the standard that must be satisfied to obtain release requires the individual to show both that he or she is neither a flight risk nor a danger to the community, which a forensic evaluation can persuasively and effectively support.

An individual qualified to seek adjustment of status, who previously committed fraud or misrepresentation, may require an application for a hardship waiver explaining the circumstances underlying the violation of immigration law, including cultural factors influencing prior conduct, which can be supplied by a forensic evaluation. Similarly, an individual qualified for an immigrant visa, who has resided unlawfully in the U.S. for certain periods of time, may need to establish hardship to a family member, which can be amplified and explained by a forensic evaluation.

In the context of a marital relationship, there may be a need to corroborate the proposition that the marriage was not entered into solely to obtain an immigration benefit, which a forensic evaluation can readily support. Likewise, if the marriage must be dissolved, a forensic psychological evaluation can provide support for the justifiable reasons for the dissolution.

An individual seeking cancelation of removal is required to prove the existence of exceptional and extremely unusual hardship to a qualifying family member, which can be established at least in part through a forensic evaluation of the relative. In the context of either the defense or waiver of criminal law violations, matters such as potential recidivism and rehabilitation are central concerns, and forensic psychological evaluation has an important role to play in verifying remorse and recovery from any underlying difficulties, as well as cultural factors that played a part in the criminal conduct.

The use of psychological and psychiatric expertise in establishing an individual's eligibility for immigration benefits or relief from removal is an evolving component of immigration practice. The evidence produced through the process of forensic psychological assessment constitutes an independent expert opinion that corresponds to the qualities of objectivity and impartiality that are found most persuasive by adjudicators and immigration judges.

Forensic psychological assessments are recognized by the Federal courts as both relevant and reliable forms of evidence that may be provided by an expert witness. The Federal Rules of Evidence, 5 Rule 702, 'Testimony by Experts,' provides that subject to certain conditions,

[i]f scientific, technical, or other specialized knowledge will assist the trier of fact to understand the evidence or to determine a fact in issue, a witness qualified as an expert by knowledge, skill, experience, training, or education, may testify thereto in the form of an opinion or otherwise.

When properly submitted to an immigration official or introduced in Immigration Court, the information developed through forensic psychological assessment methods, backed by solid scientific literature, can provide valuable and often crucial evidence.

The role of the forensic psychologist in the context of immigration proceedings is unique; he or she cannot be considered an advocate for a party in the proceedings as a therapeutic psychologist or social worker might be. As an expert who uses a variety of established investigative techniques and testing to obtain objective results that are supported according to scientific standards, the forensic psychologist is truly an independent evaluator, and, in many ways, more akin to a 'friend of the court' than a witness for one side or the other.

Although he or she may be retained by the applicant's attorney, the forensic psychologist properly insists on conducting the assessment with no result in mind, and proceeds on the condition that he or she will exercise independent professional judgment on all aspects of the evaluation. As a result, the assessment that is ultimately submitted is likely to be given a great deal of credibility and significant weight by the adjudicator or immigration judge.

Interestingly, immigration judges tend to welcome the participation of forensic psychologists. The decisions that must be made in asylum and other removal proceedings often present life-or-death choices. Although an immigration judge will properly insist on reserving the ultimate conclusion regarding the immigrant or refugee's eligibility for themselves, most treat the findings of the forensic psychologist, even those relating to credibility, with respect.

The role of the forensic psychologist can be one of great significance, especially taking into account the unavoidable barriers imposed by the 'otherness' of the immigrant or refugee appearing before an adjudicator or before the Immigration Court. Accordingly, the special skills and talents of the forensic psychologist contribute a unique component to the elements that make up a fair hearing and produce a reasonable outcome.

The Honorable Lory D. Rosenberg (Ret.) served on the Board of Immigration Appeals from 1995 to 2002 and is highly regarded for her many appellate opinions that helped shape immigration law jurisprudence. She is currently CEO of IDEAS Consultation and Coaching, providing expert legal mentoring and transformational business and personal coaching, and is a senior advisor and attorney at the Immigrant Defenders Law Group.

Notes

1. *See* 'The Other', *The New Fontana Dictionary of Modern Thought*, 3rd edition, (1999) p. 620 (also Otherness, Othering), a concept originating with the eighteenth-century philosopher Georg Wilhelm Friedrich Hegel's introduction of self-consciousness, and appearing in the later writings of Franz Fanon (post-colonization and race), Simone de Beauvoir (gender and sex), Edward Said (Orientalism), and many others to describe subordinated and differentiated populations and relationships.
2. As defined in the *Oxford English Dictionary*, the word 'alien' is used as a noun, meaning '[a] person belonging to another family, race, or nation; a stranger, a foreigner.'

Acknowledgments

Together, we would like to acknowledge and applaud all the forensic psychologists and other mental health assessors who provide psychological assessment in Immigration Court (IC), especially those using systematic and evidence-based methods. Working in the IC context has become increasing tough and we hope this book will provide you with substantive help in fashioning high-quality and effective evidence for immigration matters, which at times revolve around issues of life and death.

Special appreciation is due to our competent and patient Routledge book editors. This book became reality under George Zimmar's watch. Barton has had the pleasure of collaborating with George on three books, the idea for two of which emerged out of our annual conversation at the Society for Personality Assessment. George's professional and personal support and good-hearted approach to the reality of business over the years has been deeply treasured. As with many good people, George moved onto a different position at Routledge and introduced us to our current editor, the capable and understanding Lillian Rand. Lillian has more than met the challenge of taking up this book project mid-stream, providing excellent advice and bearing patiently to the longer-than-desired process of getting this book to press. In particular, Barton and Giselle sincerely appreciate Lillian's flexible approach to the life circumstances we faced during the writing of this book.

Barton Evans' appreciations are many, though special gratitude must go out to several special people. When George Zimmar and I decided that this book needed to be written, I immediately asked Giselle Hass whether she might join me as the co-author. It was my, and now your, great good fortune that she said yes. What a joy it has been to collaborate with Giselle! Giselle leads with her unassuming, supportive, and collaborative approach and backs this up with her remarkable sharp mind as well as her superior experience and weighty knowledge of immigration work, psychological assessment, and social justice. Lory Rosenberg is a legal *mensch* without peer. I consider the opportunity to learn from, and work with, Lory to be one of the highlights of my long career. Without her early support of my work in IC, my ability to write this book is unimaginable. No appreciation would be complete without thanking Karl Goodkin, M.D.,

Ph.D. (a psychiatrist and clinical psychologist!), Chair of Psychiatry and Behavioral Sciences. Karl afforded me many opportunities during my tenure at ETSU College of Medicine, not the least of which was carefully guarded time to write in the midst of heavy academic and service demands. Karl is that all-too-rare academic chair who marks his success by how well he facilitates good works in others. Personal thanks go to my dear friends Rick Ferris and Dr. Adrienne Ferris, who are always there with words of wisdom and kindness. And of course, the Beautiful Judy! Judy Maris is my soul mate who has provided me with more love, personal support, and kindness than anyone has the right to deserve.

Giselle Hass is feeling grateful and indebted as we are finishing this book. Writing this book was particularly arduous emotionally because it happened during a zeitgeist where immigrants have become vilified and expulsed from the country, and refugees rejected and left to survive on their own. Much of the energy and time I had for this book had to be transferred to dealing with these cruel realities. Trying to educate decision-makers to maintain the humanistic trend that had characterized the United States became my priority. I am thankful to those who pushed me to pour my commitment and passion for the field into this book in order to share with others our experiences and find common ground. First of all, I thank my co-author, Barton Evans. Barton was already a friend and a mentor, and in this project he showed an enormous patience and flexibility to guide and encourage me to the end. His inquisitive mind helped me sharpen my observations and maintain focus. Second, I am thankful to my dearest peers in the immigration field, especially attorneys Leslye Orloff, Sonia Parra, Gail Pendleton, Eunice Cho, Leticia Salgado, and Fabienne Chatain, who continuously help me grow professionally. We have spent countless hours discussing theoretical and case-specific issues in immigration law, and they have been invaluable consultants on many of my papers and reports, and have always shown an amazing sensitivity and humanity. Third, to those colleagues who are in the trenches of immigration evaluations with me, including Gloria Morote, Gustavo Rife, and Joe Gorin, I owe you my sanity, as you have been a wonderful ear when I struggle. Finally, and most importantly, I have to acknowledge my husband, Steve, and my daughter, Amanda, whose unconditional love and nurturing grounds me so I can fly and fulfill my professional dreams.

Introduction
Our Personal Journey

Forensic psychological assessment for Immigration Court (IC) is a relatively new subspecialty within forensic psychology, though some practice areas such as the forensic assessment of torture have dramatically grown in the past 20 years. We have been powerfully drawn to this area of forensic practice, where the confluences of societal forces are played out in legal proceedings, often with very real, even life-and-death, consequences. It represents not only a sizeable commitment in our professional careers, but also a personal journey where there were initially few markers to guide us. This book is an attempt to draw together our knowledge about forensic psychology, psychological assessment, traumatology, family processes, and national and international political forces to present an approach to effective and ethical practice of forensic psychological assessment in IC. We hope that this book spurs future work on this challenging and complex area of forensic practice. Our introduction takes a more personal approach than many forensic psychology texts, if, for no other reason, than to emphasize the deeply moving nature of the work with vulnerable immigrants, while respecting the various serious challenges faced by IC judges, immigration attorneys and USCIS administrative law administrators.

My story (FBE) begins in 1994 when Washington, DC-based immigration attorney David Garfield, an innovator in the use of forensic psychological evaluations in his legal representation of immigrants, first approached me to conduct an assessment of a young woman from Ethiopia seeking political asylum. I found no professional literature on this area of forensic assessment, so I courteously refused his request, not once but twice, before relenting to the third, realizing that my expertise in assessing and treating psychological trauma could be useful. If it were not for David's persistence and willingness to educate me about immigration matters, I doubt I would be writing this book. I was just beginning to practice forensic psychology as an expert in psychological trauma and, while I had taken some training in forensic assessment, nothing had prepared me to take on the assessment of torture victims. I very soon found out that nothing I had ever done prepared me emotionally for this endeavor.

Because there was no guidance that I could find in the psychological literature, I agreed to conduct the assessment as it had been done by this attorney's prior psychologist – essentially a careful interview with my own addition of a posttraumatic stress disorder (PTSD) based semi-structured interview (see Meek, 1990). What followed was nearly a disastrous result. During my testimony in IC, the competent and ultimately compassionate IC Judge Paul Nejelski challenged my findings as too subjective, without proper basis, and unconvincing. I strongly believed the young Ethiopian female torture and rape victim who just recently escaped the horrors of imprisonment during the Mengistu regime, but, as I came to see quickly, my evaluation did not meet the IC judge's evidentiary standard. The judge provided me an opening and I opined that the young woman was not psychologically able to provide the level of detail required for IC. I then suggested that she receive a year of trauma-focused psychotherapy before testifying again about the details of her persecution. The judge humanely decided to take my advice, allowing the respondent to appear again in a year after the treatment was complete. She was then able to tell her story without decompensating, and was granted asylum at that time.

What followed was one of the most important experiences in my now long career as a clinical psychologist. In spite of the difficulty with my initial IC evaluation, the attorney was very pleased with my work and wanted to me to do more. I was not so pleased, so I began to seriously research how to do such evaluations with greater rigor and probative value. I reexamined the existing psychological literature and again found a paucity of guidance. There were good resources about the experience of torture victims (for example, see Basolgu 1992), but I found essentially nothing to help me develop a comprehensive model for conducting these evaluations. To give context, Frumkind and Friedland's (1995) seminal article on the areas of practice for forensic assessment in immigration had not been published and the Istanbul Protocol was submitted in 1999 and published in 2004 (United Nations Office of the High Commissioner for Human Rights, 2004). Mollica et al.'s (1992) Harvard Torture Questionnaire was recently published, but available only for Indochinese torture victims and with no indication on how to conduct forensic evaluations in IC asylum proceedings.

Without a clear assessment protocol to use, I sought the most adaptable model I could find. I was most fortunate to have taken two workshops on forensic psychological assessment of psychological trauma in personal injury with the late Stuart Greenberg (see Greenberg, 2003). Greenberg's clear explication of the psychological assessment of proximate cause – actions sufficiently related to a legally identifiable injury that are the cause of that injury – served as a good model to assess signs and symptoms of torture in the context of an asylum claim. Under the U.S. Refugee Act of 1980 (Public Law 96-212), non-citizen immigrants arriving to, or already in, the U.S. may apply for asylum, or protection from persecution. A forensic assessment of psychological signs and symptoms of torture and other mistreatment could therefore help establish the nexus of events proximately causing asylum seekers' well-founded fear of persecution. I developed an initial protocol that fit the psycholegal and evidentiary requirements of IC, moving beyond the use of simple interviews as had been done in the past to a model more consistent with standard forensic practice. The result was to provide immigration attorneys representing legitimate claims from asylum seekers with forensic psychological assessment that was highly useful as part of their comprehensive submission of evidence.

By 2004, much happened quickly regarding forensic assessment in IC, indicating a clear need for direction on how to conduct these evaluations. I presented many workshops around the U.S. and internationally, consulted to a leading center of refugee services, and lectured in the immigration law course at the Washington College of Law. I presented this forensic assessment model to staff attorneys of the U.S. Department of Justice's Immigration and Naturalization Service (INS) as well as the Board of Immigration Appeals, offering to provide evaluations for them as well as immigration attorneys representing their client. Interestingly, in the 20+ years of my practice in immigration matters, I have never been asked to provide an independent forensic evaluation for the INS, or as it is currently called, the U.S. Citizenship Immigration Service. Most importantly, I met and soon collaborated with a consummate immigration law scholar, Board of Immigration Appeals Judge Lory Rosenberg. Lory soon became my Rosetta stone for understanding immigration law as I developed a deeper understanding of the intricacies of psycholegal issues in this area and refined my assessment protocols accordingly. With the guidance of Lory and other excellent immigration attorneys in Washington, DC I was able to expand forensic psychological assessment to other practice areas such as extreme hardship, criminal matters, and VAWA assessments.

Over these years, I also collaborated with fellow psychologists who deepened my understanding of psychological trauma and of the horrific impact of persecution and torture. For me, Dr. Jeffrey Jay set the standard for understanding psychological trauma. His excellent article, 'Terrible knowledge' (Jay, 1991), helped me focus more clearly on the meaning of psychological trauma that devastates fundamental life beliefs and personal identity rather than on simply describing psychiatric symptoms and physiological reactions. I owe much to Jeffrey and Therapeutic Assessment creator Steve Finn (Finn, 2007) in my development of a compassion-based approach to writing forensic reports and in giving IC testimony. In turn, this led to my critique (Evans, 2005) of the forensic psychology canon of neutrality as a skeptical stance (see Greenberg & Shuman, 1997), especially for forensic assessment of torture victims. Dr. Beatrice Patsalides and, especially, Dr. Uwe Jacobs of Survivors International of Northern California, and major contributors to the Istanbul Protocol, deeply enriched my understanding of torture victims. To my knowledge, our two articles (Jacobs, Evans, & Patsalides, 2001a, 2001b) were the first in-depth publications about applying forensic psychological assessment principles to the documentation of torture in IC asylum and Convention Against Torture proceedings. It was also my great pleasure to collaborate with Dr. Giselle Hass in forensic assessment in IC and to watch as she has taken this work into new areas, such as relief from victimization in applications in U visa and T visa matters. Our delightful collaboration presenting a recent workshop on forensic assessment in IC for the Society for Personality Assessment was the impetus for this book.

My path (GAH) to conducting immigration evaluations came from the education and training in my graduate school, Nova Southeastern University. I was taught about trauma by Steven Gold, and about research and evaluation of family violence at the Domestic Violence Clinic with Mary Ann Dutton. Naturally, being an immigrant myself, my focus turned to the impact of trauma and domestic violence on immigrant families. This training gave me a strong foundation in the assessment of trauma, which has been a cornerstone of my entire professional practice since I graduated in 1992. In my professional practice, I became a forensic evaluator for criminal and family court cases, and I focused a lot of energy on obtaining postgraduate training in this field through the University of Virginia Institute of Law, Psychiatry and Public Policy, and the American Academy of Forensic Psychology. Around 1996, Dr. Mary Ann Dutton and Leslye Orloff invited me to participate in a research project that involved an analysis of data from immigrant, mostly undocumented, women. The findings of this project (Ammar, Orloff, Dutton, & Hass, 2012; Dutton & Hass, 2004; Dutton, Orloff, & Hass, 2000; Hass, Ammar & Orloff, 2006; Hass, Dutton, & Orloff, 2000; Orloff, Dutton, Hass, & Ammar, 2003) revealed the reality of immigrant women and the extensive traumatization in their background, and set a new standard through which to understand their needs. Our findings were remarkable, and our legal partner, Leslye Orloff, presented them as an advocacy tool to support the expansion and improvement of the Violence Against Women Act in Congress in the year 2000. I have a debt of gratitude to my co-researchers who, for the past 20 years, have been a source of learning and support as we continue to expand our understanding on the psycholegal issues of immigrant battered women.

It was easy to transfer my knowledge from the forensic field and trauma knowledge to conducting VAWA evaluations, especially given the research and theoretical work that helped me understand the underpinnings of the VAWA. I continued to update my training in the assessment of trauma and legal issues with several legal assistance organizations (AILA, AYUDA, Legal Momentum, NIWAP, Tahirih Justice Center), and I was also fortunate to receive training from people outstanding in the personal injury, trauma, and immigration fields, such as Stuart Greenberg, Randy Otto, Mary Ann Dutton, Christine Courtois, Nancy Kaser-Boyd, Judy Okawa, and Barton Evans.

When the first massive Immigration and Customs Enforcement (ICE) raid of undocumented immigrant workers happened in Postville, Illinois in 2008, a huge number of workplace abuses were exposed and I was asked to assemble a team of assessors to conduct the evaluations supporting their U visa cases. A group of friends, colleagues, and acquaintances offered to help. After an intense training we completed evaluations of all minors and women involved in the case. With the help of immigration psychologist Joe Gorin, we developed a framework and model of evaluation that I have continued to use and that has been expanded to present in this book. It did not take long when I was approached to look into the psycholegal issues of the U visa with another legal team (Cho, Hass, & Saucedo, 2015).

From focusing on those two areas of immigration practice, I quickly moved on to T visas, as immigration raids exposed large numbers of victims; the law firms that have hired me for U visa cases contacted me again for these. However, it took me a while to feel comfortable taking on other immigration cases, including asylum and extreme hardship cases. My friend Barton encouraged me to continue expanding my immigration assessment practice. His help and support were essential to my comfort moving into other aspects of this field.

As I worked more and more with the immigrants in the U.S. who are subjected to all types of abuses and indignities, my personal journey paralleled a different level of consciousness regarding my own identity as an immigrant. I was confronted with both my disadvantage and my privilege. I came to the realization that, independent from the traumatic experiences that may have brought us to the U.S., our lives in exile were still full of discrimination and oppression that did not abate regardless of our healing and drive to succeed. This led me to the urge to become an advocate at the macro level.

Along my journey conducting assessments for immigration evaluation, I had to be careful to balance my role as an assessor and my advocacy interests. Outside the clinical office, I have been a strong advocate for improvement of immigration laws, elimination of immigration detention, and protection of human rights for undocumented immigrants. I have written numerous amicus briefs, presented at different conferences, and also at the U.S. Congress. I have written about the unfairness of our immigration system and social xenophobia and racism. I have coordinated with numerous human rights organizations and participated in several workgroups, including an NGO consultation group with ICE.

I believe that the two roles of assessor and advocate are not incompatible. Through my clinical and research work, I have acquired knowledge that helps me see the connection with public policies and the need for systemic change. I have entered the public debate out of a deep awareness of injustice and the belief that education can help shape the policies that are congruent with the humanitarian values of our society. I believe that advocacy is the best way to avoid burn-out in the forensic work. Working only in individual forensic assessment cases forces us to face frustrations with the rigidity and antiquated norms of the system, and may lead to a sense of helplessness. When we look at the bigger picture, we understand that we have knowledge that allows us to be agents of change.

In addition to the incomparable Lory Rosenberg, Giselle and Barton have been blessed to work with superbly talented and deeply dedicated immigration attorneys who shared with us their knowledge of immigration law and who helped us broaden our practice of forensic assessment in IC to issues of extreme hardship, criminal issues, various relief from victimization claims, and competency issues. These attorneys include Jan Pederson, Bruce Hake, Thomas Elliot, Fabienne Chatain, Karen Grisez, Leslye Orloff, Gail Pederson, Sonia Parra, Eunice Cho, Leticia Salcedo, and of course David Garfield.

Forensic psychological assessment in IC has become an increasingly utilized area of practice. We still see many reports and hear of many testimonies based essentially on clinical interviews without taking into account the special needs of the IC for comprehensive neutral, objective, and corroborated assessments. While this purely advocacy-based approach arises from an understandable and admirable desire to be of assistance to vulnerable immigrants, we have found in practice that IC judges and USCIS administrative adjudicators frequently accord limited weight to what is essentially hearsay testimony. Based on our experience with IC triers of fact welcoming a more comprehensive psycholegal approach, we believe the time has come for a higher standard of practice. That is the aim of this book.

We begin with three chapters on Conceptual Foundations. The first addresses a perspective on basic principles of forensic psychological assessment as they apply to IC. Next, the especially critical concerns of cross-cultural, gender, and language issues will be elaborated. Last, a discussion on the special ethical concerns and issues of assessment of credibility and malingering rounds out this part of the book by describing ethical standards in this complex area of forensic practice and addressing the vexing problem of impression management in forensic immigration assessment.

The next part – Areas of Forensic Practice – provides in many ways the core of the book for forensic practitioners by offering numerous applications of forensic assessment approaches to common areas of immigration law practice. We begin with an overview of forensic assessment for asylum and Convention Against Torture claims, the most widely known and developed area of practice. Next, we move on to forensic assessment in matters concerning legal relief from immigrant victimization, including self-petitioning for legal permanent resident status under statutes including the Violence Against Women Act (VAWA), and U and T visas. Third, we address when and how forensic psychological assessment can be useful in the broad area of IC hardship waivers, including family impact statements regarding the likely effect of deportation of the IC-involved immigrant. Last, we address specific issues in which forensic assessment can be probative in criminal matters in immigration cases, including concerns about rehabilitation, assessment of dangerousness risk, and flight risk. We also review the critical subject of competency to represent self in immigration court, a frequently overlooked concern that has special implications in IC proceedings.

The last part – Special Topics – offers perspectives on two issues pertinent to forensic psychological assessment in IC – the use of psychological tests and methods and report writing and expert testimony for IC. The first chapter in this part explores principles of diagnostic interviewing in this specialized setting, the use of trauma-specific instruments that can provide empirical support and incremental validity to interview findings, as well as the use of comprehensive self-report instruments, such as the Minnesota Multiphasic Personality Inventory (MMPI-2, MMPI-2-RF) and the Personality Assessment Inventory (PAI), focusing on the benefits and risks of these omnibus psychological methods in IC. The following chapter examines use of performance-based methods, such as the Rorschach and TAT, in forensic psychological assessment in IC, emphasizing their special contributions in multi-method assessment in complex matters as well as the broad international and cross-cultural utility. The final chapter focuses on presentation of assessment findings in reports and expert testimony and provides recommendations on how to integrate the multiple sources of information necessary for a comprehensive forensic assessment.

Part I

Conceptual Foundations

Chapter 1

Forensic Psychology and Immigration Court

Basic Concepts

The use of forensic psychological mental health experts in immigration matters is a developing and evolving area of practice (Evans, 2000; Frumkind & Friedland, 1995), which has increasingly provided attorneys with valuable and, at times, essential evidence in representing their clients before the U.S. Citizenship and Immigration Service (USCIS) and the Immigration Court (IC).[1] Yet, mental health assessments adequate in clinical settings or forensic reports based solely on clinical treatment frequently fail to address the more stringent standards of objectivity and neutrality required for psychological assessment in the legal setting (see Melton, Petrila, Poythress, & Slobogin, 2007; Weiner & Otto, 2014) and the particularities of IC (Frumkind & Friedland, 1995). Without a clear understanding of how psychological and mental health expertise and practice intersects with the relevant legal system, clinically focused interviews run the risk of being unhelpful or even discounted. The price of this lack of understanding can be measured ultimately in terms of deportation of vulnerable immigrants with a solid foundation for legal relief from removal.

The purpose of this chapter is to introduce psychologists, other mental health practitioners, and immigration attorneys to the principles of forensic psychological assessment with particular reference to matters before the IC. After a basic introduction to forensic psychology, we address the areas of practice in the IC and the required professional expertise to provide opinions and professional boundaries with referring attorneys. Our goal is to share our knowledge of effective practice in immigration matters and to increase the value of forensic psychological assessments for immigrants, attorneys, and the IC.

Principles of Forensic Psychology[2]

While the psychological literature offers valuable information relevant to immigration claims, such information must also be carefully placed within the legal context of IC. Often the professional psychology practices may appear to irreconcilably conflict with the stringent legal criteria set forth by the court. For example, well-meaning psychologists may describe well the horrors told to them by victims of political persecution or domestic abuse, yet quite competent clinical evaluation may fail to address the more stringent standards of objectivity and neutrality required in the legal setting (Melton et al., 2007). Psychological experts must conform their clinical information to the evidentiary standards set by the court (for example, the Specialty Guidelines for Forensic Psychologists; American Psychological Association (APA), 2013) and judicial concerns about the possible bias of the psychological expert toward advocacy over neutrality must be overcome.

Psychological assessment using the principles of forensic psychology can improve the value of expert psychological testimony in IC proceedings. Unlike clinical evaluations, forensic evaluations must include the assessment of deception and malingering and pre-morbid (pre-trauma) psychological functioning. As a consequence, such assessments require the increased need for corroboration of claims. Without this proper foundation, psychological evaluations may provide little in the way of useful information to the trier of fact, such as the IC judge or IC administrative officer. Ultimately, it is the immigrant seeking relief who suffers from the failure to reconcile psychological knowledge with legal standards. Forensic psychological procedures can powerfully integrate the dictates of the IC, by addressing the relevant psycholegal questions in a neutral and objective fashion, which balances the court's requirements for verification and assessment of credibility with the needs of the immigrant respondent's need for psychological documentation of his or her suffering or hardship. This chapter clarifies these principles of forensic psychology and how they are relevant to the IC. Additionally, other chapters address our suggested guideline for how to conduct such assessments and for how to establish expertise to provide psychological cogent reports and testimony in the IC.

There are fundamental differences between the forensic assessor and the mental health clinician (Greenberg & Shuman, 1997). The most important difference is that the forensic assessor must take an objective, neutral stance in the evaluation. The forensic assessor holds the statements of the examinee in a state of suspended belief and disbelief and requires immigrant respondents to corroborate their statements to the degree possible. The stance of the neutral forensic expert is different from the supportive, accepting, empathic, and confidential relationship critical to good clinical treatment. This difference in role arises from the fundamental difference about who is the client in a forensic evaluation. For forensic assessors, the client is the attorney who retains the forensic assessor to conduct the independent psychological evaluation (or by the Court itself, though in practice we know of no instances where an expert has been retained by an IC judge or USCIS attorney). This arrangement also holds a particular advantage for the attorney's client. Because client–patient privilege is forfeited when the immigrant respondent puts her or his mental health at issue before the court, the immigrant's attorney can invoke attorney work product privilege if the assessor's findings prove unhelpful to the case. The unfavorable evaluation would not be entered into evidence and the attorney could go forward on the merits of the case without it, thus better protecting her or his client's legal rights.

In our experience, this crucial distinction between forensic and clinical evaluation is often not well understood by assessors, attorneys, and judges. The forensic assessor's job is to provide an independent, neutral, objective evaluation of the relevant psycholegal question at hand and to share that information with the attorney retaining the assessor, whether or not it is beneficial to the examinee's case. An example of such a question is, *whether or not* the respondent in IC asylum proceedings shows indications of psychological trauma that are consistent with, and supportive of, her claims of rape and torture and that appears proximately caused by persecution. Therefore, it is of critical importance for the forensic psychologist to understand legal questions to be answered and how the information from a psychological evaluation fits in the evidence. As such, evaluations should be functionally based, not diagnostically based (Frumkind & Friedland 1995; Melton et al., 2007) – that is, tailored primarily to the legal question.

The presumption that the psychological expert must arrive at a psychological diagnosis, or even that a formulation of a diagnosis is necessary, often obscures the actual question before the IC. It is possible that the establishment of a diagnosis may be necessary in some, though not all, cases such as extreme hardship based on a mental disorder of a U.S. citizen spouse or child in a suspension of deportation proceeding. Even in these cases, the diagnosis may be necessary, but certainly not sufficient, for a forensic assessment. The diagnosis must be linked to the actual hardship experienced by the qualifying U.S. citizen through an understanding of the relationship between the impact of her mental disorder and the deportation of her immigrant spouse. For instance, it is entirely possible that the condition of an individual suffering from a diagnosed mental disorder would be unaffected, or even improved, by the deportation of a spouse.

As with all forensic evaluations, the assessor must go beyond the requirements of a clinical evaluation to: (a) evaluate the credibility of the respondent by formal assessment of malingering and, wherever possible, third-party corroborative information; (b) assess proximate cause/nexus issues; and (c) determine preexisting conditions and post-event experiences to rule out other causes for psychological findings.

All forensic evaluations must consider the problem of potential fraudulent reporting, where there is secondary gain for doing so (Rogers, 2008; Simon, 2008). Because the issue of credibility lies at the heart of most, if not all, IC proceedings, a professionally supportable assessment of malingering, deception, exaggeration, withholding of information, and secondary gain is essential and must be explicitly addressed in forensic psychological reports and testimony. Such an evaluation must go beyond 'clinical judgment,' as such judgments are notoriously unreliable (see Garb, 1998). For example, Bourg, Connor, and Landis (1995) showed that experienced forensic psychologists, as well as experienced clinical psychologists, demonstrated good accuracy in differentiating malingerers from non-malingerers, when sufficient information is available. Such information includes, in addition to clinical interview, psychological testing when possible, assessment of malingering, and collateral information from third-party sources.

Perhaps there is no area that calls more for the creativity of the expert assessor in obtaining collateral information than immigration matters. Sources of collateral information can include, where possible, the attorney's USCIS documentation (including any affidavits), collateral interviews with friends and family, whether it is safe to the immigrant, and country profiles on human rights violations from Amnesty International and the U.S. Department of State. For example, many credible claims, and more than one fraudulent claim, of torture in an asylum proceeding have been aided by simply examining the methods of torture claimed by the respondent and those used by the existing regime at the time of the respondent's report. We go into detail about assessment of malingering and credibility in Chapter 3.

Expertise in Forensic Psychology in IC

The kinds of evidence provided by psychological experts varies according to area, reflecting different information probative to the court. Additionally, as a general rule, each kind of case will call for different kinds of psychological expertise and therefore perhaps different experts. It is also important for forensic assessors to understand what constitutes expertise from a forensic assessment perspective. It is not simply enough to be a licensed psychologist or mental health professional to claim expertise that is relevant to the IC. Specific graduate training leading to relevant licensure may qualify the mental health professional to provide diagnosis and treatment of mental disorders, but such training is insufficient when entering the forensic psychological assessment arena. We recommend that individuals considering providing expert assessment and opinions for the IC get a good grounding in the legal definition of expert opinion. We provide a quick overview below and recommend chapter 1 in Melton et al. (2007) for a more detailed discussion.

While IC judges have broad discretion in deciding about admission of expert testimony, an excellent benchmark is the Federal Rule of Evidence 702 (FRE Rule 702, 2011):

> Rule 702. Testimony by Expert Witnesses
> A witness who is qualified as an expert by knowledge, skill, experience, training, or education may testify in the form of an opinion or otherwise if:
>
> (a) the expert's scientific, technical, or other specialized knowledge will help the trier of fact to understand the evidence or to determine a fact in issue;
> (b) the testimony is based on sufficient facts or data;
> (c) the testimony is the product of reliable principles and methods; and
> (d) the expert has reliably applied the principles and methods to the facts of the case.

Unlike fact witnesses, who are limited to testifying about what they know or have observed, expert witnesses have the ability to express opinion because, as their name suggests, they are presumed to be 'experts' by having scientific, technical, or other specialized knowledge 'beyond the ken' of the tier of fact. Expert testimony is 'beyond the ken' of the IC judges or USCIS administrative review officers when the expert can demonstrate factually supported special knowledge that is beyond that of the trier of fact. The legal rationale is that judges cannot be expected to be knowledgeable in all areas of human activity and count on experts to provide specialized knowledge relevant to the matter before the Court. In reality, many cases before the IC are greatly aided by, and may even turn on, access to opinions based on specialized, fact-based scientific knowledge and application of reliable assessment methods.

For our purposes, expert witnesses are called upon to testify in the IC on matters of mental health requiring both scientific and clinical expertise, and may include other areas of expert knowledge such as social, experimental, cognitive, or developmental issues. For IC proceedings, immigration attorneys do most, if not all, expert witness recruitment. It is important to emphasize that, regardless of who calls in the expert, it is the IC judge who determines the acceptability of the expert witness and the probative value of her or his report and testimony. As such, it is a good approach to conduct an expert forensic psychological assessment as though it ultimately addresses the needs and interests of the IC judge rather than the retaining attorney or immigrant respondent. All ethical expert witnesses must be able to resolve the issue of being a neutral expert in the case or being an advocate for the immigrant. They must decide between a careful adherence to factual application of their field of expertise or to the outcome of the case. While being an advocate for the immigrant is compelling and morally appealing, our experience is that IC judges quickly ascertain the difference between a forensic psychological assessor who provides neutral, fact-based expert opinions and an advocacy-based assessor who frequently bases opinions on clinical interview and little else. As the Discussant of my (FBE) presentation on forensic assessment in IC, the Honorable Judge James R. Fujimoto of the Executive Office for Immigration Review in Chicago (Fujimoto, 2000) noted that the neutral, objective, fact-based approach espoused above was an important corrective to advocacy-based testimony. He termed this latter approach 'the regurgitation model' of expert testimony, which was of limited probative value to the IC. Having reached an opinion through ethical methods, the assessor is free to advocate for his or her opinion in the report and testimony.

Because the practice of immigration law addresses a broad and diverse set of legal issues, the following areas are most pertinent for the application of psychological expertise (Evans, 2000):

1. The assessment of torture and rape for asylum and Convention Against Torture (CAT) claims.
2. The assessment of physical, sexual, and psychological abuse and extreme mental cruelty in claims for permanent residence of a battered spouse or children of a U.S. citizen under Subtitle G – Protections for Battered Immigrant Women and Children of *the Violence Against Women Act of 1998* (VAWA).

3. The assessment of extreme hardship to a qualified spouse, child, and parents in suspension of deportation proceedings.
4. The assessment of recidivism and dangerousness for exceptions to mandatory deportation for aggravated felony and for parole from indefinite suspension.

Since then more IC forensic areas have developed, such as forensic assessment in U and T visa cases. Each of these areas calls for different psychological expertise, including an understanding of the underlying psychological research literature for each and the use of different psychological methodologies appropriate to the assessment of each of these issues.

In addition to professional and scientific knowledge, it is essential that the forensic psychologists have a working understanding of the legal issues relevant to each IC area. Gathering, weighing, and presenting psychological assessment information for the IC is significantly different from standard clinical protocols. The most important differences between these role is that the forensic assessor must take an objective, neutral stance in the evaluation, though, especially in the case of the assessment of torture and psychological trauma, neutrality must be understood in a broader context (Evans, 2005).

Relationship Between the Immigration Attorney and Forensic Assessor

One of the most important sources of understanding the legal issues is from the referring immigration attorney, though there are now good introductory books on immigration law that can provide guidance (see Aleinikoff, Martin, Motomura, & Fullerton, 2011; Johnson, Aldana, Hing, Saucedo, & Trucios-Haynes, 2015; Scaros, 2007; Weissbrodt & Danielson, 2011).

A key practical aspect of conducting forensic assessment is the establishment of a clear framework of the evaluation resulting in a mutually signed expert–attorney agreement. Providing and agreeing to the 'ground rules' of forensic psychological practice through written informed consent is an essential first step to conducting an assessment. This agreed-upon foundation will hopefully later remove important questions and doubts in the mind of the IC judge regarding issues of neutrality and in the mind of the immigrant regarding confidentiality and disclosure of interview information.

Generally, a referral begins with a phone call from either the immigration attorney or the attorney's client. If the attorney's client calls directly, it is essential that she or he be tactfully and clearly informed that the assessor must speak directly with the attorney before any information about the immigration matter is discussed between the assessor and immigrant respondent. Otherwise, such communications are not covered by attorney work product privilege and are discoverable. It is our experience that most attorneys will call the forensic assessor directly and that a deviation from the approach may foretell a difficult relationship.

When an immigration attorney calls directly, our experience is that many attorneys will begin by trying to give a detailed account of the case. Naturally, the attorney will be representing the best interest of their client and cannot be fully depended upon to give an unbiased view of the case. For this reason, we recommend finding out what the matter is before the IC (e.g., asylum, hardship, VAWA) and what questions the attorney would like the forensic assessor to address, before going into the details of the case. Not infrequently, attorneys will ask for a diagnosis to present as part of the evidentiary basis of the claim. This provides the forensic assessor with the opportunity to ask how this finding would be useful in relationship to the legal question or questions. The assessor can collaborate with the attorney to refine the inquiry from one of psychological diagnosis to a functionally based assessment, tailored primarily to the legal question. For example, it is helpful for all concerned to reframe a request for a diagnosis of PTSD in an asylum case to providing an assessment of psychological signs and symptoms consistent with immigrant's claim of being tortured as part of establishing a well-founded fear of returning to her or his home country.

Based on our experience doing many forensic psychological assessments for IC, we have found in working with experienced and competent attorneys that their cases are well developed before getting an assessment. Such attorneys have themselves been careful regarding the credibility of their clients, informing them about the problems of not being candid and open, and thorough about the foundation of the claim. As such, our request for collateral information comes as no surprise and it is usually already available. There are other cases for which the attorney refers the case in order to get more information that the client has not been able to provide, and the evaluation becomes the core of the legal case. This method can be very risky for the assessor.

One of us had an upsetting experience in which the immigration attorney had not done a thorough development of her case and had not been clear with her client about the risks of not providing credible information. The immigrant respondent claimed that she had been tortured in a prison in her country, but it became clear to the assessor that her story was vague and inconsistent with known torture methods. Eventually, the young woman admitted that she had not been tortured, but was told by a fellow countryman in exile in the U.S. to make this claim to get a green card. The examiner asked her why she really left her country and the young woman shared in believable detail how her family had been arrested for political reasons and never returned. She was told that she should leave as soon as possible and individuals arranged for her to stow away on a cargo ship. When she arrived in the United States hungry and sick, she was able to connect with ex-patriots from her country who cared for her and found her an attorney. Clearly, if corroborated, her actual reasons for leaving her home country fell well within acceptable asylum regulations. When I shared the information with her attorney, she asked that I only report the information helpful to the case, but I made it clear that I had to include the young woman's initial non-credible claim. The attorney decided that she did not want a report from me and acknowledged that she had not interviewed her client in detail, hoping to use the information from the forensic evaluation as the primary data in writing the immigrant's Declaration.

The next step is establishing the ground rules for the forensic assessment. Prior to an agreement to conduct an independent psychological evaluation, the immigration attorney and his or her client must understand and agree to the condition that the forensic assessor will approach the assessment with no particular result or opinion in mind. Further, the assessor must exercise independent professional judgment in all aspects of this evaluation. This independent judgment means that the assessor will not accept limitations on the information she or he requests. This includes, but is not limited to, available medical and mental records; arrest records; legal documents including applications and declarations; and collateral information in support of the claim, including all country conditions reports from the U.S. Department of State and Amnesty International. The assessor makes it clear that he or she may ask for additional information as the assessment progresses and that failure to provide the information will cause the assessment to end.

It must be clearly understood that the payment of fees is not connected to the contents of any report or consultation or any particular finding or recommendation on the matter at question. In practice, this means that the attorneys will contract on behalf of their immigrant clients to get a neutral evaluation, which may or may not be helpful to their cases. Practices such as contingent fees violate the forensic psychologists' standards for practice (APA, 2013). Further, payment following the release of a forensic report can give the appearance of contaminating the neutrality of the expert's opinion. The ultimate goal of these fee practices is to show clear neutrality to establish credibility to the trier of fact, who is generally either the IC judge or USCIS case assessor. This practice also frees the forensic assessor from a conflict of interest that a treating therapist would have with the respondent. Additionally, it must be clearly understood by all parties, through informed consent with the attorney and the respondent, that the forensic assessor cannot offer the examinee the protection of client–patient privilege, as is expected in a therapeutic relationship. Naturally, it is important for the forensic psychologist to clearly explain his or her role in the evaluation to both the immigration attorney and the respondent and obtain informed consent before proceeding.

Neutrality Reconsidered in Forensic Assessment in Immigration Court

As we have stated, a central tenet of forensic psychology in any court-related setting is maintaining a neutral stance, different from a therapeutic stance. The classic paper outlining these differences is Greenberg and Shuman (1997), which has become accepted canon in the forensic world. The authors outline ten fundamental differences between therapeutic and forensic roles, which as general statements are fundamentally sound. They also take an extreme position that there is an irreconcilable conflict between therapeutic and forensic roles. Among the ten fundamental differences, three warrant discernment in working with traumatized and vulnerable forensic populations such as immigrants in IC proceedings. First, Greenberg and Shuman indicate the forensic examiner should be neutral, objective, and **detached**, as opposed to **empathic**, supportive, and accepting. Second, the basis of the forensic relationship is evaluative, and third, critical judgment is unlikely to cause serious emotional harm.

As Evans (2005) pointed out, while forensic assessment requires a more explicitly factual basis and concern for malingering and deception than clinical work, it does not follow that forensic assessment should be practiced with greater human detachment. As a result of his assessment experiences with torture victims, he strongly recommends reconsidering forensic psychology as a human process. He cautions that the concept of neutrality held by many forensic psychologists is in fact not neutral. Forensic psychologists frequently see their stance in evaluations as similar to scientists. Scientists are by nature skeptical and doubting, wanting tangible proof of phenomena, thus taking an exclusively scientific view of neutrality in forensic assessment is a de facto acceptance of skepticism and disbelief as neutrality. As such, the forensic examiner underestimates the impact of skepticism and disbelief in the interpersonal realm, which can substantially skew information gathered in a forensic assessment. Mollica and colleagues worked with severely traumatized Indochinese refugees (Mollica et al., 1992; Mollica, Wyshak, & Lavelle, 1987), and shared that such skepticism can in fact be absolutely toxic to torture victims and others who have suffered from interpersonal violence (see also Herman, 1992; Kassindja & Miller, 1998). On the other hand, psychopathic individuals are often quite highly adept at interpersonal maneuvers designed to neutralize skepticism (Hare, 1993). Naturally, an attitude of unquestioning belief and acceptance of what we are told, what is best called naivety, is equally problematic in forensic assessment.

Smith and Evans (2017) go further and state that, whether or not the forensic assessor chooses to recognize it, he or she is a participant-observer during the forensic assessment, and therefore a purely detached and neutral position is not only impossible, but also fails to utilize critical evidence of great value to the final forensic opinion. Smith (1990, 2005) points out that the idea of strict neutrality is a fallacy. The interpersonal dynamics in any psychological interview are such that the examiner will always be in reciprocal role relationships with the subject in ways that are often outside of awareness. The point here is that a strict inquisitorial or uncritically advocacy-oriented approach is not, in fact, neutral. Given this reality, Smith and Evans believe that an ongoing examination of the forensic examiner's inevitable countertransference should be an important part of the evaluation process.

To illustrate, one of us (FBE) was asked by a government attorney during cross-examination in an asylum case, 'Isn't it true, Doctor, that you are biased?' He acknowledged that, yes, it is true that he was biased against the practice of torture and then explained to the judge how review of records, formal assessment of malingering, and the use of psychological testing all serve as ways of checking this bias. While an assessment approach that over-emphasizes sympathy toward the immigrant's plight runs the risk of over-identification and a loss of objectivity, a strictly detached stance runs the opposite risk: that the examiner can be experienced as an adversarial interrogator, which can trigger terror and avoidance in torture survivors. It is good to remember that Sullivan's (1954) development of the concept of participant-observation was indeed an application of common anthropological and sociological research methods of his era and an early model for both clinical and forensic applications.

There are others in the practice of forensic mental health who raised similar concerns about balance in forensic assessment. Sadoff (2011) also differentiated between the role of the treating clinician and that of a forensic psychiatrist, who makes assessments as an expert witness. At the same time, though, he said the forensic psychiatrist had a responsibility to protect vulnerable patients from being exploited by skilled professional adversaries in the court system. Further, Griffith, Stankovic, and Baranoski (2010) indicated that forensic psychiatric writing is grounded in the discipline and relies on both ethics-based principles of respect for persons and truth-telling, while using narrative language that is persuasive to the legal audience. Griffith (1998) notes that compassion lies at the root of forensic assessment, especially where social context suggests possible injustice toward individuals from the non-dominant cultures has a long history.

As Evans (2005) posited, true neutrality in forensic practice is where the assessor strives at the same time to be totally skeptical *and* totally open. As practiced by many forensic examiners, maintaining a position of only skepticism and suspicion is therefore fundamentally biased, and the value of personality tests as de-biasing is undercut by an all-too-wary and negative predisposition toward disbelief. The concept of neutrality is, in fact, to be neutral in which a deep openness to the experience of the person evaluated is leavened with a desire for facts and the knowledge that people naturally wish to escape painful and dangerous experiences or desire other secondary gains. This attitude of balanced openness is closer to Wilfred Bion's (personal communication, Spring 1976) warning about the impact of preconception in interpersonal relationships and his recommendation to approach interviews 'without memory or desire.' Although we will need all the memory we can muster when testifying and in our desire to do competent work, a fundamental attitude of what Edith Weigert (1970) called 'benevolent neutrality,' when applied to forensic practice, allows the forensic examiner to balance an alert openness to experience with various methods including, especially, psychological testing to further open the forensic examiner to experiences otherwise not considered. It is very instructive that, as we increasingly approach forensic assessment with benevolent neutrality, we are also better able to ferret out deceptive reporting and malingering to the degree that in some instances, individuals have shared blatantly fraudulent reports to the INS of being the victim of torture. In our experience, this balanced approach produces rich, 'truth-telling' narratives in forensic reports and expert testimony that are appreciated by IC judges, who in turn give considerable weight to forensic findings.

Notes

1. Immigration Court also includes the Board of Immigration Appeals (BIA), all of which are administratively under the purview of the Department of Homeland Security.
2. While we refer to forensic psychology, these principles can be adapted to other mental health professions as well.

Chapter 2

The Cross-Cultural, Gender, and Language Perspective

Human rights are often violated on account of factors such as the individual's race, language, ethnicity, culture, religion, gender identity, sexual orientation, disability, or socioeconomic class; or because they are indigenous people, migrants, displaced, or refugees (United Nations (UN) Declaration of Human Rights, 1948/2015). Mental health professionals working in immigration cases are keenly aware that these violations are the reason why we have migration between countries and need protective laws for immigrants. The reason why we continue to encounter a system of human exploitation and abuse in the world is due to the systems of domination and subordination that create experiences of social inequity. Gender, age, sexuality, gender, socio-economic status, class, ability, religious/spiritual orientation, education, voca-tion, nationality, race, and ethnicity have been utilized to marginalize, oppress, and victimize others and prevent them from achieving the equal opportunities and meaningful lives they deserve. These intersecting identities play a role in the migration, are further impacted by the migration process, and powerfully influence a person's functioning in the new environment (Reid, Lewis, & Wyche, 2014).

When a mental health professional provides services to immigrant or refugee examinees, whether they are recent arrivals or they have resided in the host country for a long time, it is critical to understand these individuals' own worlds and experiences to better serve their needs (American Psychological Associ-ation, 2002, 2003). Factors at the cultural, individual, familial, community, and societal levels interact in a reciprocal manner to shape the risks and protective factors that affect immigrants and refugees (Bronfenbrenner, 1977). Examiners need to consider these interactions.

Mental health professionals who choose to work in this field usually possess a strong desire to connect with human suffering, have generosity of spirit, and value how culture provides meaning to life. These values are more relevant than ever when working in immigration evaluations, because the exact nature of this practice is to interact with someone different from the examiner, and the cul-tural, gender, and other individual difference issues are often at the core of the human rights violations that makes them eligible for immigration relief.

Assessing and reporting on the damage and dangers to which the immigrants were exposed on account of their intersecting identities and circumstances in their countries of origin or in the new society is essential to the mental health evaluations supporting petitions for immigration relief. In particular, examiners for immigration cases need to explain how these social identities intersect and 'shape the meaning, experiences, and expressions of one another in an inextricably interlocking and irreducible fashion' (Greenwood, 2012, p. 104). The examiner's task is to integrate the subjective, objective, and unique ways in which the examinee experiences and interprets the causes, solutions, and legitimacy of the human rights violations committed against them. The goal of an immigration evaluation is to provide a picture of the individual that honors their psychological reality and that also serves as a pathway for healing and empowerment; this is why thinking in contextual and intersectional terms as examiners is a valuable approach.

It can be a challenge to understand and integrate into a comprehensive analysis of the immigrant examinees' identities, values, lifestyles, and nuances of their worldview and psychological functioning in the detail-oriented and ethical manner required in forensic evaluations for the Immigration Court (IC). Typically, to become competent when evaluating immigrant respondents, examiners need the competences outlined in Figure 2.1.

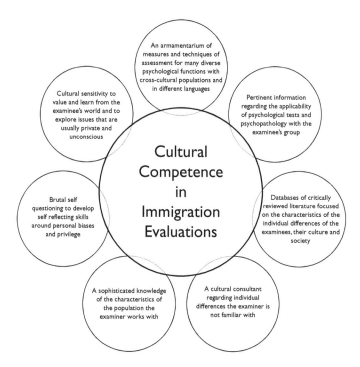

Figure 2.1 Elements of Cultural Competence in Immigration Evaluations.

While cultural competency is usually understood as the product of education, training, and exposure, to be truly sensitive an examiner needs to also have a 'critical consciousness' (Freire, 2005, p. vii). This requires self-reflection that leads to an awareness of differences in power and inequities inherent in social relationships. This consciousness leads to a transformed perspective focused on social justice and an understanding that social, cultural, and economic systems shape people's actual and existential experiences. This is a way of knowing and 'reading the word and the world' (Freire & Macedo, 1987, p. viii), that allows examiners to understand how cultural politics serve to empower or disempower people. Using this framework, we can assume that examiners with this level of expanded awareness are able to carry themselves with a reduced psychological distance between themselves and their immigrant evaluees. Increased consciousness around racism, sexism, and homophobia in both themselves and society, combined with a critical sense of empathy and social justice, will prevent forensic assessors from falling into the trap of pitying their examinees or seeing them as inferior, but rather acting with the benevolent neutrality described in Chapter 1.

A framework for assessing all these individual differences has been developed by Hays (2008), and is known by its acronym, ADDRESSING. This word stands for:

- Age and generational influences
- Developmental disability
- Disability acquired later
- Religion
- Ethnicity
- Socioeconomic status
- Sexual orientation
- Indigenous heritage
- National origin
- Gender

Although we list them individually in this model, it is the intersection of these identities and not the aggregation of them individually which concerns us. When assessing the examinee's diverse identities, their context, and how they intersect, the best evaluation tool is to ask. However, questions about these identities are delicate. Some examinees may get offended; they may think the answer is obvious; or they may be reminded of past experiences when their identities were used to discriminate against them. It is best to start with general questions that address the overall issue and then ask for more details from there. One can ask: *Tell me about the family you grew up in,* and follow up with questions such as: *How was [specific characteristic(s)] seen by the extended family ... and in your community?* And then: *Did ... [specific characteristic(s)] ever cause you or your family frustration, or problems in life?*, and so on.

For example, with an examinee who spoke about being raised by a single mother and suffering from stark poverty, this line of questioning led to an understanding of what it meant for him. Through open-ended questions he explained that his extended family and community marginalized his mother for having five children with three different men, and for having left all her partners. He said nobody helped them because they thought she deserved her predicament. However, the examinee said he was proud of his mother for leaving those men, who were abusive alcoholics, and that having all the children work with her selling shrimp in the local market was smart and caring. As the oldest boy, he was happy to take on the responsibility and did not care about missing school to work with her and care for his siblings. This information tells the examiner the depth of his empathy with his mother and pride about his family, and how a disadvantage can also be a source of resilience and personal strength.

The information gathered regarding the respondent's ADDRESSING characteristics, and how they intersect into a matrix to make up the person's internal world, is utilized in two ways:

1. to understand how they connect with the basis for immigration relief and how it shaped the persecution or abuse; and
2. to understand their inner world (customs, traditions, values, beliefs, practices, gender role, family structure, parenting practices, language, and modes of expression) and its meaning to the respondent in the foreign environment.

This information helps forensic assessors form accurate and balanced conceptualizations, including how the integration of culture-specific (emic) and universal (etic) factors shape their personality development as well as trauma experience and expression of physical and mental problems.

The way respondents will navigate the journey of an immigration relief petition, which in many cases takes years, will be a product of the ADDRESSING matrix. If we do not identify and incorporate this knowledge into our work, we may encounter a minefield of problems as we work with respondents in the journey of their immigration case. To begin with, we may miss valuable information that could have strengthened their cases, or we may fail to establish a relationship of trust due to a missed opportunity to value their individual differences. Problems due to failure to properly take these issues into account can happen at any time. To name a few issues:

- Some examinees may have difficulties with standardized tests or be completely illiterate even in their own language.
- Other examinees may not cooperate with law enforcement due to past traumatic experiences.
- Still other examinees may conceal parts of their stories for fear of being misunderstood or judged, and their need to control the narrative for the rest of the process gets them into all kinds of trouble.

- Other examinees may refuse to continue in the psychotherapy they desperately need and is being used as a major factor in a hardship case.

Based on an intersectional conceptualization of the case, we can prevent misunderstandings or provide solutions to these dilemmas in many such situations. In some cases, educating and supporting the examinee to find adequate alternatives may solve the problem. In other cases, referring the immigrant to therapy to work on those issues may help; in other cases, enlisting the support of a helpful and safe relative or partner can be valuable. In all instances, forensic assessors try to educate the trier of fact regarding critical cross-cultural issues.

This ADDRESSING knowledge also helps us appreciate behaviors and attitudes unfamiliar to us but coherent in the evaluee's own context. For instance, a Russian asylum applicant was hesitant to disclose to his family back in Russia that he is gay in order to enlist their help to get evidence of the persecution he suffered. A battered woman from India applied secretly for VAWA without separating from the abuser. A Muslim man seeking a VAWA visa due to extreme cruelty reluctantly revealed that his wife was not as religious as she pretended to be when their families arranged their marriage. A Salvadorian minor who does not understand that the contract he paid for in his country to work in the U.S. was part of a human trafficking network and he is now an unemployed and undocumented crime victim. These attitudes and behaviors make perfect sense when understood from the context of the immigrant's worldview, and it is critical information that we can pass to her or his attorney and the trier of fact.

An important matter to take into consideration is the role of the ADDRESSING matrix in the examinee's expression, meaning, and experience of trauma. Immigrants and refugees may belong to all walks of life, and their individual experience of trauma may vary widely. For instance, Brown (2008) explains that social class and social status interact with trauma in that persons of the middle and upper classes may have had little or inconsistent trauma in their lives and thus they may be more challenged to deal with it. This framework can be applied to understanding the wide range of presentations of victims of the same massive trauma (e.g., natural disaster, civil unrest, workplace abuse) even when they shared the same geographic, ethnicity, cultural group, and other such characteristics. Another issue is the presence of insidious trauma, which includes the cumulative devaluation of individuals with identities different from those in power (Root, 1992), which activates survival responses. This framework explains long-term consequences of systematic sexism, racism, heterosexism, ageism, and classism that progressively denigrate a person's self-worth.

Trauma impacts identity (Root, 1992) and examinees may engage in a transitional life identity to make sense of their experience (Brown, 2008).

Myrna, a deeply religious Muslim adolescent from a wealthy background, was brutally gang raped and her parents sent her to the U.S. 'to study' because of the shame it brought to the family and to prevent an honor killing by other family members. Once in the U.S., she underwent a number of identity transformations, such as wearing revealing clothes, drinking, and partying with college peers. Her presentation was incongruent with the story of her traumatic experience, and which, if not explained by the impact of trauma on her cultural identity, would have raised flags in IC regarding her credibility.

Race, Ethnicity, and Culture

Race technically refers to a biological subgroup in which people share similar physical characteristics (Gray-Little, 2002). Ethnicity refers to structures such as religion, cultural values, language, and customs. Persons of different races may belong to the same ethnic group and people of different ethnic groups may belong to the same race. When members of a racial or ethnic group are differentiated from others in the same society and occupy a subordinate position, they are considered minorities. Assignment to an ethnic group can be a matter of personal choice; thus a person may claim membership in several ethnic groups.

A person may belong to a protected group based on racial, ethnic, or cultural persecution, but any individual can be persecuted by communities or groups when one or more of these characteristics are not shared with the majority. For instance, indigenous or ethnic minority individuals may be discriminated in any culture and social milieu, including their own. Discrimination and violence on account of race, ethnicity, and culture occur all over the world. For example, as reported by Amnesty International (2015):

- In Paraguay, the Sawhoyamaxa Indigenous community has been subjected to a great deal of discrimination and abuse, including attacks on their cultural heritage, attacks on their right to self-determination, and being forcibly removed from their ancestral lands.
- In India, Dalit women and girls continue to face multiple levels of caste-based discrimination and violence. Self-appointed village councils issued illegal decrees ordering punishments against women for perceived social transgressions.
- In Central and Eastern Europe, the discrimination of Roma has been widespread, and persistent. It has not only included violent attacks and social exclusion, but also discrimination of Roma in housing, education, and employment, together with forced eviction from informal settlements.

Implications for Immigration Evaluations

In immigration evaluations, the value of identifying the examinee's ethnic and racial identity lies in our ability to study the interaction of these factors with other contextual and individual differences that play a role in the examinee's experience of marginalization, discrimination, persecution, or abuse. Even in cases when there is institutionalized violence against people from different ethnic or racial characteristics, the individual experience is essential to our assessment. In such cases, attaching country conditions documents and integrating this information in the report with the manner in which the examinee specifically experienced such violence can be extremely helpful to support the examinee's allegations, especially when other collateral data are lacking.

Race, ethnicity, and cultural identification are individual characteristics that often but not always can be explored with the respondents. However, the way a person has been socialized, their insight, their identity development process, and their own internal biases, leads to different levels of awareness and consciousness about these personal identities. Moreover, race, ethnicity, culture, and acculturation are entangled with socioeconomic status (SES), education, social class, and contextual social factors, which often confounds the development of a coherent theory on how exactly each factor impacts the individual (Gray-Little, 2002).

A sound understanding of the respondents' cultural, racial, and ethnic identity is essential because these issues are key to their social identity, social acceptance, or social rejection. Analyzing these issues allows us to not only define the individual, but also the arguments regarding the request for protection through immigration relief on those bases.

> A Guatemalan girl from an indigenous rural and poor community, Yukary escaped from brutal physical and psychological abuse by her parents, and entered the United States as an unaccompanied minor at age 15. During the asylum's psychological evaluation requested by Child Protective Services, Yukary reported that she was the youngest in a family with eight children and the only child who was abused. She reported that, among other abuses, her father would tie her to a tree and hit her with a twig for what seemed to her to be hours. She had the scars to prove it, but no matter how battered she looked, neither teachers nor law enforcement ever cared because it was 'a family matter.' She could not explain why she was the only one abused and she described herself as an obedient child. Psychological testing did not find evidence of issues that often make a child a target of parental rejection, such as mental deficits, autism, hyperactivity, or oppositional behavior. In fact, her personality was of a timid, passive, and people-pleaser teenager. Yukary was of Mam ethnicity and she explained that she was proud of her ethnic heritage. She never saw herself differently from her siblings in physical or behavioral characteristics and lived in a community of Mam peoples. The mystery of her being individually targeted was resolved when I interviewed her cousin by phone. Her cousin disclosed that Yukary had a lighter skin tone and hazel eyes and Yukary's father thought that she was not his own. These characteristics were directly related to the discrimination and abuse in her family, as well in their community, as Yukary was brutally bullied by peers and

neighbors. Yukary's mother felt helpless to protect Yukary from the husband's abuse and she was also especially harsh when punishing her because, otherwise, her husband would think she was protecting her out of guilt for having strayed sexually. At one point, Yukary's mother felt such pity that she encouraged Yukary to leave home and establish herself far away from home. Clearly, this careful exploration revealed that Yukary fell into a protected category of victims.

You may wonder: Why was not just reporting the brutal childhood abuse, which had significant medical evidence, enough for the psychological report? The motivations for the abuse are important because I (GAH) wanted to fully honor Yukary's life story and obtain an integrated understanding of her experience. Understanding and documenting the reason of her victimization may help Yukary in her healing process. Additionally, because without this reasoning her story was incomplete and may appear unreliable. Cases are stronger when we tie the markers of the story in a reasonable and contextual manner so the trier of fact can understand and empathize with the examinee's plight and understand her vulnerabilities and need for protection. Reporting the subjective aspects of the victimization history creates a human connection with the adjudicator and increases the reliability of the allegations.

Similarly, ethnicity, culture, and social status are essential to understand in other types of immigration relief. For instance, undocumented immigrants who qualify for U visa petitions on the basis of qualifying crimes committed at the workplace have been subjected to employer–employee relationships plagued by power disparities. While there are always power disparities between workers and management, usually immigrant workers have vastly larger differences in legal status, race or ethnicity, language, acculturation, socioeconomic status, and culture vis-à-vis their employers and supervisors, and this makes them particularly vulnerable to abuse and exploitation. Moreover, certain cultural groups profess values that demand deference and obedience to superiors and employers, particularly if they are men. Young workers or women may be especially vulnerable to this prescription of compliance (Waldinger & Lichter, 2003). Some abusive supervisors or employers may exploit this power dynamic to exert abuse and exploitation either directly and aggressively, or through pseudo-friendly, flirtatious, or paternalistic behavior (Cho, Hass, & Salgado, 2015). Qualifying crimes that occurred in those environments may be directly related to an abuse of this cultural power differential.

In a case of a group of Mexican minors who were victims of abuse and labor law violations in their workplace, they reported that the verbal abuse, raging, yelling, and threatening were most hurtful when white supervisors called them 'brutos indios' (brute indigenous), 'monos' (monkeys), 'ilegales' (illegals), 'mojados' (wetbacks), 'cholos' (of uncertain origin), among other slurs. This language reflected their employer's racism and xenophobia, and constituted psychological abuse because they were humiliating and cruelly dismissing them as human beings, while at the same time using and exploiting their labor and skills. Abuse to a person's race, ethnicity, and culture is the more damaging because it targets immutable conditions that are at the core of a person's identity.

Mental health professionals conducting immigration evaluations are encouraged to assess and document the change in social status as a result of coming to this country for immigrants and refugees, and the level of stress related to acculturation (American Psychological Association, 2003). The emotional impact of abuse and discrimination on account of race, ethnicity, and culture is further aggravated when immigrant workers in the United States, forced by necessity, accept jobs of lower status than they could have in their native countries. For instance, physician and engineer immigrants who can be found driving taxis in our large cities have shown sharper declines in their mental health than immigrants who are in jobs suited to their education, experience, and expectations (Institute for Work & Health, 2011). Immigrants often arrive to the United States with large debts from the money they borrowed to make the journey and also have the added responsibility to support economically and pay for the trip for other family members. This situation makes them strongly dependent on a job and income. Settling for menial jobs due to necessity may lead to a loss of identity and status, and lowers a person's sense of personal power and value, which further prevents them from responding constructively to new traumas such as workplace abuse. Feeling powerless and trapped in abusive conditions leads to greater psychological harm (Grandey, Kern, & Frone, 2007).

To the mental health assessment of the distress generated by racism, racial discrimination, xenophobia, and other types of intolerance, we want to add the contribution of acculturation stress on psychosocial functioning. Not only social and interpersonal discrimination, ethnic oppression, and racial violence are damaging, but so are the stresses of having to adjust to a different language, different methods of social affiliation, foreign cultural knowledge, and different preferences and options in many aspects of daily living, such as foods, dress, etc. Learning new information in an often-unwelcoming environment is an added source of stress that compounds the many challenges faced by immigrants and refugees. However, we do not want to lump them together and rather we need to understand the specificities of their situation. The challenges of acculturation are different depending on where the immigrant came from, why they came, where in the U.S. they are settled, and whether they are young or old, men or women, and if they have certain identities that cause privilege or oppression in the U.S. We also want to carefully analyze the immigrants' difficulties to navigate the adjustments successfully in cases in which the examinees are expected to adapt fairly well, given their education, intelligence, exposure, and acceptance of the new culture. This diminished adjustment from what is expected if there is a supportive environment may cue the examiner to possible symptoms of their debilitated psychological state. As such, assessing and integrating this information in the immigration report can be very helpful.

One of the more troublesome aspects of providing forensic assessment in the IC is the question of the applicability of psychological measures to immigrants who have lived in the U.S. for years. One aspect of the issue has to do with limited English proficiency and acculturation, which is unfortunately rarely assessed in forensic assessments (Canales, Kan, & Varela, 2017). Weiss and Rosenfeld (2012) noted that acculturation, the process and degree of adaptation from a foreign culture of origin to a new host culture, might be more relevant for mental health professionals than cultural, ethnic, or racial context. Beyond language proficiency by itself, acculturation is a significant variable when considering the interpretability of English-language psychological tests. The importance of measuring acculturation when relying on English versions of psychological assessment methods is significantly multiplied in the forensic setting. As a rule of thumb, Butcher (1996) recommends being in the U.S. for five years when considering achieving acculturation to a new country on the validity of the MMPI, but many immigrants live in communities within the U.S. where their home country mores and values are little affected by the surrounding U.S. culture. In some instances, an immigrant may be well or poorly acculturated to the U.S. or maintain a bicultural adaptation.

A measure of acculturation is useful in IC forensic assessments. Fortunately, such measures of acculturation do exist, in either a culture-specific format – for example for Hispanic evaluees (see Canales et al., 2017) – or a broader measure such as the Stephenson Multigroup Acculturation Scale (SMAS; Stephenson, 2000). Where questions under cross-examination in IC might arise about the validity of psychological assessment measures, including a measure of acculturation can assist the IC judge in deciding the probative value of test results. If the client is not acculturated and does not fit the assessment instrument standardized population, a more valid, fair, and culturally equivalent instrument needs to be utilized (Butcher, Hass, Greene, & Nelson, 2015).

Gender, Gender Identity, and Sexual Orientation

A person's gender, gender identity, and sexual orientation are part of their identity, and are related to the manner in which they are perceived and treated in society and their own sense of power or powerlessness. Equally important are those issues related to how society shapes social roles and identities by the expectations, the punishment of non-conforming individuals, and the use of these factors in the establishment of a social hierarchy. Examiners will need to assess how these gender and sexual orientation identities interact with a person's other identities, because of their significant differences in the psychological meaning for the examinee.

Violence against women and lesbian, gay, bisexual, transgender, and queer (LGBTQ) individuals is a human rights violation and there are international conventions, resolutions, and treaties designed to protect abused women and

LGBTQ individuals and provide them refuge (United Nations, 2011, 2013). Being female or LGBTQ in this and other societies is a risk factor for abuse and exploitation. Social beliefs about the inferiority of women and LGBTQ individuals are so pervasive that they fuel interpersonal violence and a culture of discrimination within the protective institutions. In turn, this prejudice may lead to negligent investigations and a failure to sanction perpetrators (Amnesty International, 2015). Unfortunately, not all countries have laws to protect women and LGBTQ individuals from violence, while some countries may have laws that are ignored and violated with impunity.

Some of our asylum applicants and petitioners of other types of visa have been targeted on account of their gender, gender identity, or sexual orientation. For instance, in many cases of asylum, the individual's rights were violated in their home country due to the society's homophobic, transphobic, and misogynistic values. In these cases, the examiner studies the country conditions and the social context in relation to the nature of the abuse the examinee reportedly suffered in his or her home country (reviewed in Chapters 4 and 6). Other cases may present gender violence suffered in the U.S., which forms the basis of a petition for immigration relief (i.e., U visa). Here, the examiner similarly examines the context and nature of the hate crime (as reviewed in Chapters 5 and 6).

However, there may be cases when these issues are not the focus of the immigration relief petition at all, but still exert a great deal of pertinent influence in the experience of the examinees, and may have a role in understanding the nuances of the qualifying crime committed against them. For instance, in many cases of U visa petitions based on labor abuse, LGBTQ individuals have reported that they were especially vulnerable to being more viciously victimized in the workplace (Cho, Hass, & Saucedo, 2015). In many cases, LGBTQ immigrants were subjected to discrimination, abuse, sexual harassment, sexual exploitation, sexual assault, and discrimination that heterosexual cisgender employees in the same abusive work environment did not experience. The careful questioning and analysis of information regarding the examinee's gender identity and orientation, and the experiences related to these factors, are critical to understand the psychological picture.

In many immigration evaluations, explaining and documenting the country conditions regarding human rights violations on account of gender, sexual orientation, or gender identity is essential. Country conditions and cultural literature are evidence that the respondent was (in cases of asylum) or will be (in cases of extreme hardship) likely persecuted, targeted for violence or abuse, and not safeguarded by protective legal and social systems in the native society. However, this information needs to be meaningfully integrated and individually applied to the case in order to be effective.

Men and women immigrants applying for visas may have been psychologically harmed by the gender bias that discriminated and targeted them for violence. This gender bias may range from what we may see typically in our societies, such as women who are pregnant or have children being discriminated at work, in social institutions, and in the community, to vicious gender violence such as torture and murder of LGBTQ individuals. The following are the most likely issues a forensic examiner will encounter in the context of immigration evaluations.

Homophobia and Transphobia Violence

It is recognized (United Nations, 2012) that LGBTQ persons have a right to legal identity, the right to health, the right to bodily autonomy and integrity, and the right to protection against discrimination. However, there are many countries and situations excluding them from legal protections. In addition to the widespread discrimination and prejudice against LGBTQ people, there are extreme violations of their human rights in certain parts of the world. For example:

- In Cameroon, Gambia, Senegal, Uganda and Zambia LGBTQ people are persecuted or criminalized for their real or perceived sexual orientation (Amnesty International, 2015).
- In Brunei, the Penal Code imposes death by stoning as a possible punishment for consensual sex between people of the same gender (Amnesty International, 2015).
- In Russia, LGBTQ activists are not allowed to organize public events, and legislation prohibiting the promotion of homosexuality among minors is used as a repressive tool. At the time of this writing, the torture of gay men by law enforcement and security agency officials in Chechnya was the news of the day (*New York Times*, 2017).

Implications for Immigration Evaluations

Violence on account of a person's gender identity and gender orientation can be devastating to a person's sense of self. When the message from society is that these characteristics are an illness or aberration, it makes a person question the value of their own existence. In my anecdotal experience evaluating a large number of LGBTQ examinees for asylum, it is the group where I most frequently find a history of suicide attempts and ideation. This is congruent with the statement by the National Action Alliance for Suicide Prevention (2012) that has named LGBTQ individuals among the high-risk groups. There is a range of mental health consequences related to violence caused by homo- or transphobia (American Psychological Association, 2012b), whether the individual suffered isolated incidents of violence or a persistent abusive environment.

In evaluations of asylum on the basis of persecution due to sexual identity or orientation, examiners need to remember that well-founded persecution may include not only significant violence such as imprisonment, torture, confinement, corrective rape (rape of a homosexual person by a person of the opposite sex with the purpose of 'converting' the homosexual person to heterosexuality), but also threats and other less violent forms of oppression. If a single incident does not constitute persecution, the totality of multiple incidents may rise to the level of persecution.

In cases of asylum, U visa, T visa, and VAWA, we want to assess whether LGBTQ examinees may have suffered homophobic verbal and emotional abuse, including microaggressions such as jokes, slurs, ridicule, and discrimination. LGBTQ examinees have the right to control the disclosure of their sexual orientation or gender identity, and violations to this privacy by employers, friends, or relatives are additional forms of abuse and violation of boundaries. In settings such as blatantly discriminatory workplaces, LGBTQ individuals may force themselves to go along, or pretend they fit a traditional gender role, in order to keep their jobs. This coping strategy can be very costly to these individuals' sense of dignity and personal integrity.

When a person is pervasively harassed, mistreated, and coerced into repressing their freedom, they may use self-protective mechanisms such as cognitive adjustment to deny the abuse or even provoke it to gain a sense of personal control over the stressful situation (Ragins & Cornwell, 2001). Trauma caused by persistent abuses of one's identity can be very damaging and debilitating to a person's psychological functioning. We should not forget that, if the victim was forced into extreme self-protection and dissociation, they may deceive some examiners into thinking that there is no psychological impact from the abuse.

> Kathy, a Vietnamese lesbian adolescent who was enslaved into sex traffic, was rescued during a sting operation, and during the evaluation she made fun of the irony of her enslaved sex work and bragged about her faked sexual skills. It took several months of psychotherapy for her to come in touch with her true feelings and her deep traumatization.

Sometimes gender identity development interacts with the oppression and persecution in the home country, trauma, and ethnicity influencing the manner in which a person seeks support, including immigration relief.

Examining these issues with an examinee demands a great deal from the examiner as there are formidable cultural taboos about exposing these intimate experiences with strangers. Many transgendered immigrants experience intense shame when discussing serious violations of boundaries around sexuality. Moreover, human sexuality is a fluid and multidimensional experience and examinees themselves may not have full awareness of their processes to explain it. The examiner cannot solely rely on the examinee to understand their gender identity and sexual orientation, and this needs to be clearly explained in the report and to the trier of fact.

> Dmitry, a man from Russia, was persecuted in his country of origin and brutally assaulted because he was perceived as gay. However, he never thought

of himself as being gay and, in fact, was highly homophobic. During our interview he insisted that he was heterosexual because he did not have sex with men but only with transgender women. Dmitry had never had sexual relations or relationships with heterosexual women and was attracted to men. At the time of the evaluation, he stated that he was disgusted at the thought of a romantic relationship with a man and he believed that transgender women were not gay men because they were 'feminine.' Dmitry identified himself as heterosexual. but had homosexual thoughts and feelings and was exploring outside the gender binary. He felt that he was unfairly persecuted but felt very strongly that the asylum petition should not mention his sexual preferences or orientation.

In consultation with his attorney, Dmitry was advised to delay submitting his application until after completing a course of psychotherapy, during which he made peace with his inner homophobia, fears, and shame. At that time, Dmitry accepted that the application for asylum be made for persecution on account of his gender orientation.

Female Genital Mutilation/Cutting

Female genital mutilation/cutting (FGM) is a brutal form of gender violence that involves the partial or total cutting of female genitals. Because FGM is the removal of healthy sexual organs without medical necessity and results in harmful physical and psychological consequences, it violates the human rights to non-discrimination, health, and bodily integrity. Even though FGM is a cultural practice and not undertaken with the intention of inflicting harm, its damaging physical, sexual, and psychological effects make it an act of violence against women and children (Center for Reproductive Rights, n.d.). Further, FGM can be life-threatening to girls and women, thereby violating their human rights to life, liberty, and security of the person (United Nations Children's Fund (UNICEF), 2016).

It is estimated that about 100–140 million women worldwide have undergone FGM, with an additional three million girls and women undergoing the procedure every year (Center for Reproductive Rights, n.d.). UNICEF reported that there are vast disparities regarding the type of ablation performed, the contextual factors of this practice and the characteristics of affected groups. Although there has been an overall decrease in the prevalence of FGM in the last 30 years, it continues to be a serious social problem with grave health and psychological consequences for women worldwide (UNICEF, 2016). Some of the statistics as a reference point are as follows (UNICEF, 2016):

- The top countries where, from 2010 to 2014, girls ages 0–14 years experienced FGM are: Gambia, Mauritania, Indonesia, Guinea, Eritrea, Sudan, Ethiopia, and Nigeria.

- The top countries where girls and women ages 15–49 were subjected to FGM from 2010 to 2014 are: Somalia, Guinea, Djibouti, Sierra Leone, Mali, Egypt, Sudan, Eritrea, Burkina Faso, Gambia, Ethiopia, Mauritania, and Liberia.

Of note is that in Europe, Australia, and North America, the practice also occurs among immigrant groups from countries practicing FGM (Baldas, 2017). There are many countries where this problem has not been quantified and the human rights community believes that, even in countries where less than 1 percent of girls or women are affected by this practice, it is too prevalent.

Implications for Immigration Evaluations

It is important for the assessor to have knowledge about all the aspects of FGM both in general and individually, including the type of cutting and the medical issues for the examinee. Naturally, the impact of FGM for the specific examinee and the group to which she belongs are also paramount. FGM experiences are diverse and take on different meanings depending on the culture, ethnic group, age, social support, and other factors, as well as individual differences. The assessment of women who undergo FGM lends itself well to the interactive theory that links the experience of FGM with the social context. Assessors need to take into account that, aside from the health consequences in the short and long term, the psychological consequences are significant even when girls submit voluntarily to FGM and accept it as a cultural norm (Compton & Chechile, 1998) or when it was conducted by a surgeon under anesthesia. Immigrant females who undergo FGM and then migrate to a culture with different values often show a delayed response of trauma as they become aware of differences in the appearance of their genitalia, lack of sexual enjoyment, and may feel deeply embarrassed, angry, guilty, ashamed, or inadequate when under-standing from a different point of view the gratuitous damage to their bodily integrity (Whitehorn, Ayonrinde, & Maingay, 2002).

Long-term psychological consequences include feelings of incompleteness, anxiety, depression, chronic irritability, frigidity, loss of self-esteem, feelings of victimization, loss of trust, psychosomatic disorders or symptoms, feelings of worthlessness, embarrassment, inferiority, shame, and guilt (Compton & Chechile, 1998; Whitehorn et al., 2002). Typically, sexual contact and inter-course will be unpleasant because of its strong association with the mutilated genitals and the physical and emotional pain of the FGM procedure. Childbirth, medical exams or procedures, menstruation, and menopause also may stir up the traumatic memories (Whitehorn et al., 2002). Many girls experience a loss of trust in their caregivers because they were coerced and forced to submit to this cruel tradition. Even when they receive family and social support immediately following the procedure, many girls feel betrayed that their family allowed them to be submitted to such cruelty. Some girls and women find it hard to feel safe and trust caregivers when they were hurt by the persons who were supposed to protect them from harm.

Although the severity of psychological trauma seems to be related to the extent of the FGM procedure, the feelings of humiliation, submission, and fear experienced by these girls and women have been equated to those following rape (Bengston & Baldwin, 1993). Moreover, dissociative amnesia, dissociation, and depersonalization should be evaluated in these cases, as testimonies of FGM survivors have often expressed symptoms of loss of memory about the procedure, disconnection from their bodies, experience of being in a dream, or experience of observing themselves from far away (Getachew, 2004). Not being able to fully describe the FGM experience may need to be explained in the report or testimony as a consequence of the trauma, as well as self-protective dissociation.

Examiners need to pay attention to whether the cultural message from FGM – that women must get used to enduring pain, suppressing their emotions, becoming timid and acquiescent, and accept their inferior status in their society – was internalized by the examinee. In some cultures, the message is that women's sexuality has to be controlled because otherwise her sexual urges would run amok. The FGM procedure defines the women and where they belong, and takes away their option to define themselves as the human beings that they want to become. This message leaves its imprint in the victim's personality and may bring irreversible psychic changes that would impact the way they see themselves and the impact they have in the world.

Feeling repulsion and loss may occur at any point after the procedure, maybe many years later (Lightfoot-Klein, 1989). There are respondents who dismiss the distress of the practice, adducing that it was normal at the time and all their relatives and friends had it, but also acknowledge that in the new society where they live now they feel mutilated or deformed. These women often do not feel free to enter a spa naked, go to lengths finding an OB-GYN from a culture that uses this practice, are afraid of engaging with sexual partners that are not from their culture, and overall feel self-conscious about any potential situation that would expose their scars. Moreover, if they have to face the danger of deportation and they have daughters, women who have experienced FGM feel terror at the possibility that they will have to relocate the family in their home country.

Amara's attorney requested an immigration evaluation of extreme hardship to stop the deportation of this 45-year-old mother of two girls, eight and six years old. Amara migrated 24 years earlier from Burkina Faso. Amara underwent FGM at age four or five. She said that her mother refused to consent, so women from the village kidnapped her and her sister. After being captured, they forcefully circumcised Amara, brutally and without anesthesia. Amara said that these women kept her for three days, and she still remembers her terror. She said that the vaginal parts that they cut grew back again in a strange way. When she was 14 years old, her parents married her and, when her husband forced intercourse, she ended up in the hospital.

Her resulting injury was such that she regularly suffered during menstruation and intercourse and had several miscarriages. Amara thinks that it is a crime to submit a child to such a cruel tradition and she does not want her daughters to undergo this type of mutilation. She said that she came to understand that this tradition is part of the low status in which women are held in her culture and how women's feelings are not considered. She said her culture taught her to think of herself as only valuable when she was being useful to others and following the rules without complaining, which did not prepare her to live on her own, especially after her husband's death five years ago. Amara is under deportation proceedings and she is agonizing about the potential fate of her daughters if she takes them to live in Burkina Faso. Because her FGM happened without her mother's consent, Amara fears that she would have to supervise her daughters night and day, and still may fail to protect them. If deported, not only would she be going back to the place where she was physically mutilated, felt worthless as a human being, and lacked power or control over her life, but her daughters would be at risk of suffering the same fate. Amara raised her daughters to become independent, strong, assertive, and self-protective females who feel powerful and able to fulfill their dreams and to reach their potential. Her fear of deportation is also based on the belief that back in her country she would not be the strong woman that she was in the U.S. to continue parenting and protecting her daughters.

Interviewing and assessing examinees around their FGM experience requires a great deal of sensitivity, as revealing memories can be re-traumatizing and trigger deep shame. Victims not only feel shame about having undergone this practice, but also about reporting the subsequent complications, such as their sexuality problems or needing fertility procedures to have their children. The examiner may want to consider preparing some grounding techniques that are culturally appropriate to help the immigrant survivor in case she becomes overwhelmed with emotional material during the interview.

Domestic Violence

Domestic violence is the most common and insidious form of violence against women and girls (Kapoor, 2000). Nearly one in three adolescent girls aged 15–19 (84 million) worldwide who are in formal unions have suffered emotional, physical, or sexual violence at the hands of their husbands or partners (UNICEF, 2014). Countries in sub-Saharan Africa, South Asia, Latin America, and the Caribbean have the highest rates of intimate partner violence. Among the examples of violence against women (UNICEF, 2014), the following stand out:

• In India, Mozambique, Nepal, Pakistan, the United Republic of Tanzania, and Zambia, over 70 percent of girls and women named their current or former husbands or partners as the perpetrators of physical violence against them.

• 'Honor killings' have been reported in both Afghanistan and Pakistan.

• Afghanistan has laws to protect women, but family members of victims and perpetrators are barred from testifying against the perpetrators, thereby making intra-family violence, and forced and child marriage impossible to persecute (Amnesty International, 2015).

The fact that legislative bodies and law enforcement do not protect women, and in fact even write laws to de-criminalize violence against women, is very alarming. Women from many countries flee from domestic violence perpetrated by spouses, partners, or family members, because the law enforcement and judicial bodies fail to protect them and rather empower the abuser.

Implications for Immigration Evaluations

Immigrant women escaping from intimate partner violence in their countries or after their migration to the U.S. may apply for immigration relief based on this violence. Immigrant battered women often suffer from significant medical and psychological problems or disability resulting from the violence, and their limited access to healthcare aggravates their medical conditions. Luckily for the forensic evaluator, there are many resources dedicated to the evaluation of the psychological impact of this tragic form of violence against women, which will be reviewed in Chapter 5.

In addition to the range of psychological consequences of domestic violence for women and children, domestic violence has been implicated in poor health outcomes such as chronic disease, disability, somatic syndromes, injury, chronic pain, sexually transmitted diseases, gastrointestinal disorders, and changes in endocrine and immune functions (Breiding, Black, & Ryan, 2008). Direct and indirect injury due to domestic violence leads to long-term health problems even years after the battering has stopped.

Paulina, a 24-year-old woman from a rural town in Ukraine, married a 56-year-old American man after meeting him through a mail-order-bride agency followed by six months of correspondence and one in-person meeting. Paulina was looking for stability in her life and forming a family, after having been raised as an only child in a broken home and having had several bad romantic experiences. She felt safe taking her trip to the U.S. to marry her fiancée based on the excessively favorable marketing of this man done by the agency. This man was fun and charming until the moment they got married. From that moment on, he made it clear that he expected her to serve his every whim and be dutiful and submissive. He stated in clear terms that he was the master of his house and she was there to serve him. Paulina said that her husband's attitude shifted from Dr. Jekyll to Mr. Hyde. Paulina reported that the beatings would start for anything, such as not having fresh coffee, not ironing his shirts to his taste, or not washing the rugs to his specifications. She estimated that he beat her at least twice a week. In addition, there was jealousy, isolation, and psychological abuse. He threatened her with not filing for her visa application and sending her back to Ukraine. Paulina was able to report the abuse during a medical visit after her husband broke her jaw, and the doctor asked her husband to step out from the consulting room. Paulina was an immigrant-bride and the battering and psychological abuse amounted to extreme cruelty. Collateral documents provided evidence that she entered the marriage trustingly and with honorable intentions. Psychological assessment revealed that she met the criteria for post-traumatic stress disorder and major depression, and that her clinical presentation was consistent with having experienced stress of extreme proportions. She had the right to self-petition for residence in the U.S. through a VAWA visa without the help of her husband.

Examiners may encounter cases in which domestic violence is at the core of the immigration relief petition or is an additional victimization the examinee suffered or is still experiencing. The impact of the violence is aggravated when the immigrant victim lives under the stress of poor socioeconomic status, limited social and economic opportunities, or social discrimination (Hass, Dutton, & Orloff, 2000). If the examinee is a new arrival, she may lack a social network or English-language skills. Other individual differences that may be a source of discrimination (ability, age, ethnicity) can also be risk factors for intimate partner violence, create high levels of stress, and lessen resilience. Those aggravating factors, as well as previous trauma, rob the victim of resources to cope and multiply the impact of the violence, adding to the psychological sequelae (Lockhart & Mitchell, 2010).

Immigration evaluators may encounter cases of women fighting deportation due to fear of being the victim of honor killing or assault. Usually, in these cases of gender violence the fear for their life and shame is imposed on top of the psychological sequelae of the crime committed against them and that makes them dishonorable. Women may be have been determined to be disgraced in the eyes of their family or society, for reasons such as being raped or any sexual misconduct as determined by their moral codes, often where the woman was a victim. These brutal assaults and often humiliating socially sanctioned practices (Sidahmed, 2001) may constitute a realistic and frightening prospect for women from certain parts of the world. The examiner must carefully assess the country conditions and victim's exposure and background that makes the fear credible and terrifying.

Sexual Violence

Sexual violence against women and girls is in general a serious social problem and in some countries this problem is highly prevalent and insidious (Amnesty

International, 2015). Forms of sexual violence include rape, sexual assault, sexual slavery, exploitation, international trafficking of women and children, forced prostitution, and sexual harassment. For instance:

- In India, rape within marriage is still not recognized as a crime if the wife is over 15 years of age (Amnesty International, 2015).
- Islamic State (IS) forces in Syria and Iraq have killed Yezidi men and boys in execution-style killings, and abducted hundreds of Yezidi women and girls into slavery, forcing many to become 'wives' of IS fighters (Amnesty International, 2015).
- In Egypt, groups of men attacked and sexually assaulted women protesters in the streets around Cairo's Tahrir Square (Human Rights Watch, 2013).

Sexual violence and other forms of violence against women are a hideous symptom of cultures and societies that have failed to properly value women's role and traditional work, or provide opportunities for their education and employment (Tiefenbrun, 2002). Those social ills keep women marginalized and in a subordinated status. Some cultures and societies hold harmful stereotypes of women and condone all types of inequalities, discrimination, and violence against girls and women.

Implications for Immigration Evaluations

Asylum cases that involve sexual violence may emotionally challenge the examiner unaccustomed to the heinous actions the perpetrators inflict on their fellow human beings. These cases often suffer from lack of evidence about what they have gone through because perpetrators were seasoned sex offenders or were part of organized crime networks. The assessor may be in the best position to opine not only about the psychological damage but also the credibility of the victim.

CNN reported the case of a human trafficking activist who was a victim herself (Romo, 2015). Karla Jacinto lived in a small rural community in Mexico. Karla was lured at age 12 by a man who befriended her and convinced her to go with him. For three months, he was attentive and bought her clothes, chocolates, flowers, and shoes. Shortly thereafter, he made her captive and trained her into sex work, including what positions to use, how to talk to men, and how to treat them well to get more money. He took Karla on the road. Changing cities every few days in brothels, road-side motels, streets, and homes, Karla was sexually exploited, abused, and battered. Her trafficker was jealous and accused her of falling for the clients. Karla gave birth at age 15, and her trafficker used her daughter to control her even more by taking her baby away from her for a year. Karla was finally rescued in an anti-trafficking operation. She estimated that she was raped 43,200 times as she was forced to sexually serve 30 men a day, seven days a week. Karla testified before the U.S. Congress and her testimony was used as evidence in support of H.R. 515, or Megan's Law, that mandates U.S. authorities to share information when child sex offenders attempt to travel abroad. CNN went to great lengths to corroborate Karla's story before publishing, and they independently verified significant portions of her story. The article's author emphasized that he personally experienced how the clandestine nature of the human trafficking business makes it extremely hard for the victims to obtain evidence to corroborate their story.

When asking about a lifetime history of sexual violence, examiners need to remember that sexual violence can also be perpetrated against LGBQT individuals, boys, and men, as well as girls and women. The journey of migration to the U.S. is a particularly dangerous time for women and children who are vulnerable to being raped by any of the many unscrupulous people they may come into contact with. It is important to assess the cultural and social issues from the evaluee's background that may have provided a risk factor for sexual victimization. Risk issues include the role of shame in cultures that socialize boys to be hyper-masculine and that sexualize girls (Fontes & McCloskey, 2011), lack of sexual education, or being raised by relatives or others due to fragmentation of the family. There is literature documenting the risks and impact of re-victimization (Messman-Moore & Long, 2003), and this can help the examiner make a case for the psychological impact of the crime relevant to the visa application.

In evaluations for U visas, examiners may encounter cases of both men and women who may have been sexually abused or exploited in their jobs, or suffered date, acquaintance, or stranger sexual violence, or so-called corrective rape. Women and LGBTQ individuals are particularly at risk of sexual harassment, sexual assault, and rape (Bauer & Ramírez, 2010) in male-dominated workplaces where the abuse may be associated with a sexualized environment that devalues them. There are cases in which employers or supervisors require sexual favors and compliance with sexual demands as a condition of employment or job-related opportunities (Fitzgerald, Swan, & Fisher, 1995), taking advantage of the employee's desperate economic dependence on a job.

It is important to assess the obstacles that the victim encountered when trying to report the crime or seek help. Victims of sexual violence may be locked into relationships or kept captive, and they are unable to access systems of care or protection. Many victims are very hesitant to report the crime due to issues including fear of retribution, avoidance of the upsetting memories, fear of being re-victimized by the judicial system, fear of losing their social status, fear of damage to their reputation, fear of being labeled, or fear of having their gender identity or sexual orientation exposed. It is important to understand and report these obstacles and the debilitating effect of this type of violence in order to counteract any potential bias on the adjudicator's part about blaming the victim, questioning credibility, or being too horrified to connect emotionally.

Examiners need to take into consideration that, as hard as it may be for the victim to speak about those experiences in the evaluation, it will be harder to testify in IC about it. In the report, the examiner may explain from the clinical findings why the examinee may be fearful, hesitant, or unable to speak coherently about her past traumatic experiences in the courtroom because of self-protective mechanisms over which she has little control.

Child Marriage

Boys and girls worldwide are married before they reach their 18th birthday, with girls disproportionally comprising the majority of these victims.

* The marriage of girls is most common in South Asia and sub-Saharan Africa, but South Asia accounts for almost half (42 percent) of all child brides worldwide.
* The number of child marriages in India is one-third of the global total.
* Niger has the highest overall prevalence of child marriage in the world, but Bangladesh has the highest rate of marriage of girls below age 15 (UNICEF, 2013).

Even within the countries with very high rates of child brides, the level of risk is different depending on the region, ethnicity or cultural group, socioeconomic status, and the region's level of development (UNICEF, 2013). For instance, in Ethiopia the rate of child marriage is three times higher in Amhara (75 percent) than in Addis Ababa (26 percent), the capital; in West and Central Africa, Latin American, and the Caribbean, the prevalence of child marriage in rural areas is about twice the level found in urban cities. As a result, a detailed knowledge of the cultural context of the immigrant being assessed is especially important during these immigration evaluations.

Girls may be forced into marriages by their family in order to alleviate the family's poverty, compensate for a debt, in exchange for food or resources, to resolve a conflict with another family or their tribe, or because they are orphans (International Center for Research on Women, 2016; Steinhaus, Gregowski, Stevanovic Fenn, & Petroni, 2016). Sometimes girls are kidnapped and forced to marry the perpetrator; others are forced into marriages by traffickers. These girls are at a high risk of being exchanged or kept as work- or sex slaves (UN, 2013).

Girls and women escaping from child marriage or having been a child bride forced into marriage are a protected group who may receive asylum in the U.S. on account of this human rights violation. In addition, escaping from forced child marriage or being forced into marriage as a child is very relevant when this has made the woman vulnerable to sex trafficking, domestic violence, workplace abuse, or other victimization that qualifies for a humanitarian visa.

Implications for Immigration Evaluations

Examiners need to collect information regarding the age and level of development when the marriage was forced, whether her consent was sought or not, family poverty, being in a rural community or culture where this practice was normalized, whether there were other wives, and all types of abuse she may have suffered. Information about the groom is also relevant, particularly factors such as the groom's age and social status differential with the examinee. Even when the examinee was not brutally coerced and when many aspects of the forced marriage seemed favorable, the negative consequences can be significant and pervasive. Marrying a young girl may rob her of an important developmental period in which she should be allowed to grow psychologically before taking on adult responsibilities.

Girls who marry young can become socially isolated, especially if they are cut-off from family, peers, and other social supports, have limited opportunities for education, and have low employment skills (International Women's Health Coalition, n.d.). Due to their young age, social naiveté, and underdeveloped judgment, child brides are often unable to effectively negotiate safer sex and are highly vulnerable to sexually transmitted infections, including HIV, and early pregnancies. Child brides usually end up with many children to care for while still young and are also less likely to receive proper medical pre-natal care, despite the fact that they and their babies are at high risk because these women are usually not physically mature enough to give birth easily. Child brides are also vulnerable to domestic violence, because they are in a subordinate role with their spouses and their spouses' family. The chain reaction of all these disadvantages that she will carry throughout her lifetime (and will extend through generations) can also be explained in the report, as it is a powerful argument for fully understanding her plight. Documenting this information to explain to the adjudicator the examinee's need to be protected so she can heal physically and psychologically is one of the most important tasks for the examiner.

Language

The most authoritative catalog of the world's languages, Ethnologue (www.ethnologue.com), lists 7,099 distinct known living languages. Languages are developed to communicate within a community and learning language is thus a social task that is highly dependent on context and culture (Evans & Levinson, 2009). As linguists and psychoanalysts have emphasized, language shapes the way we process our thoughts, feelings, and perceptions. Language not only shows the person's intelligence, education, and socialization, but also their personality and state of mind (Weiner, 2014b). Language is a large part of who we are, how we project ourselves, and connect with others.

We make a number of judgments based on the examinee's use of language. We pay attention to the characteristics of the language, such as vocabulary, fluency, and grammar, because they give us cues about the individual's tendency to be pedantic, profane, informal, humble, condescending, or solicitous (Weiner, 2014b). As clinicians, we are used to assessing our evaluees' wordiness, cryptic style, or brevity and concreteness, as signs of their engagement and level of trust. However, with immigrants from other cultures, we need to revise this understanding. Regarding non-verbal communications, we also need to expand our frame of reference in order to understand diverse modes of expression that immigrants may utilize.

Because we will be exploring a potential history of trauma, we want to take into consideration that the examinee's logic, reason, and coherence may be compromised when speaking about difficult subjects and we want to have a culturally appropriate strategy to deal with this eventuality. However, the examiner's job is to anchor the story of the examinee in a psychological frame while portraying the story of the examinee in his or her own words (Salton, 2017). Balancing those two goals demand from the examiner attention to both the content and details of the story, as well as the psychological narrative that accompanied the relating of the event or crime (directly linked to the visa application) then and now.

Limited English-Language Proficiency

It is important to take into consideration the significant impact that limitations in proficiency with the English language and limited literacy has on the lives of immigrant respondents. Depending on the accommodations that may exist in their community, this limitation may interfere with their acculturation, their employment, and their ability to interact with community services. Additionally, language barriers can exist when communication with service institutions such as children's schools, physicians, and police are required. The immigrant's ability to understand critical documents can be compromised in activities such as contracts to rent a house or buy a car, as well as their ability in the workplace to read guidelines and to understand their salary details and benefits. Immigrants may need help with interpretation or translation, which sometimes is done by well-meaning but less-than-ideal people, such as their children, or not so well-meaning individuals such as employers and supervisors. In any case, chances are high that those interpreters fail to fully convey the meaning of the communication. These experiences can be very frustrating for immigrants and can be the cause of extremely distressing experiences. This limitation may have caused the immigrant to be exploited, manipulated, or robbed. Exploring these potential events may help to understand a number of difficulties the examinee may have had seeking information, better conditions, or failing to question bad advice.

Limited English proficiency also makes it difficult to seek help or protections related to the crimes committed against immigrants (Kandel & Parrado, 2005; Qaundt et al., 2006). Language isolation creates a barrier to an immigrant's ability to voice complaints or report abuse when living in the host country. It is important to inquire about these experiences, their impact, and their willingness to or comfort using an interpreter in forensic mental health evaluations.

Examiners may need to specifically assess lack of language proficiency in certain situations. Licensed psychologists are authorized to submit a Form N-648, Medical Certification for Disability Exceptions, on behalf of an applicant. The immigrant may request an exemption for the English-language requirement and take the Civics test in their native language. Another option is to apply for a Medical Disability Exceptions to English and Civics, in which the person provides evidence that he or she is unable to comply with these requirements because of a physical or developmental disability or a mental impairment (USCIS Policy Manual, 2017). In these cases, a psychological evaluation describing the examinee's specific impairment is necessary.

> Marta was a 65-year-old woman from Bolivia who has been in the U.S. for 45 years. She has three U.S. citizen children, five grandchildren, and three great-grandchildren. She has never been in trouble with the law and is an esteemed member of her religious and civil community. She only finished third grade of elementary school in her own country, and in the U.S. Marta has worked hard and did not further her studies. She works from midnight until 6 a.m. in a department store, putting the clothes and items stranded all over the store by customers back on their hangers, racks, and shelves. Marta has her U.S. residency but wants to obtain her citizenship based on the awareness of a growing anti-immigrant sentiment in the U.S. However, Marta does not think she can pass the naturalization exam. She had trouble reading and her memory was impaired after a car crash in which she suffered a concussion. She also does not speak or understand English. A neuropsychological evaluation in this case was needed to address Marta's limitations in order to request a waiver for the Civics exam. If the results of her reading, comprehension capacities, memory skills, and executive capacity supports her claims, Marta may submit this report to request accommodations, a waiver, or exception depending on her needs.

Using Interpreters

When working with immigrants, it is almost inevitable that we encounter examinees who do not share our language or languages. In the words of Lisa Fontes (2017, para. 12), 'When examinees do not speak the clinician's preferred language, the burden is on the clinician to adapt and accommodate – just as we would do to a client's age or disability.' The use of interpreters in mental health has been a necessity for a long time, because there are not sufficient bilingual and culturally diverse clinicians and our ethical standards mandate that we serve our examinees preferably in the language of their choice (American Psychological Association, 2003). An examiner who lacks linguistic and cultural understanding runs the risk of missing important aspects of an examinee's issues, including their notions around mental health symptoms, which may lead to a misdiagnosis or normalizing a mental health problem (Alegria, Atkins, Farmer, Slaton & Stelk, 2010).

The need to offer the examinee a choice of language is important even with examinees who speak English, if this is not their native language. Given the wide variety of languages that immigrants and refugees may use, it is important for the forensic assessor to develop relationships with interpreters, create a database of translated documents, and train in the manner in which communication with our immigrant examinees through an interpreter can be productive, comfortable, and effective. These steps are essential to a successful practice in forensic immigration evaluations, but will most importantly prevent mistakes, frustration, and burn-out on the part of the assessor.

Most examiners feel apprehensive about working with an interpreter in general, and especially with immigrant examinees who may need to communicate traumatic experiences. For some assessors, the decision to work with an interpreter may not be easy and they overprepare; for others the decision can be exciting and they may underprepare. Either way, what matters is to have the right preparation and to understand that it is a learning process and, over time, it usually becomes an enriching learning experience.

Similarly, for the examinee, using an interpreter can be very intimidating and it constitutes a leap of faith (Tribe & Sanders, 2003). One's native language carries a great deal of emotional attachment, since it is part of our identity and it has been part of our life experiences and internal dialogue. Many immigrants and refugees may have been silenced by authoritarian regimes, oppressive cultural values, or plain xenophobia in their host country. Having to speak through an interpreter may resemble these limitations about being heard and expressing their own voice. All these issues need to be taken into consideration by the examiner and, when appropriate, discussed to alleviate any concerns that may interfere with the immigrant's engagement in the evaluation or testimony.

Because a language is not just a means of expression, but also a form of thinking and experiencing, it is not unusual that individuals who are bilingual manage to use language as a tool to modulate their emotions. For instance, some may prefer to speak in their native language about intimate subjects, because they feel more in touch with the emotional aspects of the story (Guttenfreund, 1990), while others may want to speak in English or their second language when they want an emotional distance from distressing material that can be overwhelming (Marcos, 1988). The examiner needs to manage the affects of both the examinee and the interpreter in order to maintain a stable and grounded environment that is not re-traumatizing for the examinee or vicariously traumatizing for the interpreter (Salton, 2017). Table 2.1 offers guidance on using interpreters.

Table 2.1 Recommendations When Using Interpreters

1. Find out the examinee's first language and particular dialect and any other languages he or she may speak fluently ahead of the evaluation session. The first or native language should be your first choice for an interpreter. Give priority to an interpreter of the same nationality or cultural group. Another issue is to match on age and gender depending on the issues to be discussed and the culture, if possible. If you do not have much referral information, a telephone interpreter can be utilized to obtain this information in a very concrete manner in order to have enough information to hire a professional interpreter.

2. Avoid telephone interpreters and, whenever possible, try to use a certified interpreter. Give preference to those bicultural interpreters with experience or training in mental health interpretation. Make sure that the interpreter does not have a dual role with the evaluee.

3. Do not use translators of convenience and do not ask the examinee to bring their own translator. Never use family members. The most effective interpreter is one who behaves, acts, and appears neutral.

4. You can find a professional interpreter at interpreting agencies or by asking in the local courts or at the embassy. If you find one you liked working with, develop a good and trusting relationship with this person.

5. The interpreter needs to integrate verbal and non-verbal communications within the cultural context. Needs high proficiency in both languages, and to know the ethics of both interpretation and the assessment (you need to tell him or her about evaluation ethics).

6. Schedule at least twice the amount of time you usually need for a regular evaluative session in order to accommodate translation.

7. You need to have a pre-meeting session, so schedule the interpreter to arrive earlier or meet before the evaluative session. During this pre-meeting session: (a) familiarize the interpreter with your work, (b) explain specifically the goals you are trying to accomplish during the appointment with the examinee, (c) describe the methods you will use, (d) explain areas to be covered, including sensitive topics, (e) discuss attitude of the interpreter and potential problem areas, including any technical terms that may pose a problem, (f) emphasize need for accuracy, (g) emphasize the need for confidentiality regarding what is going to transpire. In evaluations involving psychological trauma, educate the translator about the intensity of the evaluation.

8. Your interpreter is also a source of information and can tell you about cultural matters relevant to the examinee and to the strategies and methods you are planning to use.

9. Consider moving the furniture around for a three-way conversation in which everyone can see everyone else. You will talk to the examinee and not to the interpreter [or the interpreter can sit behind the examinee and act as his or her voice and talk in first person].

10. You need to choose the style of interpretation, whether to know only the gist of what the examinee said or every detail, depending on your goals.

11. You may not want to have the interpreter formulate any questions you did not ask, unless he or she is a mental health professional and seeks approval from you.

12. Remember that having an interpreter as a mediator makes you dependent on another person, and this alters the dynamic of the interactions. Therefore, make clear to the interpreter the strategies you may need to use if you feel that you need to regain control of the meeting.

13. Do not leave the interpreter alone with the examinee at any time. Even when they are honorable, interpreters are put in a very difficult position when this happens.

14. Do not expect all meanings and thoughts to be conveyed perfectly. Language is not a set of formulas and words with meanings associated, but a whole way of conceptualizing. Do not become impatient with the interpreter if they take longer than it seemed was necessary.

15. Allow the interpreter and examinee to introduce themselves, and then re-introduce the interpreter in your own words. Tell the examinee that the interpreter is independent, is not there to make any evaluations, has no decision power and is bound by confidentiality policy.

16. Speak as if the examinee is understanding you, use a normal tone of voice, use genuine facial expressions, be careful with gestures because they may be offensive or trigger posttraumatic reactions.

17. Remember that you need to slow down your pace. If you speak for too long this makes it hard for the interpreter to remember, but if you speak in too short bursts the thought becomes fragmented.

18. Try not to use any technical language. Avoid using proverbs and sayings. Avoid using double negatives. Avoid leading questions, try to let the examinee use her or his own words.

19. Pay attention to the examinee's non-verbal behavior and paralinguistic behavior, including cries, laughter, sighs, stuttering, reactions, gestures and facial expressions, take note to clarify at some point. If the examinee looks confused try to determine what is going on immediately instead of later.

20. Provide sufficient breaks during the session.

21. Do not discuss with the interpreter issues that do not require translation.

22. Spend a few minutes with the interpreter after the interview and ask the interpreter his or her impressions of the meeting. You can also clarify cultural issues and seek meaning for anything that was not clear during the meeting.

23. Allow the interpreter to provide any feedback about your approach or attitude, even if you do not agree with him or her. Discuss your own observations of the interpreter's performance.

24. Give the interpreter ahead of time any written material for the examinee that needs to be translated (consent to the evaluation, confidentiality statement, etc.). You may also consider another interpreter to do this if you want independent sources of information or to preserve confidentiality for the examinee.

25. In general, do not ask the interpreter to interpret large inventories (above 20 items). This method is not reliable. Try to find the translated version of the test.

Source: Adapted from Tribe and Sanders (2003); Salton (2017); Warrier et al. (2005).

Use of Translations

Wherever possible, it is important to have key documents (e.g., confidentiality, releases of information) translated into the language of the examinee (American Psychological Association, 2017). Psychological tests can be found in a number of languages, and they can become an important part of a forensic examiner's armamentarium (see Chapters 9 and 10). When giving the examinees translated documents, make sure the language is simple and devoid of too much formal or legal language, but faithful to the original in English. Give the examinee the translation along with the original English that you use with English-speaking examinees, so they can compare or ask someone to compare them. Allow the evaluee to take it home to consult with someone before signing and to keep a copy for themselves after signing.

Religion

Religious intolerance and discrimination has been pervasive in many countries, and authorities can be either complicit or fail to combat it. For example (Amnesty International, 2015):

- Blasphemy laws in Pakistan and Indonesia repress religious liberties and are linked to vigilante violence, with law enforcement failing to protect the victims.
- Sri Lanka has experienced violence against Muslims and Christians carried out by armed groups, and police have failed to protect them or to investigate incidents.
- Ethnic Tibetans continue to face discrimination and restrictions on their rights to freedoms of thought, conscience and religion, expression, association, and peaceful assembly in China, including being shot by police in the Sichuan Province when a crowd gathered to protest the detention of a village leader.

When evaluating whether an immigrant suffered discrimination on the basis of religious affiliation, examiners need to consider that religion and spiritual orientations convey not only the belief system but also ritual practices, codes of conduct, and other types of responsibilities (Brabender & Mihura, 2016). Immigration evaluators may need to pay attention to religion and spirituality as a significant part of a person's identity. This is an identity that, depending on the degree of adherence, may involve significant life experiences and perspectives that have been found to increase levels of health and wellbeing (Maselko & Kubzansky, 2006). Attacks to this aspect of one's identity can be extremely distressing and psychologically disorganizing.

Strengths, Resilience, and Hardiness

We want to briefly discuss that the ADDRESSING matrix is also a source of strength, resilience, and hardiness that is important to take into consideration in our immigration evaluations. Individual differences, culture and ethnic heritage are a wellspring of benefits that we also want to understand and integrate in our conceptualization of the immigrant's life story and psychological landscape. Given the right supports and conditions, the immigrant's behavioral functioning and wellbeing can increase as a result of migration (Pumariega, Rothe, & Pumariega, 2005). A strong work ethic, aspirations, desire to be law-abiding citizens, healthy intact families, ethnic pride, a cohesive community of fellow immigrants from the same country of origin, strong family ties, and a sense of family obligation are among the many characteristics that we have found in immigrants and refugees. These are the forces that have made a country of immigrants like the U.S. outstanding.

In a study of 292 unaccompanied immigrant minors in the U.S. (Sabet et al., 2016), resilience was found in their focus on a better future, motivation to get ahead, faith, returning to their country, being with their families, and helping others. Research has documented that immigrants have positive values regarding education and family support (Suárez-Orozco & Carhill, 2008). Immigrants have been found to be interested and quick in learning English (Foner, 2002). Young immigrants entering the U.S. educational system have shown better attendance, higher grades, greater engagement with their teachers and school, and a closer attachment to school than second-generation youth (Colls & Marks, 2012; Fuligni, 2001).

Adult immigrants have positive attitudes about hard work, are driven, and have high aspirations (American Psychological Association, 2012a). Although immigrants suffer from discrimination, social oppression, and systematic inequities, they trust U.S. institutions (Lopez & Taylor, 2010). While they value collectivism, immigrants work toward self-sufficiency (Balgopal, 2000). First-generation immigrants have numerous positive outcomes when compared with peers from their native countries or American-born people (Vega & Amaro, 1994). All-in-all, immigrants bring richness and complexity to the fabric of our society, and when we help them reach their potential we are also enriched and privileged.

Chapter 3

Ethical Standards and the Assessment of Credibility and Malingering

Let's start with the question in many people's minds when the issue of psychological evaluations for Immigration Court arises. As stated by Morgan (2007, p. 26): 'Is it ethical practice or advocacy?' Clinicians engaged in this field will be confronted with this question by other professionals, attorneys representing the U.S. government in immigration cases, and even lay-people. Surely, every professional who practices in this field has deeply considered where the boundary lies between these two issues and how to balance one's practice of assessments in areas of social justice without falling into unethical behavior.

The response that fits better our approach to this dilemma is that it is both. Lustig (2007) argues that advocacy and ethical behavior are not opposites. This means the examiner can be impartial and fair without being insensitive. Pope and Vasquez (2016) argue that we do not live in a vacuum, and when faced with ethical dilemmas we should think about the meaning of our professional actions and the ethics of social justice. Specifically, Pope and Vasquez state that we should

> open our eyes to how discrimination, hatred, injustice, beatings, slavery, jail, starvation, torture, or genocide – based on factors like race, religion, culture, gender, sexual orientation, politics – affect us, our clients, our supervisees, and the world we live and work in. We search for the most ethical response to social injustice. We don't shrug our shoulders and turn away.
>
> (p. 5)

In the field of forensic evaluations, advocacy means that we stand behind our opinion once we have reached it to the best of our knowledge and skill. In immigration cases our opinion, obtained through ethical methods, could serve to support the ability of individuals who meet the law requirements to obtain immigration relief. There is nothing professionally unethical about this. Mental health evaluators can be objective and caring by practicing the benevolent neutrality (Evans, 2005) mentioned earlier in this book.

Mental health professionals are bound by several stringent ethical guidelines and standards that ensure that, if we practice within these parameters, our work can withstand scrutiny and adhere closely to the truth. Rather than reviewing them here, the reader is advised to become very familiar with these guidelines pertinent to their profession from the following list. This list includes many, but not all, the guidelines that educate us about the relevant issues and potential themes that may come up in evaluations for Immigration Court. Of these, the APA *Ethical Principles of Psychologists* (American Psychological Association, 2017), especially the assessment section and the Code of Conduct, and the APA Specialty Guidelines for Forensic Psychology (American Psychological Association, 2013) provide the most relevant information for the practice of forensic evaluations in Immigration Court (IC). All the following codes can be found at the website of Ken Pope (www.kspope.com/ethcodes/index.php):

- American Academy of Child & Adolescent Psychiatry (AACAP): Practice Parameter for the Assessment & Treatment of Children and Adolescents with Posttraumatic Stress Disorder (PTSD).
- AACAP: Practice Parameter for Child & Adolescent Forensic Evaluations.
- American Academy of Clinical Neuropsychology (AACN): Policy on the Use of Non-Doctoral-Level Personnel in Conducting Clinical Neuropsychological Evaluations.
- AACN: Policy Statement on the Presence of Third Party Observers in Neuropsychological Assessment.
- AACN: Practice Guidelines for Neuropsychological Assessment and Consultation.
- AACN: Position of the American Academy of Clinical Neuropsychology on Ethical Complaints Made Against Clinical Neuropsychologists During Adversarial Proceedings.
- American Academy of Pediatrics: The Evaluation of Sexual Abuse in Children.
- American Academy of Psychiatry & Law: AAPL Practice Guideline for the Forensic Psychiatric Evaluation of Competence to Stand Trial.
- American Academy of Psychiatry & Law: AAPL Practice Guideline for the Forensic Evaluation of Psychiatric Disability.
- American Academy of Psychiatry & Law: Ethical Guidelines for the Practice of Forensic Psychiatry.
- American Board of Examiners in Clinical Social Work: Professional Development & Practice Competencies in Clinical Social Work.
- American Board of Independent Medical Examiners: Guidelines of Conduct.
- American College of Legal Medicine (ACLM): Guidelines on the Ethical Conduct of the Expert Witness.
- American College Personnel Association: Statement of Ethical Principles and Standards.
- American Counseling Association: 2014 Code of Ethics.
- American Mental Health Counselors Association: Code of Ethics.
- American Psychological Association (APA): Ethical Principles of Psychologists and Code of Conduct.

- APA: Guidelines for Assessment of and Intervention with Persons with Disabilities.
- APA: Guidelines for Psychological Practice with Girls and Women.
- APA: Guidelines for Psychological Practice with Lesbian, Gay, and Bisexual Clients.
- APA: Guidelines for Psychological Practice with Older Adults.
- APA: Guidelines on Multicultural Education, Training, Research, Practice, and Organizational Change for Psychologists.
- APA: Record Keeping Guidelines.
- APA: Report of the American Psychological Association Presidential Task Force on Psychological Ethics and National Security.
- APA: Resolution on Appropriate Therapeutic Responses to Sexual Orientation.
- APA: Rights and Responsibilities of Test Takers: Guidelines and Expectations.
- APA: Specialty Guidelines for Forensic Psychology.
- Association for Lesbian, Gay, Bisexual, and Transgender Issues in Counseling (ALGBTIC) Competencies for Counseling with Lesbian, Gay, Bisexual, Queer, Questioning, Intersex and Ally Individuals.
- National Association of Social Workers: Code of Ethics.
- National Board for Certified Counselors: Code of Ethics.
- National Latina/o Psychological Association (NLPA): Guidelines for Mental Health Professionals Working with Unaccompanied Asylum-Seeking Minors.
- National Organization of Forensic Social Work: Code of Ethics.
- World Professional Association for Transgender Health: Standards of Care for the Health of Transsexual, Transgender, & Gender-Nonconforming People.

In addition to seeking guidance in these guidelines, we need to develop what Pope and Vasquez have termed 'ethical intelligence' (2016, p. 2). The authors argue that ethical norms cannot replace the continuous critical questioning and awareness of our ethical responsibilities, which should inform our practice at all times. Because ethical guidelines could never cover all the potential complexities of difficult cases and, because we cannot practice clinically on the defensive, we need to develop an ethical decision-making approach. This approach is particularly relevant in IC evaluations because of the risks, complexities, and uniqueness of the cases. The area of practice of IC evaluations is also poorly regulated and, both in the legal and clinical arena, there is a minefield of blurred situations. More importantly, in immigration work we deal with a population that is usually vulnerable and often uninformed regarding the legality and ethics of the professionals serving them – thus we need to exercise the highest standards of practice and ethics in order to protect them.

Finally, mental health practitioners need to be familiar with the state board regulations for their profession that have been developed for the state in which they practice. This issue may be somewhat ambiguous. IC evaluators need to have a state license and they need to see the examinee where they hold their license and within the professional activities defined by their license. Some immigration evaluators may have examinees who are in detention and are transferred to a jail in a different jurisdiction before the evaluation is completed, or may have clients who live in another state, or the examiner may need to testify in courts located in a different state. Many state boards have regulations regarding what forensic activities, and in which conditions, can out-of-state expert witnesses do and not do, sometimes including that the expert acquire a license in such state. Unfortunately, we do not have a standard set of rules to cover each situation, so examiners need to painstakingly take the time to evaluate the regulations in the state where they may conduct a forensic activity in order to remain within their licensing obligations. Failure to do so may incur charges of practicing without a license, which could result in civil and criminal penalties, and even possibly voiding of malpractice coverage.

Ethical Minefields in Immigration Evaluations

Although most of the ethical codes and practice standards that we follow in our clinical practice are applicable in forensic evaluations for IC, there are significant differences that appear when compared with other fields of mental health practice.

Practicing Without Proper Training

The newness of this field presents the following significant problems:

1. limited empirical and scholar writings;
2. very few mental health professionals have received adequate training as part of their graduate education;
3. little guidance to consumers;
4. poor regulations to the field; and
5. few mentors and supervisors available.

Therefore, clinicians may be tempted, for various reasons, to enter this IC forensic evaluation without enough preparation. They may see this booming field as a potential way to expand their practices or they may be moved by a deep desire to work on issues of social justice, or attorneys and their immigrant clients may pressure a mental health practitioner to take on this role. This field of practice should not be taken lightly, because the weight of expert opinion in IC is very high and requires a specialized competence. In fact, immigration attorneys and their clients do not usually have deep knowledge of the expertise required for these IC evaluations, the differences between a clinician and a forensic expert, or the various areas of specialization required for specific forensic IC evaluations.

The alert forensic assessor is aware of the litigious nature of forensic work in IC and understands that there are important differences between clinical and forensic assessment (Greenberg & Shuman, 1997). In addition to the training and experience, forensic evaluators are *not* the examinee's therapist, which is precisely a foundation for their ability to be objective. Many well-meaning mental health providers have been drawn into complex and contentious legal matters, making expert opinions without a proper basis that are readily and successfully attacked by skillful USCIS attorneys and IC judges. Such experiences are often painful and humiliating for the treatment providers and may lead to a loss of status in the professional community and even to malpractice suits. Even worse, it can undermine the credibility of an otherwise worthy application for asylum and rob the asylum seeker and the attorney of the quality expert opinion they deserved. It is our advice that mental health treatment providers always ask on intake whether the client is involved with or anticipates being involved with a legal matter related to their psychological state in IC. If this is the case, we strongly advise developing a policy regarding the forensic assessor's willingness to participate in such matters, to weigh the implications for the therapy process, and to only become involved in such matters with extensive and rigorous training and supervision in forensic assessment.

To conduct IC evaluations, a good education includes familiarity with the clinical issues of culturally diverse populations, cross-cultural psychology and psychopathology, the plight of undocumented immigrants and refugees, diagnostic and assessment methods, trauma psychology and stress responses, acculturation, immigration law, the intersection of legal and judicial arenas with psychological knowledge, and good writing and testifying skills. It is good practice in immigration evaluations for the new forensic assessor to be supervised at the outset and to have a mentor at hand for challenging situations. We worry after seeing in professional listservs some students and clinicians asking for tips or an evaluation template to do immigration evaluations while acknowledging complete ignorance about the field. Mental health professionals are advised to not practice outside of their areas of competence, because it does a tremendous disservice to the clients and the profession, and leads to liability and licensing board actions.

A correlate of this concern with practicing outside the area of expertise relates also to the use of assessment methods and techniques for which the examiner has not been properly trained. Psychological tests and methods such as bonding evaluations, structured interviews, neuropsychological methods, and risk assessments have protocols of administration, coding, and interpretation that require specific knowledge, skills, and qualifications. Forensic examiners need to make sure that they use techniques they are qualified to perform and refer to another professional for information they are not competent to obtain themselves but need to incorporate in their evaluations.

Clinicians who want to enter the field are better prepared when they have training and experience closely related to the immigration field. For instance, competence with forensic psychological evaluations and work with trauma and diverse populations is an asset from which a clinician can build the other skills required for immigration evaluations. On top of this foundation, clinicians can acquire specialized knowledge by attending workshops, lectures, reading articles and books on the subject, and finding a supervisor or consultant. More and more of these services are becoming available and accessible as the field expands.

Forensic examiners in the immigration field, which is characteristically complex, constantly changing, and deals with a very vulnerable population, will benefit from having a consultant or consultation group of professionals proficient in the field of immigration evaluations that can provide helpful feedback. In particular, it is important to also confer with a consultant who is culturally competent and, whenever possible, speaks the language of the examinee in order to understand the nuances of the language and culture. Much can be said about the effects of desensitization and burn-out that can compromise clinical judgment. Pursuing and following the feedback of a peer consultant is one of the factors taken into consideration by experts when having to determine if the mental health professional complied with the standard of care (Pope & Vasquez, 2016).

Notification

Because many of the immigrants who are referred for a forensic evaluation have minimal experience with forensic psychology or even with clinical evaluations or therapy, it is always a good idea to go beyond the basics when explaining our credentials and experience, the purpose of the assessment, the nature of the evaluator's role, the limits of confidentiality, and that a forensic evaluation is not psychological treatment. The applicant needs to know that the report will be given to his immigration attorney and, at the attorney's discretion, it could be released to other professionals involved in the case. Examinees need to have an opportunity to read and correct any errors on the report and discuss inconsistencies during the feedback session. However, the forensic examiner's client is the attorney who retained him or her and the report goes to the attorney. It is the evaluee's attorney or legal representative who decides if a copy of the report will be given to the applicant. If the evaluee decides to change attorneys, which often happens, their new attorney will request from the previous attorney the entire file, which would include the expert report.

The IC applicant needs to know that the report will include the story that they tell us, in all detail, and the clinical interpretation we make of their emotional state. Sometimes victims may not be ready to have others hear the most horrific forms of abuse they endured, as victims may be overwhelmed by shame, which may be a symptom of their posttraumatic state (Herman, 2011). In particular, because in some cultures the process of immigration relief is of interest to the entire family, they may want to protect a parent, spouse, child, or someone they love dearly from hearing the painful experiences they suffered. Examinees may need to work through these concerns before they feel comfortable to fully engage in the evaluation process.

The examinee also needs to know the level of involvement the examiner may have over time, since the case may stretch for several years. They need to know about any future meetings or charges that may occur, or updates to the evaluation if too much time passes between the evaluation and application or court hearing. They need to understand if expert testimony is required, whether this is charged separately and if waiting court time, preparation, and travel is charged. They need to have all information to be able to contact us, and we have to make ourselves accessible to the attorneys who hired us.

Examiners need to go over carefully with the examinee in his or her native language, whenever possible, the fee for the evaluation and any other charges and payment procedures, such as whether credit cards are accepted, charges for missed appointments, how the billing is conducted and if collections agencies are commonly used in your practice (Knapp & VandeCreek, 2001).

Confidentiality

The confidentiality in immigration evaluations may be more stringent than for other types of forensic evaluations, because for most of these types of immigration relief the applicant is a victim of a crime. Confidentiality is built into the laws of immigration processes. For instance, the Department of Homeland Security (DHS) is obligated to keep VAWA and U visa applications confidential, and information about a case can only be accessed by individuals authorized for a legitimate, statutorily prescribed purpose (Orloff, 2014). Examiners are wise to do the same.

It follows that mental health professionals working with these cases also need to abide by a strict level of confidentiality. This highest level of care is rooted in the risk that the abuser or someone linked to the perpetrator may try to find the victim to intimidate or seek revenge, or to interfere with the victim's ability to obtain immigration relief. In VAWA cases, victims are allowed to apply while still living with the abusive husband. In cases of asylum, trafficking, or labor criminal activity, the abusers may be highly organized and influential, and may have means and resources to silence the victim who is a witness in a criminal case against them. In these and other cases, these abusers may pose a grave risk to the safety of the victims, their families, and the professionals working with the victims. DHS personnel are not allowed to contact the abuser or the relatives of the abuser in these forensic cases. In fact, if the perpetrator of the crime or any of his or her family members provide information to the DHS about the crime victim, the DHS is precluded from relying solely on this information to initiate or take any part of an enforcement action against the victim (Rosenberg, 2006). Mental health providers should consider that perpetrators do not have the best interest of the victim at heart and be sure to protect the applicant and themselves.

Confidentiality also includes not accusing other people in crimes unrelated to the focus of the immigration relief, such as mentioning who specifically brought, smuggled, or paid to bring the examinee to the U.S., because, in addition to the fact that this is hearsay, it has possible legal ramifications. We also need to be careful about discussing motivations for the behavior of abusers when we have no real basis to determine their inner motives. We can write what the examinee believed was the cause of the words and actions that the abuser used, reflecting their motivation (e.g., racial slurs or using intimidation only with women), but lacking this information our opinion may appear biased since we have not personally evaluated the perpetrator.

For those forensic examiners who in other aspects of their clinical practice are regulated by the Health Insurance Portability and Accountability Act of 1996 (HIPAA), the Privacy Rule's requirements apply to these immigration evaluations as well. This means that all uses and disclosures of protected health information, regardless of the purpose for which the protected health information was created, is subject to privacy requirements. Understand that confidentiality still applies in a forensic practice, and information about the examinee is to be released only pursuant to an authorization or by state or Federal law (Vanderpool, 2016). With this said, when retained by an immigration attorney, IC expert reports may be subject to attorney work product privilege and therefore shielded from discovery.

Even though the relationship of the examiner and the evaluee is not a doctor–patient relationship, courts, state licensing boards, and professional associations regulate forensic activities and provision of expert testimony. Examiners are wise to study and understand their role, duties, and expectations from IC, licensing boards, and professional associations. Vanderpool (2016) recommends three steps to protect your practice: (1) ensure your compliance with state laws, especially licensure and expert witness activities; (2) discuss your concerns about the case with the attorney that retained you; and (3) confirm your professional liability insurance policy covers all of the forensic services you wish to provide.

Professional Boundaries

Although the issue of professional boundaries is extensively addressed in professional ethical guidelines, these are additional issues in immigration evaluations that examiners need to consider. In certain cultures, the boundaries between professionals and their clients are much more flexible. In fact, in many societies, people are used to conducting business with friends and family, or seek the professionals they need through family or friend networks. In some cultures, people may greet the professionals who serve them with hugs and kisses, bear gifts to their appointments, and, after their case is resolved, they may want to offer gifts, dinners, and even invitations to the celebration party. In some other cases, they may want to meet outside the office, such as at a café. Some evaluations outside the office are appropriate, such as home visits in cases involving the evaluation of children (e.g., extreme hardship) or when the applicant is extremely incapacitated or incarcerated in a detention center; the examiner always needs to be careful about protecting confidentiality and the professional relationship. Some respondents may offer to provide services or to engage in business with the examiner, as a way of showing appreciation or because they sincerely get along with you, but this is likely to be inappropriate. Examiners need to refer to the APA Ethics Code 6.05 (American Psychological Association 2017): 'the acceptance of goods, services, or other nonmonetary remuneration from clients/patients in return for psychological services [can occur only if]: (1) it is not clinically contraindicated, and (2) the resulting arrangement is not exploitative' (p. 9).

While it is very hard to say no to examinees who are eager to thank us because they may feel offended, rejected, and invalidated, the examiner needs to be careful to not let the boundaries erode. Examinees may need a thorough explanation of the way professional relationships function in the U.S., as well as our Code of Ethics. They also need to hear of the immense satisfaction we derive from our work and their success, without the need for other demonstrations of their gratitude.

Credibility and Credible Evidence

Immigration judges must consider the totality of circumstances when making a credibility determination (8 U.S.C. § 1158(b)(1)(B)(iii)). It is the responsibility of the applicant and his or her legal representative to present a clear and consistent case in court or to the decision-making body. However, collecting evidence of the criminal activity is extremely hard for victims who are struggling to survive or maintain emotional stability in the midst of significant abuse, especially because most perpetrators go to lengths to protect themselves. Immigration cases can be denied immigration relief when they are found to lack credibility, especially in cases that rely heavily on the victim's testimony and have minimal relevant collateral evidence. Issues such as inconsistency, implausibility, and vagueness of account may be weighted heavily by IC adjudicators in the asylee's testimony or the applicant's affidavit. When there is doubt regarding the veracity of the applicant's story, the IC adjudicators look at the rest of the evidence. Collateral evidence that is extremely general, such as a professional letter without basis for the opinion, or a general affidavit about the topic (but not about the applicant), country conditions found in Wikipedia, and other such non-individualized materials may not only be unhelpful, but can hurt the case. This is especially true when taking into consideration that accounts of criminal activity by the victim are always at risk of being flawed due to the symptoms of the traumatic experience. Trauma literature has found that undergoing a traumatic experience affects recall, and that avoidance of the topic or any triggers (such as having to collect evidence and having to retell the story) can be a symptom of posttraumatic stress disorder (Herlihy, Jobson, & Turner, 2012).

Forensic examiners can be extremely helpful in assisting the victim to recall or collect pertinent evidence, as well as explaining to the adjudicator the manner in which the psychological disorder interferes with the proper recall and retell of the details of the criminal activity or torture committed against them. Forensic examiners can also provide social science literature that supports issues such as: victims of intimate partner violence reluctance to call the police or seek help; the inability of victims of human trafficking to obtain evidence due to the strict surveillance they endured; or how frequent it is that victims of torture or persecution leave their country with only the clothes on their back and why they are reluctant to contact family or others in their country of origin to obtain evidence for fear of putting their family or themselves at risk.

Another way in which a forensic examiner can support the assumption of truthfulness in an applicant is by describing how on previous occasions he or she told the truth even when it was inconvenient or not beneficial to their case or status, including during the evaluation, and how they have not shown previous behaviors expressing an intention to deceive or manipulate others, or antisocial behavior. These types of statements from the expert, when true and consistent with the psychological data, help the adjudicators decide whether the applicant will uphold the oath they take on the stand to say the truth.

Malingering and Deception

The issue of malingering and deception can be dealt with at the outset in two ways. First, the forensic examiner informs the attorney and applicant that the evaluation will be conducted only on the condition that the examiner approach it with no particular result in mind and exercise independent professional judgment in all aspects of the evaluation. It is important to notify them that the payment of fees is not connected to the content of any report or consultation or any particular finding or recommendation on the matter in question. In fact, it is better practice to have the payment completed before the report is written. If they raise any concerns about this requirement, we can tell them to compare it to the medical field, where this is a customary practice. Our physicians give us an opinion that is not dependent on the payment and they do so using their independent professional judgment and expertise. Likewise, we can assure them that, if the attorney conducted a screening of the respondent, then he or she must be confident that the client is a good candidate for the immigration relief they are seeking, and that, if by any chance the forensic exam is not in their favor, there would still be relevant information that would help them become ready to apply later or explore other options.

Second, the examiner may want to tell the respondent that the most important form of collaboration they can adopt in the evaluation is to be completely honest, without misrepresenting, embellishing, or exaggerating events or the way the evaluee is functioning emotionally. It is also prudent to ask if they received advice from people in their ex-pat community, if their attorney coached them, if they looked for information on the web about immigration evaluations or tests, or perhaps consulted a 'story shaper' – people who take their story and make it fit what they believe would be more credible and bullet-proof for whatever immigration benefit they are seeking. Examinees need to know that misrepresentation would be the single most serious problem with their application, because immigration authorities may find the truth – if not now, maybe later. In fact, the penalty for submitting a false asylum application is a permanent ban from any U.S. immigration relief. Fines and imprisonment are also potential consequences, including for the people who help them, such as the lawyer and interpreter, who may be tried for immigration fraud. A legal permanent resident can lose their green card if it is discovered they lied in their application, and they could even be 'denaturalized' and lose their U.S. citizenship if a fake story is discovered. When you have a good relationship with the attorney who hired you, you may ask them to prepare their client for the forensic evaluation by explaining this issue to them.

Most applicants are honest when showing intense distress that they do not suffer in their daily lives, because during the evaluation their trauma memories and processes are activated. There may be some applicants who believe or have been told that they need to exaggerate their psychological problems. Some of these applicants exaggerate their distress, because so much time has passed between the traumatic incident and the forensic evaluation that the shocking, upsetting, and intense feelings have begun to dissipate with time and the retelling of the story. Thus, the applicant may try to recapture the initial emotional shock at this later time by dramatizing how they currently feel. Others may embellish the abusive events, because they want to make sure the intensity of the abuse meets the immigration relief criteria. However, not knowing the specific psycholegal concepts may incline them to tell outlandish or dramatic stories that fall apart under scrutiny.

Overreporting psychological disorders is not unusual when there is a secondary benefit. For example, Frueh et al. (2003) found up to 50 percent significant overreporting of symptoms among veterans evaluated for PTSD who were seeking disability compensation. Rosen (2006) cautions that overreporting of PTSD in compensation cases is so common that it raises concerns about inflating rates in the epidemiological PTSD database. For immigrants who fear being deported to countries they escaped due to horrendous conditions or death threats, the fear of having their immigration application rejected can be so consuming and terrifying that they may underestimate the impact of using some dramatic measures to prevent this from happening. This desperation, together with their lack of familiarity with immigration law, English language, and U.S. society, may make them prey to exploitive or well-intentioned but uninformed advice.

There are other applicants who received help to completely fabricate an event that never happened, including explaining accidental injuries as scars from torture or beatings that never occurred, and reciting stories of persecution that are taken from other individuals. Asylum officers and immigration judges are schooled in recycled stories and are hypervigilant when it comes to spotting inconsistencies in applicants' statements. In our experience, most people who fabricate stories often had a case for immigration relief – if not in the type of immigration relief for which they were applying, then possibly for another option. Unfortunately, once they take the route of changing the truthful story, they find it almost impossible to keep the account straight for the length of the case and everything begins to unravel when they have to produce evidence and provide oral testimony.

When the examiner provides a thorough explanation of the process of evaluation and methods, the examinee will learn that instances of criminal activity or torture and the times before and after will be discussed in detail. It is the entire picture that will make sense, so they should not worry about trying to make sense of things themselves, but just report as they best recall or feel. I also like to give the assessee a dignified way to save face by saying that this is the time when they can make 'corrections' to the story they told their attorney so they can start the process in the best possible way.

One of the major errors a forensic IC examiner can make in immigration evaluations is a failure to think critically about the examinee's story and presentation. While being caring and not re-traumatizing the examinees, we cannot simply take their account as fact without probing, questioning, and looking at their story from different perspectives. Philip Resnick (1997) has written extensively about credibility and malingering in forensic examinations. He has provided some guidance to assess an evaluee's credibility in their narration of the critical event, which is especially useful when psychological tests cannot be administered. Specifically, with posttraumatic symptoms, Resnick has reported that examinees who are faking it tend to exaggerate current symptoms or extend genuine current symptoms to when the criminal activity happened. For example, people exaggerating posttraumatic stress report extremely intense emotions, while people with bona fide PTSD may deny emotions or suffer from numbing. Individuals who suffered traumatic experiences are reluctant to talk about it, while people who malinger may take every opportunity to recount their alleged trauma in excessive detail.

Other ways to assess potential malingering offered by Conroy and Kwartner (2006) include:

1. answers become less disorganized with fatigue;
2. endorsement of obvious symptoms rather than more subtle ones;
3. inability to consistently sustain the affective and behavioral correlates of the disorder;
4. overplay and call attention to their psychological problems;
5. endorse many symptoms indiscriminately, including rare and improbable symptoms with extreme or unusual severity; and
6. discrepancy between reported and observed symptoms.

The examiner needs to keep in mind that the presence of one or more of these factors does not guarantee that the individual is malingering, and the final decision requires a multi-method approach to corroborate the assessment. In particular, when assessing psychological trauma, a forensic assessor needs to be alert to potential problems of overreporting and outright malingering of posttraumatic symptoms, while taking into consideration the specific influence of trauma in memory and emotional management.

In immigration cases, an individual may erroneously believe that exaggerating the emotional impact would make the case clearer and stronger to ensure that they receive the immigration relief they are seeking, or may present him or herself as beyond reproach and in perfect mental health in cases of extreme hardship where the consideration is their role in the family. In both cases, the examiner needs to be careful to distinguish the actual psychological state from the exaggerated or deceitful presentation. For this, examiners need to rely on a multi-method assessment because our clinical judgment is fragile.

The credibility of the examinee's report can be formally evaluated with psychological tests. Results of psychological tests can provide evidence that the evaluee was honest and forward, thus strengthening the credibility of the report. Psychological tests such as the Trauma Symptom Inventory (TSI-2; Briere, 2010) have validity scales, and more specifically focus on malingering of PTSD. Other such tests include the Minnesota Multiphasic Personality Inventory (MMPI-2; Butcher, 2010; Butcher, Dahlstrom, Graham, Tellegen, & Kaemmer, 1989), Personality Assessment Inventory (PAI; Morey, 1996), and Millon Clinical Multiaxial Inventory (MCMI-III; Millon 1977). There are specific tests for malingering, such as the Miller Forensic Assessment of Symptoms Test (M-FAST; Miller, 2005) and the Structured Interview of Reported Symptoms (SIRS-2; Rogers, Sewell, & Gillard, 2010). However, the evaluation of the examinee's credibility ultimately involves a multi-method strategy in which the interview, a battery of tests, third-party reports, and collateral evidence contribute to the full picture.

Moreover, we cannot forget the impact of cultural issues in the methods we use to determine credibility, which are based on Western notions of response style. Certain cultures may express psychopathology in different ways, including presenting symptoms that may appear bizarre or fabricated. In some cultures, the manner in which a person retells a story is oblique, obfuscated, with circular thinking, and they have difficulty answering simple questions with concrete information. These and other cultural idiosyncrasies need to be taken into consideration before we can say with certainty that a person is likely deceiving or malingering.

Evaluating Examinees with Inadmissibility Issues

Immigration relief is not available when the applicant has committed certain serious crimes such as genocide, an act of torture, or extra-judicial killing. There are other crimes for U and T visa victims, as well as asylum seekers, which may preclude their ability to obtain immigration relief if they are not waived upon a showing of extraordinary circumstances (Rosenberg, 2006).

It is recommended that forensic examiners screen from the very beginning of a case for any potential inadmissibility issues and other adverse issues that may complicate the case in order to discuss this information with the respondent's attorney (Sullivan & Orloff, 2013). It is good practice for the forensic examiner to raise the issues with the attorney and respondent as a warning that proceeding further implies that these issues will impact the expert report and opinion.

There may be other cases in which the forensic examiner discovers that the evaluee is committing a reportable act (e.g., child abuse), which had not come to anyone's attention earlier. In these cases, the forensic examiner must communicate with the attorney and the respondent about his or her obligation to report such abuse, and that they need to plan for the complications this situation will bring to the case. Cases in which the forensic examiner discovers a serious level of malingering or deception that casts doubts about the overall credibility also should be reported to the attorney or legal representative of the applicant.

Colluding to disguise or manipulate unfavorable facts is both an ethical and criminal violation for forensic examiners. The examiner needs to resist any influence to conceal the facts or write false statements. However, the forensic examiner may be very helpful in assessing for mitigating factors that lessen the impact these negative factors may have in the case. In our subsequent chapters that review the immigration relief for victims of crime, we explain how victims are not going to be perfect, because the nature of their psychological disorganization may incline them to use more or less dysfunctional coping mechanisms when are trying to survive in a difficult environment. Forensic examiners can analyze the arguments that place those destructive behaviors in context and explain how those behaviors may have made sense at a time of crisis, if that was the case.

Additionally, forensic examiners can devise treatment plans to help the respondent heal and correct negative behaviors or adverse situations that may improve their chances to present their best case. For instance, respondents with substance abuse issues, self-harm and suicidal behavior, antisocial behavior, past criminal charges, and other such difficulties may have a better chance if they engage in mental health treatment and specialized interventions that address those issues or prevent recidivism if they occurred years ago. Even when the application needs to be delayed or dropped, it is always in the best interest of the attorney and respondent to come clean because the consequences of misrepresentation are very serious to all involved.

Relationship with the Retaining Attorney or Legal Representative

Just like in other forensic activities, the examiner in immigration evaluations is retained by an attorney who in turn becomes the examiner's direct client. The relationship between the examiner and the retaining attorney has to be close and with direct and clear communication channels. The examiner should have rapport with the attorney to openly discuss any issues that may come up and especially those that are different from the attorney or the applicant's expectations regarding the expert opinion.

If the examiner discovers misrepresentations or lies regarding the applicant's immigration documents, or if problem issues arise such as inadmissibility factors, having a sham marriage, or having a failed asylum application in another country, the examiner will let the attorney know, as soon as they arise, so that these issues may have to be factored in the psychological formulation and will appear in the report. Moreover, mental health providers have several obligations regarding reporting child abuse, suicidal ideation, and homicidal ideation, and if this comes up the attorney needs to know. Other issues such as active substance abuse, disclosure of criminal activity under a different name, or having a criminal record in their country of origin also need to be discussed with the attorney. In many cases, there may be mitigating factors to those problem situations that can be identified by the examiner and explained in the report – that is, if the attorney wants the examiner to proceed with the forensic evaluation.

Attorneys are ethically bound to not put forth any statements that they know are false. Moreover, they have to weigh their duty to disclose any falsehoods and criminal activities of their client against their duties to protect client confidentiality, and to advocate zealously for their client, while safeguarding the integrity of the judicial system. The decision about how to proceed with the case given is something the respondent and the attorney need to resolve when there is a risk of detention and deportation for the applicant if the case does not have a positive outcome.

There may be cases in which the examiner discovers issues that require a discussion with the attorney to potentially turn the case in a different direction. For instance, the applicant may have situations or experiences that qualify him or her for another type of visa; the applicant is very disturbed and requires a competency evaluation to obtain accommodations when testifying; or when there are secrets that the applicant does not want disclosed but affect the application. For instance, an applicant did not want to disclose that she left a child in her country of origin, because her current husband did not know, but not noting this in the application may mean that this child would not have legal means to join her in the U.S. in the future if needed after she obtains her immigration relief.

While close communication and a collaborative relationship with the attorney who retained you is very important, forensic examiners do not want to lose sight of the fact that the interests of the attorney and the forensic examiner may at times be in conflict. Receiving helpful feedback about the content and organization of the report, or consulting on the psycholegal concepts, discussing the examinee's capability to collaborate or testify, and receiving background information on the examinee, country, or the immigration issue may be extremely helpful, but the attorney is not the mental health expert and should not influence the examiner's opinions (Knapp & VandeCreek, 2001).

Similarly, if the evaluation cannot meet the expectations of the attorney due to issues such as lack of a specific competence of the examiner, interference of personal problems in the timely completion of the evaluation, inability to obtain the information required due to limitations on the methods, lack of cooperation of the applicant, or problems with interpreter and translation services, the examiner communicates these issues to the attorney as early as possible. In many situations, the examiner should provide alternative options such as referral to a new examiner, agree on having a conjoint evaluation with a professional who has the competence that complements the examiner's, or seek a continuance if it is allowed.

Applicants without Legal Representation

When an immigration applicant contacts the examiner directly in order to obtain an appointment for an immigration evaluation, often one of two situations are occurring: their attorney gave them one or several names to consider for the evaluation, or they are representing themselves and have received advice about hiring a mental health examiner. It is important to be aware of the many risks that taking a case in these conditions entail. There is a great deal of corruption in immigration law and the examiner has no assurance that her or his report will end up being utilized for the purposes for which it was created. In these instances, the demand on the examiner to be competent on the legal issues is enormous and engenders many professional and ethical risks.

The Importance of Self-Care

The field of immigration evaluations puts us in touch with the darker aspects of the human experience, such as abuse, maltreatment, and exploitation of vulnerable human beings. We will hear horrific and frightening stories that we could not have imagined. In order to face this task with sensitivity and care, we cannot become accustomed, automatized, or desensitized. The responsibility to care for our own mental health and professional wellbeing is essential to the optimal mental state to work in this field. There are elements that are essential aspects of our professional fitness, such as: balancing the caseload of immigration evaluations; diversifying the practice so it is not only composed of immigration evaluations; taking good care of our physical, mental, and social needs outside of the professional arena; and having a solid network of professionals to consult with. According to Pope and Vasquez (2016, p. 114),

> neglecting an ethic of self-care early on can drain the enthusiasm, joy, resilience, and meaning out of a career. It can undermine our competence and hurt our ability to practice ethically. It can sink us into discouragement, compassion fatigue, and burnout.

Part II

Applications to Forensic Practice

Chapter 4

Forensic Psychological Assessment in Asylum

While there is an absolute prohibition against torture in international law (UN General Assembly, 1984), torture and similar human rights abuses are systematically practiced with impunity in the majority of countries around the world (Huminuik, 2016), including the U.S. (see Risen, 2014). Tragically, the widespread use of torture and rape as instruments of persecution and repression is well documented (Basolgu, 1992; Dross, 2000; Sales, 2016). At the same time, immigration attorneys, USCIS asylum officers and attorneys, and Immigration Court (IC) judges are left with a bewildering array of stories and behaviors from asylum seekers that are not infrequently difficult to interpret and to substantiate. In addition, immigration judges are regularly confronted with stories of human cruelty that are torturous to hear and difficult to believe. Additionally, because the burden of proof is on the asylum seeker, he or she is faced with sharing horrific, incomprehensible, and degrading experiences in an adversarial setting (Dignam, 1992).

The most frequent use of forensic mental health assessment in IC matters involves asylum and Convention Against Torture (CAT) claims (see Jacobs, Evans, & Patsilides, 2001a, 2001b; Istanbul Protocol; United Nations Office of the High Commissioner for Human Rights, 2004). Individuals seeking asylum often arrive in the U.S. with little more than the clothes on their back, lacking clear documentation to support their claims. Forensic psychologists, psychiatrists, and social workers with expertise in psychological trauma can provide expert opinions to the IC about the impact and severity of torture and rape (and therefore the credibility of the claim), as well as the likely psychological consequences of deportation to the country from which they escaped. High-quality psychological and medical evidence can help to substantiate allegations of torture, thereby significantly increasing the likelihood of fairness and success in IC proceedings (see Lustig, Kureshi, Delucchi, Iacopino, & Morse, 2008).

Legal Concepts

To be granted asylum, the immigrant seeking relief must demonstrate that he or she is a 'refugee,' which, according to international law from the UN Convention Relating to the Status of Refugees, is defined as follows:

A 'refugee' is any person who is outside his or her country of nationality (or, if stateless, outside the country of last habitual residence) and is unable or unwilling to return to that country because of persecution or well-founded fear of persecution on account of race, religion, nationality, political opinion, or membership in a particular social group.

(UN General Assembly 1951, p. 137)

While not initially a signatory to the Geneva Convention, the U.S. subsequently signed the UN 1967 Protocol (UN General Assembly, 1967), which incorporates the Geneva Convention by reference. The Refugee Convention obliges UN members to protect refugees living within their borders and prohibits them from sending them to other countries where they would be harmed based on their race, religion, nationality, membership in a particular social group, or political opinion. With the Refugee Act of 1980, the U.S. incorporated the refugee definition into Federal law. The refugee definition is found at Section 101(a)(42) of the Immigration and Nationality Act (INA).

A claim of asylum has two grounds, both of which must be met by immigrants applying for relief. First, the asylum seeker must have a well-founded fear of persecution, which includes either fear of future persecution or the experience of past persecution of such severity that it would be inhumane to be forced to return to his or her country of origin. Next, persecution must be on account of one or more of the five qualifying grounds: race, religion, nationality, membership in a particular social group, or political opinion. While such persecution involves torture and rape, there are other grounds for asylum involving membership in an immutable group unprotected by their government, such as fear of female genital mutilation (see *Matter of Kasinga*, 1996; Kassindja & Miller, 1998) or of physical and sexual abuse and harassment of homosexuals (see Heller, 2009). For a more detailed review of the intricacies of asylum law, please see Anker's (2016) authoritative book on the subject.

Additionally, an individual meeting the refugee definition above may be granted asylum in the U.S. (a) if he or she is not barred from asylum for a number of inadmissibility issues set out in the INA; and (b) if the USCIS adjudicator decides that he or she should be granted asylum as a matter of discretion. Adjudication of asylum applications are decided either at the USCIS Asylum Office (the so-called 'affirmative' level), which first reviews all applications, or in IC by a judge, if rejected by the Asylum Office and appealed. The legal and procedural standards for asylum are the same for both the Asylum Office adjudicator and the IC judge.

The bars to asylum include, perhaps most importantly, not filing an application within the initial one-year deadline of entry, which states that a refugee seeking asylum must file her or his application within one year of the last arrival in the U.S. Fortunately, adjudicator discretion can be used to suspend this bar if the asylum seeker demonstrates that he or she qualifies for an exception to the filing deadline and that he or she filed within a reasonable time given that exception. Given the common, generalized fear of government officials and the characteristics of posttraumatic states, it may take years for asylum seekers to feel sufficiently safe and supported to begin the asylum application process.

Other bars to eligibility for asylum include indications of participation in the persecution of others in their native country; of conviction of a serious crime, which constitutes a danger to the community of the U.S., either prior to entry into the U.S. or during the application process; of reasonable grounds for regarding a danger to the security of the U.S., including involvement in terrorist activity (sometime called the 'material support bar'); or indication that the applicant was firmly resettled in another country prior to arriving in the U.S. See Musalo and Rice (2008) for a detailed analysis of bars to application in asylum matters.

> Viviana was a transgender woman from El Salvador, applying for asylum due to persecution for her self-identified gender identity, but she did not apply within the first year after arrival, as required by law. In fact, Viviana applied after three years of living in the U.S. Viviana said that she knew she was a girl trapped in a boy's body since she was five years old. Because she dislikes sports, girls' clothes, and boys' toys, and she has an affinity to play with girls, she gained a 'bad' reputation and was sent by her parents at age five to her uncle to raise. The uncle made it his mission to make her a 'man' through brutal beatings and repression of her female identity. Viviana was sexually abused by a worker at her uncle's farm since age eight. During her adolescent years, she was abused by other men, including a teacher who demanded sex in exchange for good grades. At the same time, she was bullied, assaulted, and persecuted by peers and neighbors. Finally, she escaped after a particularly brutal beating and entered the U.S. without inspection at age 18. Initially she was very ashamed of her sexual orientation and got a girlfriend to pretend that she was cisgender, thinking this would make it easier to be accepted socially and in her job in construction. After a year, Viviana decided to move to another state in search of a gay community, and then moved three more times before settling in Miami. There, Viviana felt freer and started entering the gay culture. Viviana befriended a transgender woman and this friend became Viviana's artistic mentor, helping Viviana become a member of a drag show. From dressing as a woman at night for the show, Viviana went on to transform herself into a woman, not without fear and indecision, throughout the following year. She transitioned to a female appearance because she wanted to be truthful to what she felt inside of her heart. She picked her name 'Viviana,' inspired by a character in a Spanish soap opera. Her romantic life was turbulent, and after a particularly violent beating from her boyfriend, she tried to commit suicide and was subsequently hospitalized. There, she learned that there were immigration protections available to her.

In Viviana's case, it was the task of the examiner to explain the different psychological challenges that Viviana underwent in her ordeal since her arrival and how this was connected to her efforts to deal with the past trauma, the current traumatic relationship, and the intense repression and avoidance she developed to deal with the deep shame and painful memories. Viviana was in no psychological position to find out that there was immigration relief available to her during the first three years after her arrival, but, even if she had initially known, it was unlikely that she would have been able to follow through with the application, given the turmoil in her life and struggles with her identity. The examiner explained in the report and testimony how Viviana would have had a hard time recalling all the information necessary for her application due to the severity of her emotional and mental distress, avoidance, and repression. It was only after she was urgently hospitalized and received psychological and psychiatric help that she began to feel sufficiently emotionally stable to recall and recount her traumatic experiences and finally apply for asylum.

Frequently, with an application for asylum where torture is claimed, the immigrant likely applies for an additional form of relief if she or he fears torture if returned to her or his country of origin. While asylum relief in general encompasses a broad range of well-founded fears of persecution, the asylum seeker who has been tortured in their home country may make an additional application for protection claimed under the UN Convention Against Torture (UN General Assembly, 1984), often called a CAT claim. The U.S. has ratified the international Convention Against Torture and Other Cruel, Inhuman or Degrading Treatment or Punishment, which provides that it will not expel, return, or extradite a person if this person is believed to be in danger of being subjected to torture. The assessment regarding the potential for future torture includes a determination that the fear is well-founded and that torture is systematically practiced in the country where the person would be sent. Although evidentiary requirements to be granted CAT protection are higher than those for asylum (a preponderance of evidence that the individual would be persecuted or tortured if returned) and CAT provides more limited protection than asylum does, there are advantages to applying. First, when there is sufficient evidence, it is mandatory that the IC adjudicator grants a CAT claim. Second, bars that might otherwise prevent the individual from obtaining asylum might not prevent the granting of CAT protection.

Assessing the Psychological Impact of Torture and Persecution

As stated above, the most frequent use of forensic mental health assessment in IC matters involves asylum and CAT claims. Individuals seeking political asylum often arrive in the U.S. reporting experiences of severe torture and other psychological trauma as part of their persecution. The use of forensic psychological assessment of asylum/CAT claims for IC rests on two general principles: the expert's in-depth knowledge of the psychological impact of torture and rape and her or his clear understanding of the way in which such information is germane within the legal context (see American Psychological Association, 2013; Frumkind & Friedland, 1995; Melton, Petrila, Poythress, & Slobogin, 2007; Weiner & Otto 2014). As Evans (2000) identified, in-depth psychological knowledge required in asylum/CAT claims encompasses psychological expertise in three distinct areas: (1) the impact and psychological sequelae of torture, rape, and other forms of interpersonal violence; (2) the psychological assessment of psychological trauma; and (3) the assessment of how this trauma is expressed in the context of cross-cultural issues (see Evans, 2016).

First and foremost, the forensic assessor should know the extensive clinical and research literature on the impact and psychological sequelae of rape, torture, and other forms of interpersonal violence, including posttraumatic stress disorder (PTSD) and the long-term sequelae of the experiences (see Herman 1992; van der Kolk & McFarlane, 1996). Not only is an expert knowledge of PTSD essential, but also other sequelae of psychological trauma such as complex posttraumatic disorder (Nickerson et al., 2016; Pelcovitz et al., 1997); dissociative disorder (Putnam, 1997); and a variety of other mental disorders, including depressive disorder, anxiety disorder, and substance use disorder (Heeren et al., 2012).

Since the best forensic evaluations focus on functional assessments over diagnostic studies (Frumkind & Friedland, 1995), it is important that the psychological expert understand the impact of severe psychological trauma in general and torture and rape more specifically, but additionally address issues of impaired memory, presentation style, and variation in impairment in work versus recreational functioning. For example, a severely raped and tortured woman or man could easily present with a bland affectless manner with significant gaps in memory and confusion about the details of their persecution and escape. Without some psychological information explaining how such trauma often manifests in emotional numbing and dissociation, traumatic amnesia, and the destruction of central cognitive organizational capacities, it would be easy for the asylum officer or IC judge to rule such a respondent as not credible. As such, expert psychological opinion and testimony often can go to the heart of the central concern of the court, the issue of whether the often difficult to document claim of the asylum seeker is believable and credible.

Second, the mental health expert should have familiarity with the mental health assessment of psychological trauma and, as we emphasize throughout this book, this knowledge should go beyond what can be gathered in a simple clinical interview. While clinical interviews are the cornerstone of all mental health assessments, Garb's (1998) extensive analysis of clinical decision-making suggests that research studies generally indicate that clinical judgment based solely on interview is not especially reliable scientifically. He further stated that scientifically derived actuarial approaches, which are the foundation in psychological testing, greatly increase accuracy. As we discuss later in Chapters 9 and 10, mental health assessment requires an understanding of the various empirically derived psychological assessment measures as well as relevant structured and semi-structured interviews. Assessment techniques should be selected to provide a sound description of the impact of the particular trauma evaluated, including its etiology, dynamics, and, because the courts often desire it, the diagnosis of a trauma-related disorder. For example, it is important to consider that some psychological instruments are normed for victims of rape and sexual assault. Additionally, as Jacobs (2008) has pointed out, knowledge of neuropsychological assessment can also be valuable in documenting traumatic brain injury as a result of torture.

Third, the expertise of the mental health assessor must also include knowledge of how both the psychology of trauma and the assessment of trauma operate in the context of cross-cultural issues (Okawa, 2008), including increased cultural sensitivity toward the respondent undergoing the evaluation (Pope & Garcia-Peltoniemi, 1991). Because social and cultural factors are so critical in forensic psychological assessment in IC, clinical interviews are necessary to assess the social and societal context in which the reported torture and rape occurs. It is equally true that, wherever possible, it is important to balance social context data derived from clinical interviews with scientifically reliable and valid actuarial approaches. While language difficulties may make it difficult (or even impossible) to use psychological testing, the importance of objective, fact-based information in IC strongly suggests that the mental health expert make an effort to find appropriate actuarial methods, whenever possible.

For example, the forensic assessor will need to understand how rape is perceived within the respondent's culture. In many countries from which women flee persecution, rape was seen as the fault of the woman, and a woman who was raped is shunned and ostracized for not having died in trying to protect her virginity. Comprehension of such cultural and psychological pressures can be invaluable in addressing the IC judge's concerns about the credibility of the woman during testimony. For example, knowledge that rape in general, and in certain cultures especially, is experienced as deeply shameful may help explain why the woman continually looks away during testimony. The interpretation of her demeanor in the courtroom situation may be that the woman is hiding something and she therefore may be judged not credible. In fact, the woman may be hiding something in this situation; she may be hiding her shame, not hiding from the truth.

Another example of helpful expert testimony is addressing why the asylum seeker failed to provide disclosure of her rape on her initial USCIS affidavit (not uncommon in our experience), but later claimed to have been raped during her appeal. Again, instead of changing her story to avoid deportation, the woman may have attempted to protect herself from unwanted public exposure, hoping to escape anticipated humiliation by only partially disclosing of her experiences of persecution. A woman seeking asylum may be forced to disclose her rape later only because the reality of returning to her country was worse than the dreaded humiliation. Expert psychological testimony that presents the reality of raped women's deep shame about the violation may assist the court in reconciling seeming inconsistencies.

A Model for Assessing Impact of Torture of Asylum Applications

Mental health assessment of torture in IC is a practice requiring special care because of the impact that it could have on asylum seekers' lives. Unlike counseling or psychotherapy, where the mental health professional gets to know the client through many hours of interaction, forensic mental health assessments are a more circumscribed encounter in which mistakes can be magnified by misinterpretation. Further, mistakes in forensic mental health assessment reports influence the asylum seeker's entire life. Additionally, forensic assessments can significantly influence important decisions about asylum seekers' lives, such as a need for being returned to highly dangerous and even fatal situations. As such, inadequately trained mental health assessors can cause considerable emotional and personal damage by providing incomplete, though well-meaning, opinions without a solid factual basis. What we provide below is a basic model for conducting such assessments with sensitivity toward the individuals undergoing the assessments, while taking special care to meet the requirements of the IC for facts.

An important difference from IC evaluations of psychological trauma resulting from rape and torture and other kinds of forensic evaluations is the sensitivity that the evaluator must have toward the respondent undergoing the evaluation (Stark, 1996). Far too often in forensic psychology, the terms 'objective' and 'neutral' have been interpreted as disbelieving and remote. This latter stance is anathema to women and men who are struggling to describe overwhelming traumatic life experiences. Mollica's research (Mollica, Wyshak, & Lavelle 1987; Mollica et al., 1992) strongly suggests that reliable and valid descriptions of torture and its impact cannot be obtained in an atmosphere in which the interviewer listens to the asylum seeker's story with initial disbelief and emotional inaccessibility. The assessor's stance of benevolent neutrality (see Evans, 2005), an attitude of concern and emotional connection while suspending belief as to the absolute veracity of the narrative, allows the respondent to share her or his story as she or he chooses to represent it. The assessor's other tools (e.g., psychological testing, validity checks, requirement for corroboration, attention to inconsistencies) allow for a more comprehensive assessment of the credibility of the person's story and to explore motivations other than direct truth-telling, after first giving the asylum seeker freedom to speak in a supportive environment.

Collateral Information

After getting informed consent from both the attorney and the respondent, we strongly recommend that the mental health assessor obtain and thoroughly read third-party information before conducting the initial forensic interview and psychological testing as a matter of standard practice. Such records include the legal documentation, mental health records, medical records, and, most importantly, country conditions reports. Country conditions are available through the U.S. Department of State Human Rights Reports (www.state.gov/j/drl/rls/hrrpt), Amnesty International Country Reports (www.amnestyusa.org/tools-and-reports/reports), and Human Rights Watch World Reports (www.hrw.org/world-report). It is important to note that there may be variance in the reports from the U.S. Department of State Human Rights Reports and those from independent human rights organizations. Often, detailed information, such as use of particular torture methods used by countries, can also be obtained through a careful internet search. Together this information provides both an orientation to the political and cultural circumstances of the asylum seeker as well as a validity check on his or her report. It is also important to remember that additional third-party information may be important to gather after the forensic interviews as well.

Forensic Interview

In order to both best prepare the asylum seeker for the difficulty in discussing her or his torture experience and to obtain behavioral observations of her or his demeanor in lower versus higher stress situations, we recommend at least two interview sessions. The first session involves orienting the respondent to the task and explaining the value of sharing openly to the degree possible what torture experiences she or he has experienced. The rest of the first session involves using a combination of semi-structured and structured interviews. The task of the initial session is to obtain a description of an index traumatic experience (e.g., arrest, imprisonment, torture), taking care to keep this first description brief and limited so as not to unnecessarily overwhelm the asylum seeker.

Next, a comprehensive forensic interview includes a family history; living situation before the reported trauma; current and past life situation including educational history, work history and relationships; any past difficulties or traumatic events before the index trauma; and psychological and medical history, including medications, substance abuse, family mental health history, and suicidality. Other issues explored involve the most upsetting life events other than the persecution events; what the individual has stopped doing since the events; leisure activities and whether they are done for diversion or enjoyment; and what makes the individual feel good and whether she or he is doing them currently. Next issues surveyed are current supports including emotional, social, and financial support from family, friends, work, and church, as well as current problems with family, friends, and work. Additionally, a systematic mental health diagnostic evaluation is conducted by administering a structured interview such as the Depressive Disorders, Bipolar Disorders, and Anxiety Disorders modules of the Structured Clinical Interview for DSM 5 (SCID 5; First, Williams, Karg, & Spitzer, 2015), with additional modules to be administered where problems such a psychotic disorder or dissociation disorder arise. As we discuss in Chapter 9, there are significant advantages to using evidence-based structured interviews over unstructured interviews in a court setting.

At the end of the initial interview, it is generally helpful to get the respondent's perspective on how the interview went for him or her (as well as for the interpreter if one is present). It is highly recommended that the mental health assessor make detailed notes on the demeanor of the respondent during the interview and a list of possible inconsistencies during her or his self-report and between self-report and the collateral data reviewed. An attempt to resolve such inconsistencies becomes a critical element in assessing credibility of the respondent and preserving the neutrality inherent in the forensic mental health assessor's role.

The second interview meeting works best if scheduled within a week of the first interview. Unless there are serious inconsistencies to reconcile from the initial interview, the first order of business is to obtain a detailed description of the torture event(s) experienced by the asylum seeker. By this point, hopefully the relationship between the forensic mental health assessor and the asylum seeker is sufficient to provide the asylum seeker with some measure of support to endure this excruciating task. Nonetheless, we recommend strongly that the assessor state clearly why it is necessary for the asylum seeker to undergo a painful and detailed recounting of the event; i.e., so that the assessor can relay the necessary details to the IC and depth of suffering the asylum seeker's torture caused him or her. It is not uncommon for the assessor to apologize to the torture victim for having to cause such pain of remembrance.

The assessor then carefully and compassionately walks the asylum seeker through the events leading up to her or his arrest to just before torture, including eliciting as many details of the setting and emotional reactions as humanely possible. This approach allows the assessor to support the respondent in eliciting and sharpening her or his memory of the event as well as to consider whether there is sufficient detail as part of the assessment of credibility. Next, the assessor asks the asylum seeker whether she or he can share what happened during the torture experience. Additionally, after the respondent describes her or his experience, the assessor may find it valuable to use the Survivor of Torture Assessment Record (STAR: Gorst-Unsworth, Van Velsen, & Turner, 1993), which can serve as a measure of torture severity.

It has been our experience that many respondents are able to share a mix of extremely vivid details of their trauma (i.e., 'flashbulb' memories) as well as periods of vague memory and complete amnesia (see van der Kolk, 1998). The detailed documentation of the asylum seeker's report of her or his experiences of torture provides compelling evidence for the IC as well as meets the IC requirements for elicitation of detail whenever possible. As will be discussed later, it also allows the assessor to address problems with memory and shame inherent in individuals who suffered torture (Herlihy & Turner, 2007) and to provide clinically rich, compelling, and influential IC testimony. With this said, it is critical to remember that some asylum seekers are not ready or able to share their stories and an alternate approach is necessary, such as contacting the attorney for further guidance and to indicate that treatment may be necessary before the respondent will be able to adequately present torture details often required in IC proceedings.

It is important to remember that the forensic mental health assessor is likely to experience intensely emotional (or emotionally avoidant) countertransference. These feelings arise from confronting the overwhelming horror and helplessness inherent in listening to torture narratives. In deciding whether or not to take on forensic assessment of torture victims, potential mental health assessors need to understand the critical importance of detailed descriptions of trauma events necessary for successful forensic reports and testimony, balanced with the capacity to tolerate the pain of hearing the horror of torture. Because forensic mental health assessors must maintain neutrality, they need to understand the important distinction between advocating for their assessment findings and becoming an advocate for asylum seekers, or their attorney's representation, in the IC. Another related issue for forensic mental health assessors is the difficulty of living with the gross inequity of immigration law relative to the law as enjoyed by U.S. citizens.

Psychological Testing

The question of what psychological testing to conduct, as well as when and how to do so, is highly variable to the circumstances of the overall forensic mental health evaluation. Many assessors obtain testing before interviews, though another strategy is to administer structured interviews of PTSD symptoms and other trauma presentations following a break after the in-depth assessment of the torture experience. Generally speaking, the full expression of trauma symptoms is most readily available after describing the traumatic stressor and is the strategy used with the gold standard Clinician-Administered PTSD Scale (CAPS; Blake et al., 1995) and other structured trauma interviews. It is also important to assess lifetime traumatic exposures using trauma exposure measures like the Life Events Checklist-Revised (Weathers et al., 2013) or the Trauma History Screen (Carlson et al., 2011). Issues of proximate cause of the trauma symptoms before the torture experience as well as after need to be carefully addressed to meet the requirements of the IC. In this vein, recent research by Schock, Böttche, Rosner, Wenk-Ansohn, and Knaevelsrud (2016) has helped establish that refugees and asylum seekers often experience stressful life events that can cause PTSD symptom reactivation, which in turn can be best understood as symptom exacerbation rather than a separate and unrelated traumatic event. Selection of an appropriate psychological test battery is addressed in Chapters 9 and 10.

Addressing Credibility through Assessment of Malingering and Deception

Given the USCIS and IC's concerns about credibility, addressing secondary gain issues are critical to the Court. As with all forensic evaluations, a formal assessment of deception, false imputation, feigning, and malingering is an essential component in mental health assessment of torture (see Musalo, Meffert, & Abdo, 2010). Forensic mental health assessors should take into consideration the importance of response, such as underreporting, overreporting, and inconsistent or confused reporting style in interpreting information from the assessment interviews. Without some means of evaluating response style, it is difficult to truly understand the meaning of what the respondent is saying. Without specifically addressing this concern in a systematic way, an otherwise adequate forensic assessment report may simply be disregarded by the IC adjudicator as one more example of what the Honorable IC Judge James R. Fujimoto referred to as the 'regurgitation model' – i.e., just feeding back information shared by the respondent without critical judgment or exploring the possibility of alternative hypotheses.

There are several strategies that can be used in a multi-method way to develop an informed opinion regarding the credibility of the asylum seeker. The first strategy is to make sure the self-report of the respondent is internally consistent during the interview as well as consistent with collateral information, such a country conditions reports and other factual information. When possible significant inconsistencies are present, it is important to forthrightly address them with the asylum seeker directly. A second strategy involves the use of validity scales on psychological testing methods to assess response style, wherever such methods can be legitimately used. A third strategy in assessing malingered PTSD involves attending to and attempting to elicit atypical signs and symptoms of PTSD. Perhaps the most developed example of this approach is Resnick's (2003) guidelines for assessing malingering in PTSD in which within the forensic interview he assesses eight markers that raise potential concerns about validity of the individual's self-report. For example, he notes evasiveness in responding forthrightly to the examiner's questions and inconsistency in PTSD symptom presentation as issues to be further explored. While none of these markers are pathognomonic of malingering or deception, their presence alerts the mental health examiner to look more carefully. Similarly, the application of Porter and Yuille's (1996) research on the verbal clues of deception in the interrogation context provides a similar set of useful considerations. It is important to remember that no single strategy above should be used in isolation of other information sources in developing a nuanced expert opinion about credibility. Naturally, if the forensic mental health examiner finds significant concerns about the credibility of the asylum seeker, the assessor should immediately contact the attorney to share these concerns.

On the other hand, as Lustig (2008) and Herlihy and Turner (2015) caution, it is especially important in the asylum law context to use psychological knowledge to challenge incorrect judicial beliefs and assumptions where observable symptoms of PTSD can be confused with perceived indications of deception. Such issues include memory difficulties following traumatic experiences which sometimes result in testimonial inconsistencies, which can affect credibility judgments in asylum decisions (see Rogers, Fox, & Herlihy, 2014).

Beginning with Herlihy, Scragg, and Turner (2002), the research with torture victims seeking asylum shows that discrepancies in their accounts of persecution are common. Especially for asylum seekers with severe symptoms of PTSD, the number of discrepancies increased over time, with details peripheral to the account accounting for increased discrepancies more than for details central to the account. They concluded that the assumption that inconsistency of recall means that accounts have poor credibility is at best questionable and inconsistent with what is known scientifically about memory and trauma, especially with torture victims with severe PTSD or other trauma symptom presentations.

As such, they conclude that inconsistencies in memory should not be relied on as necessarily indicating a lack of credibility. Further research by Graham, Herlihy, and Brewin (2014) found that, when clinical interviews were assessed for autobiographical memory specificity, asylum seekers with PTSD and depression recalled a lower proportion of specific memories and also more frequently failed to report any memories. This study suggested that that refugees with PTSD and depression fleeing persecution have increased difficulty with autobiographical memory, which makes them more vulnerable in IC settings where poor memory is often viewed as an indication of non-credible reporting.

Issues of Presentation in Court

Another important role for the forensic mental health professional providing assessment in asylum cases is to understand, and be able to address during testimony, the particularities of the respondent's behavior in torture and rape- and gender-based violence cases. Consistent with the research on memory, the well-prepared forensic mental health assessor will do well to testify on how memory is impacted by severe psychological trauma and depression. In particular, the assessor can prepare USCIS administrative adjudicators and IC judges on the likelihood of memory inconsistencies in general and especially in the context of IC hearings, which are likely to trigger past traumatic experiences of being interrogated. Further, where dissociation and psychological numbing are prominent in asylum seekers' symptomatic response to torture, the assessor can help explain the asylum seekers' self-representation of eerie detachment and seeming emotional non-responsiveness to horrific torture during testimony. A frequent reaction by IC adjudicators to this presentation is one of disbelief and skepticism, and careful education by the forensic assessor in reports and testimony about dissociation and traumatic detachment can address potential IC adjudicators' misconceptions.

Further, many asylum seekers will have prominent intrusive posttraumatic symptoms and intense emotional flooding that are easily triggered, especially in the context of legal proceedings. In expert reports and during testimony, the forensic mental health expert can prepare the IC adjudicator for the intensity of suffering that will likely be provoked when the asylum seeker is asked to share his or her torture experience on the stand or during affirmative interview. Witnessing this degree of suffering in others may be quite difficult as it may not be part of the IC adjudicators' and USCIS attorneys' experience. It is understandable that unconscious, powerful defenses, such as disbelief and denial, may be triggered in adjudicators, which could lead to misconceptions about the credibility of the respondent's self-representation. The forensic mental health expert can provide an explanation of the asylum seeker's likely behavior and prepare the IC adjudicator for the experience of hearing such anguish.

Another posttraumatic stress symptom presentation frequently found in asylum seekers is the dramatic alteration in their perception of themselves, especially where rape and other sexual abuse are part of the torture scheme. Such respondents may feel intense shame and self-blame, leading to reluctance to share their experiences or being unable to look at others when they do describe their torture experience. Not infrequently, there is a misconception in legal proceedings that looking away during testimony is an indication of non-credible responding, such as trying to hide something. Based on their psychological knowledge, mental health experts can help explain the power, and non-verbal indications, of shame to help provide the adjudicator with a more accurate interpretation of these non-verbal behaviors. In fact, in some instances where the asylum seeker's capacity to relate her or his account is insufficient to adequately represent herself or himself, the expert may recommend that treatment may be required before adequate testimony is possible.

The forensic mental health assessor's expertise and knowledge of the experience of the tortured asylum seeker can provide critical evidence in the IC. This expertise involves careful elicitation and documentation of the asylum seeker's torture experiences and sequelae; corroborating these experiences with collateral information and psychological testing; assessing deception and malingering to assist with issues of credibility and providing context for self-presentation of psychological trauma in the IC that may be easily misinterpreted. Indeed, the collaboration between the forensic assessor and the legitimate asylum seeker allows for psychological expert testimony that 'speaks for the torture victim' in ways that other sources of evidence cannot.

Chapter 5

Relief from Victimization
Violence Against Women Act

Congress has passed certain legislative tools to allow immigrant victims of domestic violence, sexual assault, human trafficking, and other mostly violent criminal activities to remain in the U.S. in recognition that they are: (1) vulnerable to victimization; (2) abused by U.S. citizens and Lawful Permanent Resident (LPR) spouses or parents; and/or (3) are key to providing information that aid law enforcement in investigating and prosecuting the crimes committed against them. The underlying value behind these victim-based forms of immigration relief is the knowledge that undocumented immigrant victims would not take formal actions to protect themselves, such as calling the police, filing criminal charges, or seeking a civil protection order, if they believe that these actions may lead to their deportation (VAWA, 1994, 2000). Allowing crime to go unpunished and perpetrators to get away with their crimes is a threat to the social order, community safety, and the safety of victims and their children. Similarly, victims who have suffered the trauma of crime victimization suffer great psychological harm and protecting them is our responsibility as a civilized society.

This chapter will address the Violence Against Women Act (VAWA), which is one of the three forms of immigration relief designed to help immigrant victims. The role a forensic evaluator plays in these forms of immigration relief is in assisting the trier of fact in understanding the individual circumstances of the case. Chapter 6 will address the other two victim-based forms of immigration relief: U non-immigrant status (Relief for Victims of Criminal Activity) and T non-immigrant status (Relief for Victims of Traffic).

We have found it important as forensic examiners to work closely with the examinee's attorney from early in the case, beginning with the referral, because of the very detailed, complicated, and different types of evidence required for a victim to qualify for these types of immigration relief. For instance, a person may qualify for one or more of these relief measures, and sometimes the psychological findings help the legal representative make the decision regarding which type of immigration case to file. Also, because it is not at all unusual that an immigrant has been victimized multiple times, an examinee referred for one type of evaluation may disclose victimization that meets criteria for another type of immigration case. In these cases, the legal team may decide to change the application in view of the new psychological evidence and thus the emphasis of the report may need to change as well. The best table describing these three major forms of immigration relief designed to help immigrant victims and the requirements of each was developed by the National Immigrant Women's Advocacy Project (NIWAP, 2015) and can be accessed at http://niwaplibrary.wcl. American.edu/pubs/imm-relief-forms-comparison.

The common denominator of these forms of immigration relief is that they are provided for victims of crime, and thus the forensic examiner is essentially evaluating the harm caused by the crime. Forensic examiners put the victim's story into a victim-of-crime context, as most crime victims may not self-describe as suffering from trauma or as having functional impairment when coping with basic life activities. Forensic examiners in these cases explain the victim's impairment, based on a forensically and clinically sound assessment. This is especially useful when the victim did not suffer a physical impairment. The regulations for the U visa provide an example of the types of factors that forensic examiners need to address in any crime victim-related case. These factors include (8 Code of Federal Regulations (C.F.R.) § 214.14(b) (1)):

- the nature of the injury;
- the severity of the perpetrator's conduct;
- the severity of the harm suffered;
- the duration of the infliction of harm;
- any permanent or serious harm to appearance;
- health and physical or mental soundness; and
- any aggravation of a victim's preexisting conditions.

In the evaluation by USCIS of the evidence regarding the harm suffered by the victim, the standard is 'the applicant's subjective experience' (USCIS, 72 Fed Reg.). The regulations also require that USCIS adjudicators consider the totality of the victim's circumstances and the totality of the evidence in the case in making their determinations. Therefore, the examiner evaluates the subjective experience of the victim in relation to the abusive and qualifying crime. This standard allows for a variety of abusive actions to have significant psychological impact on the victim, and the forensic examiner has the expertise to place them in the context of the victim's experiences and individual meaning.

Relief Under the Violence Against Women Act (VAWA Self-Petition and Battered Woman Waiver)

The VAWA immigration protections allow an abused immigrant or abused children to file for immigration relief without the help of their U.S. citizen or LPR abusive spouse, parent, step-parent, former spouse, intended spouse, or over-21-year-old child (NIWAP, 2015). For victims whose abuser is a spouse, the victim must also show good-faith marriage. The applicant must also demonstrate he or she resided with the abuser at some point during the marriage or the parent–child relationship. The task for the psychological examiner is to evaluate the psychological functioning of the immigrant victim, as this information contributes to the evidence regarding the allegations of abuse.

Psycholegal Concepts

The psycholegal constructs that are part of adjudication of a VAWA immigration case (i.e., VAWA self-petition, VAWA cancelation of removal, Battered Spouse Waiver [BSW]) include: a victim has suffered battering or *extreme cruelty*, having entered the marriage in *good faith* and having *good moral character* (BSW, 1990; VAWA, 1994).

While the regulations on extreme cruelty focus on any act or threatened act of violence, including any forceful detention, which results or threatens to result in physical or mental injury (8 C.F.R. § 214.14 (a)(8)), extreme cruelty encompasses all forms of domestic abuse that are not purely physical, whether they may be sanctioned by our civil or criminal system or not. Physical or mental injury means harm to the victim's physical person or harm to or impairment of the emotional or psychological soundness of the victim. Some of the acts of violence considered in this category include psychological or sexual abuse or exploitation, including rape, molestation, incest (if the victim is a minor), or forced prostitution. The regulations allow for other abusive actions under certain circumstances, including *actions that may not appear violent at face value* but that are part of an overall pattern of violence (8 C.F.R. §204.2(c)(1)(vi) 1997).

This latter concept regarding *abusive actions that in and of themselves may not appear violent* is particularly useful to account for those abusive actions that are tailored to the victim's particular vulnerabilities and cultural background, and which are not usually considered in standard definitions of battering or abuse but nonetheless have a traumatic impact to the victim (Hass, Dutton, & Orloff, 2000). For instance, psychological assaults that target particular religious beliefs, traditions, dress styles, appearance, or mannerisms.

Extreme Cruelty

The term extreme cruelty refers to any form of power and control, as experienced by the victim, and is meant to capture all the forms of abuse recognized in the domestic violence literature that is not just battery. For immigration purposes, it is not confined to the definition developed in the civil and criminal court contexts. However, there is case law history about some issues included in the definition that have been qualified as constituting extreme cruelty and that may provide examples to evaluators. Orloff, Roberts, and Gitler (2013) provide an overview of the regulatory history of coercive control. In this document, the authors analyze the various ways family courts, in the context of divorce proceedings, have found them to constitute elements of the patterns of abuse that make up coercive control. These patterns of coercive control have been deemed to be extreme cruelty by the courts, mental health professionals, and researchers.

Since domestic violence under U.S. immigration laws includes extreme cruelty for purposes of both the VAWA and U visa programs, forensic examiners have much to contribute by evaluating very carefully all the abusive actions perpetrated against the victim, explaining the evidence of coercive control in the relationship, and describing how the abusive actions constitute extreme cruelty within the context of the victim's relationship, trauma history, culture, and religious community.

Abusive Actions in VAWA Cases

The foundation of forensic assessments related to these types of crime victim-based immigration relief is the evaluation of the nature and extent of the domestic violence and the subsequent trauma and victimization. There is abundant literature addressing the strategies to evaluate psychological injury and the cultural aspects of trauma and psychopathology. However, the evaluator needs to explain clearly and directly how the specific actions of persistent abuse, coercion, and control constitute *extreme cruelty*, not just traumatic experiences.

For forensic assessors, a good place to start when assessing the violence in a relationship is with the American Psychological Association's (1996) definition of family violence and abuse as

> acts of physical abuse, sexual abuse, and psychological maltreatment; chronic situations in which one person controls or intends to control another person's behavior, and misuse of power that may result in injury or harm to the psychological, social, economic, sexual, or physical well-being.
>
> (p. 3)

Various forms of abuse tend to coexist in relationships with intimate partner violence. Abusive actions that are overt, covert, and threats are assessed as falling into the following categories.

Physical Abuse

Physical abuse is the intentional use of physical force with the potential for causing death, disability, injury, or harm. Physical violence includes physically assaultive actions, but also includes unsuccessful attempts and threats to physically harm a victim. This category alone may fulfill the VAWA criteria for battery, depending on the nature, severity, duration, and harm.

Sexual Abuse

Sexual violence includes three types: (1) use of physical force to compel a person to engage in a sexual act against his or her will, whether or not the act is completed; (2) attempted or completed sex acts involving a person who is unable to understand the nature or condition of the act, to decline participation, or to communicate unwillingness to engage in the sexual act – e.g., because of illness, disability, age, or the influence of alcohol or other drugs, or because of intimidation or pressure; and (3) abusive sexual contact (Saltzman, Fanslow, McMahon, & Shelley, 1999). Abusive sexual contact is:

> intentional touching directly, or through the clothing, of the genitalia, anus, groin, breast, inner thigh, or buttocks of any person who is unable to understand the nature or condition of the act, to decline participation, or to communicate unwillingness to engage in the sexual act (e.g., because of illness, disability, age, or the influence of alcohol or other drugs, or due to intimidation or pressure).
> (Saltzman et al., 1999, p. 43)

Stalking is also often included in this category when there is a sexual subtext to the harassment. Repeated threatening and harassing behaviors to the victim, such as following the victim, appearing at a person's home or job, harassing phone calls, leaving written messages or objects or vandalizing a victim's property all fall in this category (Tjaden & Thoennes, 2000).

Psychological Abuse

Psychological violence aims to destroy a person's feelings of self-worth and independence and involves trauma to the victim through acts, credible threats, or coercive tactics. The goal of psychological abuse is to narrow and control the victim's world by ensuring that they would not acquire social support or information that could lead to their independence or to think critically. Psychological abuse can include humiliating the victim; controlling what the victim can and cannot do; withholding information from the victim; deliberately doing something to make the victim feel diminished or embarrassed; making demeaning insults and derogatory comments; using put downs and name calling, spiteful inaction, ridiculing, blaming, and spreading damaging gossip; perpetuating psychological manipulation and lies, monitoring and checking their actions; enforcing adverse consequences for disobedience; and isolating the victim from friends and family (Browne, 1987).

A form of psychological abuse is *gaslighting* (Gass & Nichols, 1988), in which the abuser makes the victim think that things are different from what the victim intuitively knows them to be. Gaslighting causes cognitive disorientation and confusion regarding what is real and what is not and what is right and what is wrong. For instance, in immigration cases we see this strategy when the abuser who is sponsoring the victim for immigration relief based on a marriage, parental, or employment relationship portrays himself or herself as a savior and the victim as an ungrateful person.

Immigration Abuse

Immigration-related abuse can be very effective in locking the victim in the violent relationship and preventing the victim from escaping or seeking help, by threatening deportation, threatening to withdraw immigration papers filed for the victim, or actively using power over the victim's immigration status as a way of exploiting the victim and enhancing fear of deportation (Hass, Dutton, & Orloff, 2000; Orloff, Dutton, Hass, & Ammar, 2003). This abusive strategy is designed to make the victim follow the abuser's orders under the threat of deportation, refusing to sponsor a visa, or other immigration consequences such as not sponsoring the children who are back in the home country to come and join the family in the U.S.

Exploiting the fear of deportation is a particularly effective tool of violence because being sent back to a homeland the victim fled due to civil strife, conditions of intense deprivation, persecution, or violence is extremely frightening. For some it is tantamount to and experienced as a death threat. Victims who are forcefully returned to their country of origin may face risks to their safety in addition to impoverishment for them and their families. Further, having lost familiarity with their home country and suffering the stigmatization of being deported usually makes it harder for victims to seek employment and rebuild their lives, even if social conditions are better than when they left. When victims have children in the U.S., threats of deportation that are likely to effectively result in permanent separation from children are particularly potent and have significant traumatic impact on victims.

Economic Abuse

Economic abuse is another form of violence that locks someone into a relationship with an abuser for fear that their livelihood will be in jeopardy if they leave. Abusers may use tactics to force the victim into economic dependence through actions such as confiscating the victim's salary, money, or resources, exploiting them for financial purposes without compensation, withholding money or access to resources, or anything aimed at decreasing the financial security of the victim.

Other Forms of Abuse

Some forms of abuse do not fit neatly into these categories, but are also very powerful forms of abuse and coercion, such as: (1) endangering children (threats to kidnap, exposure to violence, take custody of, deport, or harm the children); (2) destruction of property; (3) threats or harm to relatives or pets (Ganley, 1989).

The way these violent actions are best evaluated is by using semi-structured instruments and interviews that allow the examiner to understand the specific abuse incidents and its intensity and frequency. For those victims with long histories of abuse, an alternative technique is to ask them to describe the first, worse, and last incident of violence in order to understand the nature and progression of the abuse. Another way of evaluating the history of abuse, especially with victims who can be overwhelmed emotionally, is to ask the victim to name the memorable experiences of victimization as 'newspaper headlines without details' (Brand, 2016) and later go over the most relevant incidents to obtain the details. The key element for the evaluation of abuse is to obtain detailed-oriented and contextualized information that provides the basis to establish whether the totality of actions rise to the level of battery or extreme cruelty.

Dutton (1992) recommends allowing victims to narrate their story without interruption and then go back to get more information and details of the incidents. The key issue here is to always get the details and guide the victim to describe the upsetting experiences rather than just naming them. As forensic examiners, we do not just accept the victim's sweeping statements without probing for specific details and context. We need details of the facts in order to develop our own opinion. It will also make it harder to determine deception if we simply allow the examinee to tell a story without looking at the factors that help us determine its reliability. However, keep in mind that, unless guided to talk about specific incidents, victims' own traumatic symptoms incline them to avoid the topic. Most frequently, they tend to forget, not have the words to label some abusive actions, or are too ashamed or frightened to mention some aspects of their abuse. It is important to remember that this part of the evaluation can be re-traumatizing and it needs to be managed with extreme care (see Chapter 3).

Coercive Control and the Escalation of Abuse

For VAWA filings, coercive control is the most important aspect of the abuse to evaluate. The concept of coercive control goes beyond emotional or psychological abuse and is central to VAWA psycholegal concepts. Coercive control is the ongoing pattern of domination in which physical and sexual violence is combined with intimidation, sexual degradation, isolation, and control (Stark, 2011). Stark (2007)'s model of coercive control includes actions such as stalking, which is a criminal offense; actions that would only be crimes if committed by a stranger, such as economic exploitation; and enforced isolation or sexual coercion. But the majority of the methods of coercive control used by abusers

> include forms of constraint and the monitoring and/or regulation of commonplace activities of daily living, particularly those associated with women's default roles as mothers, homemakers and sexual partners and run the gamut from their access to money, food and transport to how they dress, clean, cook or perform sexually.

(Stark, 2011, p. 4)

A significant body of literature documents how, once intimate partner violence begins, it will continue to escalate and is driven by coercive control (Krug, Dahlberg, Mercy, Zwi, & Lozano, 2002). However, we need to remember that there is still a risk of harm even without overt signs of escalating physical violence when one partner exercises power, control, and fear over the other. What may, at face value, appear as an isolated aggressive act may be upon closer inspection a situation in which the physical violence did not escalate, because the victim adjusted her behavior for fear of other incidents. We may not see escalation of physical violence, but the coercive control progresses and the victim organizes her life around self-protection. If the victim tries to leave the abuser or discloses the family secret of abuse, the abuser may feel a loss of power and control and the risk of increasingly dangerous and cruel abuse rises.

The extreme cruelty concept may or may not include physical violence, but it always includes coercive control. Coercion refers to inequality of the partners and oppression of one by the other because of the oppressor's sense of entitlement. Coercion includes strategies designed to retain privileges and establish domination in a partner's personal life based on fear, dependence, and deprivation of basic rights and liberties (Stark, 2007). When we gather sufficient information to understand the function and context of the abusive actions, we can determine whether the abusive actions were tools of control by one person over another, which thus constitutes extreme cruelty. This information helps distinguish a pattern of battering or coercive control abuse from fights, verbal conflict, or mutual disrespect (Dutton, 1992).

For the assessment of coercion, we look into the elements that transform a request or demand into a coercive action (Dutton & Goodman, 2005). Perpetrators set the stage to define the type of relationship they expect to have with the partner. There are four methods that they use to exert and maintain coercive control: (1) creating the expectancy for negative consequences; (2) creating and exploiting new and existing vulnerabilities; (3) wearing down resistance; and (4) facilitating attachment.

The essential element of a coercive action is that the request or demand will carry negative consequences if not obeyed and, whether the abuser makes this explicit or not, the victim knows by experience that she will be punished if she does not comply. Further, the abuser will make sure that the victim complies by surveilling for obedience and examining cues of non-compliance. The victim is not given a choice to do something different than what was demanded. Figure 5.1, based on Dutton's model (Dutton & Goodman, 2005), illustrates the elements of coercion that need to be part of the forensic evaluation and be part of a thorough questioning.

Evaluating the emotions, cognitions, and behaviors associated with the different elements of the coercive control model is important to conceptualize the psychological impact on the victim. In addition, the behaviors that the victim engages in as a consequence of coercion, which are not a product of free will, also need to be evaluated and the associated psychological meaning explained.

Figure 5.1 Elements of Coercion to Evaluate.

Why do we utilize theoretical models to assess the abuse? Utilizing a model to assess the intimate partner violence is a good way to organize the information to be assessed, to explain it in a meaningful way, and to support the data obtained from the examinee with empirical literature.

There are a number of assessment instruments that help the examinee describe the nature and experiences of violence and coercive control. Advocates, law students, and attorneys often use the Immigrant Power and Control Wheel (Domestic Abuse Intervention Project, n.d.) to document the different types of abuse and coercion typically perpetrated against immigrant women. This can help victims identify forms of power and coercive control they are experiencing and more fully describe the dynamics of the abuse suffered (the Power and Control Wheel for Immigrant Women is available at: http://endingviolence.org/files/uploads/ ImmigrantWomenPCwheel.pdf and www.futureswithoutviolence.org/power-and-control-tactics-used-against-immigrant-women). Forensic examiners need more thorough instruments because the information needed for a forensic report is more in-depth. The Psychological Maltreatment of Women Inventory (Tolman, 1999) is a tool for this purpose, and the Structured Interview Questionnaires for Immigration Cases (Dutton et al., 2013) is a very comprehensive instrument that helps gather the essential information in cases of relief from victimization, including VAWA, U-visa, and T visa, which can be found at: http://library.niwap.org/wp-content/uploads/2015/SIQI.edited.di-tb-6.15.15.pdf.

In some cases, in which the victim used violence for self-protection, it may be necessary to determine who was the primary perpetrator of abuse in the relationship. A person acting in self-defense does not aim to exert control over the other person, but rather attempts to prevent imminent serious harm. A person acting in self-defense must not be treated as, or confused with, someone in a relationship where there is mutual aggression. The forensic examiner plays an important role in providing an analysis that looks beyond the incidents themselves to assess the family dynamics and patterns of power and control. This assessment gathers information to determine if any wounds to the perpetrator were defensive (bite marks, scratches, etc.) and determines who is afraid of whom. Additionally, we look at the motivation for the violence: Was the violence motivated by retaliation, meant to punish and control, or for self-protection? Who effectively exerts control over the other person (who makes the rules, manages the money, manages the decisions, etc.)? Is the impact of violence to maintain power and control when there were challenges to that power? Who has historically been the dominant aggressor in the relationship?

Remember that the aggressor is not necessarily the person who struck first during a particular incident (Dutton et al., 2013).

Due to the popular, though erroneous, myth that a battered woman is at fault for not leaving the batterer and to increase reliability of the account, it is always important to assess whether, and what attempts, the victim made to stop the abuse. Examine the results of those actions and the factors that interfered with the victim's ability to take formal actions, such as calling the police or pressing charges, if this was the case. The risk of a batterer seriously harming or killing the adult victim and children increases when the victim tries to leave or seek out help. Citing the literature that shows that victims that leave the batterer are not necessarily safer (Campbell, 1992; Wilson & Daly, 1993) can strengthen this aspect of the evaluation. The Danger Assessment (Campbell, Webster, & Glass, 2009) is a measure of risk that can be utilized to strengthen the empirical confirmation of the danger the victim was facing.

These categories are a simplified way of organizing large and complex data regarding the dynamics of intimate partner violence in order to assess and understand it, but some cases do not fit neatly into categories. In particular, the presence of substance abuse in either the abuser, the victim, or both, may change substantially the pattern and dynamic of abuse, making it unpredictable and explosive. However, if any of these empirically supported categories fit the abuse the examinee experienced, it lends greater credibility to the forensic examiner's opinion that the abuse constituted extreme cruelty, while differentiating the case from one that was merely a dispute between a couple not getting along.

Psychological Impact of the Abuse

There are a number of empirically supported psychological measures and techniques to assess the impact of traumatic experiences (Chapters 9 and 10 review these instruments and techniques). They provide a good foundation to the assessment of the psychological impact of domestic violence.

In immigration evaluations, there has to be a proximate link between the examinee's psychological problems and the domestic violence. Therefore, knowledge of the examinee's functioning before the abuse, during the period when the abuse was occurring, immediately after, and in the long-term are important to gather and analyze. The assessment of previous functioning can be made by asking about activities that reveal social adjustment (sleeping and eating habits, work, social network, recreational activities, self-care, mood and satisfaction with life, among others) and then the assessor may ask and find evidence about how these may have changed over time as the relationship became more distressing.

The instruments used to assess the emotional impact (e.g., the Trauma Symptom Inventory-2; PTSD Checklist) look at the examinee's functioning around the time of the evaluation, which may be months or even years after the abuse occurred. Victims develop over time a series of coping mechanisms to deal with the fact that they are living constantly in fear, and after they leave the abusive situation these strategies adjust again; the end result of these transformed strategies is that they may generate miscued emotions. Numbing the fear, making the anxiety generalized to unrelated issues, splitting fear from consciousness, or turning fear into rage or desire for revenge makes it harder to link them to the specific incidents of battering and/or extreme cruelty that the victim suffered. Therefore, at the same time or after asking about the discrete events of violence and the pattern of abuse, it is important to ask the examinee:

> Tell me what were you feeling and thinking at that time?
> What did you tell yourself?
> Did these feelings and thoughts change over time and if so how?

If this knowledge is available in the examinee's awareness, it helps understand the progression of the emotions and thoughts around the incidents of abuse and to map the psychological impact of the violence. Many victims talk about how the initial reaction is of surprise or even feeling flattered. One victim said her boyfriend called her to ask what she was doing, and after she told him she was at home making dinner, he told her to open the door because he was standing outside her door. She said that at the time she thought 'Oh, how sweet that he wanted to give me a surprise!' Through this and other such situations, she later came to realize that he wanted to control everything she did and where she went, and showing up at her door was to check about whether she complied with a request he had made to always come directly home from work. Initial emotions of shock, surprise, or even feeling loved and cherished, may change into confusion, anxiety, disappointment, fear, anger, and even horror, which adds to also feeling heartbroken and betrayed. These nuances of the progression in the emotional impact of abuse are often accessed through a careful and sensitive interview.

Assessing and reporting the nature and progress of turbulent emotions around the victimization helps explain how the victim became more emotionally debilitated over time and may also help explain any seemingly unrelated or bizarre emotions that are so because they were modified over time or were influenced by cultural values. This evaluative strategy may also help when test results do not seem to reflect the true impact of the abuse.

It is important to assess and integrate information regarding the cultural values and beliefs that may have exacerbated or ameliorated the psychological impact of the battering for the immigrant victim. For instance, some cultures instruct women to be obedient and accept the authority of their husbands, which interferes with their ability to identify the abuse or seek help. In addition, the cultural value of keeping family matters in the family to prevent being seen as disloyal and bringing shame to the family may prevent some women from taking formal steps to stop, seek help, or escape from the abuse. In these cases, due to a combination of abuse and cultural isolation, the only evidence of the abuse that occurred may be the victim's testimony and the forensic evaluation. Psychological evaluations that assess the psychological impact of the battering and/or extreme cruelty are essential in providing valuable and probative evidence supporting the victim's VAWA or U visa application.

Diagnostic and Functional Findings

Although the finding of a diagnosis from the Diagnostic and Statistical Manual (DSM) is often (and perhaps erroneously) thought to be highly valued as evidence of the impact of extreme cruelty, it is not essential and may not be that helpful unless the symptoms are detailed and clearly connected to the abuse. Diagnoses that represent the impact of the traumatic events in the relationship such as PTSD, acute stress disorder, dissociative disorder, mood disorder diagnoses, anxiety diagnoses, etc. need to be well explained and detailed in an individualized way as to how exactly these diagnoses are specifically related to the battering or emotional cruelty.

It is important not to forget that psychopathology derived from traumatic abuse is varied and highly influenced by cultural factors. There are personality disorders that develop from the experience of enduring chronic traumatization, which can be noted in the expert opinion as such, as long as there is a connection with the victimization and this is made abundantly clear in the report or testimony. However, DSM is not by far the only way to judge what constitutes mental impairment. We have found the use of complex traumatic disorder (Nickerson et al., 2016; Pelcovitz et al., 1997) to be acceptable when indicated, provided that a good explanation is given as to why it is not in the DSM and adequate citations of credible literature about its validity as a diagnostic category are offered. It is important to take steps to dispel the allegations that this important and well-researched diagnosis may not be widely acceptable in the professional community.

When the examinee suffers from clinically relevant symptoms but they do not meet criteria for a diagnosis, the examiner needs to determine if these symptoms constitute a *significant* psychological impact and if so make a very strong case as to why the examiner believes so. It is not surprising that a person reading the report may refuse to acknowledge that symptoms such as stress, anxiety, and moodiness constitute evidence of extreme cruelty, because most people experience those emotions at one time or another too. If the examiner finds evidence that isolated symptoms are disabling to the victim and impairing at many levels of functioning, it should count as significant functional impairment, even if not in the DSM. Documenting these symptoms in detail, and discussing how they impact the victim's life and the level of impairment it produces, are among the most important findings an examiner can offer. This may be especially true for cases of culturally idiosyncratic symptoms.

Additional or comorbid applicable conditions need to also be provided and explained, including its interaction with their impact from trauma. For instance, developmental disorders, neuropsychological problems, or serious health conditions may be very closely linked to the impact of trauma. When there are psychological issues or diagnoses that may be counterproductive to the examinee's application, they will require additional inquiries, the examiner may find evidence that they developed as a strategy to manage emotions aroused by the abuse or were perpetrated under coercion or fraud (e.g., substance abuse, shoplifting, assault, prostitution). More about this in the next section.

Good Moral Character

Assessing good moral character is particularly demanding, because this psycholegal construct has not been clearly defined in immigration law. The legal information defines good moral character by the conditions that would contradict its presence, also called 'bars' (Musalo & Rice, 2008). Crimes such as murder, aggravated felony, persecution, genocide, or torture are considered to represent lack of moral character, and any of these issues is considered a permanent bar. Conditional bars are factors that can be waived, depending on the circumstances. These include crimes involving a controlled substance, an immigration crime, prostitution, gambling, being an alcoholic, failing to support dependents, adultery, failing to file tax returns, defrauding the government with public benefits, and others (Weissbrodt & Danielson, 2011). Where any of these unlawful acts may have been motivated by the circumstances of the examinee, this information can be of great assistance to the immigration case in demonstrating particularly the pattern of the abuse, power, control, or coercion suffered by the victim as well as how they were related to the victim's efforts to survive or escape the abuse. For instance, victims of battering may use substances to numb the psychological pain, some victims may have been forced by the abuser to engage in criminal activity (e.g., theft, shoplifting, prostitution), or they may engage in these crimes out of desperation to survive or care for their children.

Adjudicators have discretionary authority to weight those conditional bars less heavily, if those crimes were connected to the psychological state of the victim and directly caused by the abuse. For instance, it is important to assess whether the victim was forced to commit the crimes by the abuser; how the abuser used poverty, deprivation, undocumented status, and/or immigration-related abuse as part of the pattern of abuse; and whether they were struggling to survive following abuse. When the criminal acts committed were related to escaping abuse, ameliorating the effects of the abuse, or preventing future abuse, the adjudicator has the discretion to grant a waiver of a conditional bar. Therefore, when the examinee has engaged in behaviors that are listed as conditional bars, the forensic examiner needs to determine if and how they relate to the crimes committed against him or her.

When evaluating moral character, the forensic examiner needs to know if the examinee has a previous criminal record and needs to explore the specifics of those problems with the law and the victim's motivation. Problems with the law or criminal convictions in and of themselves do not equate with a criminal or antisocial personality in psychological terms, so additional steps are necessary to make this determination. For instance, if the victim entered the U.S. without inspection, he or she committed a civil violation of immigration law. The examiner should listen to see if this happened when he or she was a minor, or to reunite with family, or to escape abuse, physical or sexual violence, or extreme poverty. If the unlawful activity was to drive without a license, listen to find out if it happened because the examinee had to get to work, take care of the children, go to the doctor, escape abuse, protect himself or herself or the children, or under coercion. If the crime committed was shoplifting, listen to determine how it may have been connected with the abuse. For example, did the victim steal baby food to feed the child when fleeing the abusive home? (Dutton et al., 2013).

It is also helpful to ask whether there were consequences to the unlawful activity, such as being detained, going to court, serving a sentence or probation, or paying a fine. Assess whether the examinee understands that the consequences were warranted given the fault. If the examinee pleaded guilty, you want to know why, and if anybody advised a guilty plea but the examinee did not understand his or her rights and the consequences of such a plea (Dutton et al., 2013). These questions help to identify if there are any mitigating factors to the crime or violations that the examinee committed. It is important to assess here if the examinee assumes responsibility, feels sorry for what happened, and has the resolve and resources (psychological and otherwise) to avoid engaging in these actions again.

Keep in mind that immigration adjudicators are generally asked to *only* look at the elements of the crimes for which the examinee was criminally adjudicated. Adjudicators are, however, permitted to pursue information about any other negative facts they find in their review of the evidence in the case. If the forensic examiner provides information about behavior for which the examinee was not convicted, but could be considered objectionable, the examiner opened the door and invites an inquiry from the adjudicator that may otherwise not have been permissible or occurred, and the forensic examiner may end up hurting the examinee (Zimmer, 2013).

In order to assess a person's moral fitness, other issues in the life of the examinee need to be considered. For instance, the examiner needs to look at involvement with religious organizations, history of employment, and whether they have been fired for cause. Other factors include relationships with family, enduring friendships, relationships with employers and colleagues, ability to hold onto a social network over time, any awards or certificates received, relationship with children's school staff, volunteer work, and community involvement. Ask concrete questions so you can draw your own conclusions from this information. Normally the legal representative would ask the examinee for letters or other evidence to provide information around all these issues, but if not, it is appropriate for the examiner to ask for this evidence or question collaterals.

Additionally, during the interview, ask the examinee to tell you about the type of person they are, and the personality characteristics they are most proud of.

Then, you go back to those words and ask them for specific and detailed anecdotes when this trait showed up qualitatively. If an examinee struggles with this question, you can use your clinical and tests findings regarding the examinee's strengths to probe gently for positive attributes such as hardworking, loyal, responsible, etc.

Personality test data may provide findings that show the examinee's best qualities, such as empathy, desire to be liked, generosity, respect for authority, etc. Similarly, evidence of good moral character can show up in those areas of the evaluation that screened for problems and traits and that the examinee did not have. Clinical findings that are helpful to an examinee's ability to prove good moral character include psychological test results that the examinee is not callous or insensitive, does not have a substance abuse problem, does not show antisocial traits, etc. This is an evidence-based manner to highlight the examinee's good moral qualities.

There are other crimes for which you may need more than the interview to provide an opinion that justifies a waiver request. In order to obtain a waiver if the examinee has been convicted of a crime considered an aggravated felony under immigration law or meets the criteria for any of the categories that bar good moral character, a risk assessment may be advisable. A risk assessment that includes statements regarding future risk to the community and rehabilitation may be requested of the examiner by the examinee's legal representative. It is important to note that the immigration law definition of aggravated felony includes many crimes that under state law are misdemeanors and are relatively low-level crimes for which the examinee never served any jail time. This is a complex area of the law and there will be many cases in which victims will need help with waivers for very minor offenses and for offenses committed as a direct result of the abuse. It is important to note that risk assessments in IC matters require forensic examiners to have specialized knowledge beyond the assessment of usual VAWA parameters.

There are particular tests (i.e., Millon Clinical Multiaxial Inventory-Third Edition-Corrections Report; Millon, Millon, & Davis, 2003) and semi-structured interviews (i.e., Psychopathy Checklist-Revised, second edition; Hare, 2003) that can help with this risk evaluation in cases in which the examinee's demographics fit the standardization population of those tests. Consider that negative findings on these risk evaluations may require an extra step on the part of the examiner, which is to recommend the type of treatment or rehabilitation program that the examinee needs in order to heal and decrease risk of recidivism. While such recommendations may delay the examinee's application for immigration relief, taking the time for the examinee to receive the treatment needed and to heal can significantly improve achievement of a successful outcome in the immigration case, because it can help ensure that the examinee presents his or her best immigration case after they have been treated and healed. More about this in Chapter 4.

Good-Faith Marriage

Examinees should work with their attorney to accumulate concrete evidence regarding the requirement that the marriage was entered in good faith. The attorney may ask for this information; however, it is important that the examiner seek this information as part of the forensic exam in any immigration-related case as this evidence can be helpful in many immigration applications. Seeking this information should be part of the creation of the case hypothesis and can guide the interview. An excellent source of documents that are helpful as evidence of good-faith marriage is found in the work of Dutton and colleagues (2013).

Clinically, the examiner can assess the good faith of the marriage by asking about the story of the relationship, and tracking with questions the feelings, thoughts, and actions of the victim toward the spouse over time. Because this evaluative strategy involves judgment, it is important to avoid using Western values that may bias our opinion. It is important to ask, document, and research any cultural factors that may have played a role in the courtship, engagement, ceremony, and marriage. For instance, in many cultures falling passionately in love is not a requirement to enter a marriage; some cultures do not have a long engagement or even have one at all, ceremonies may be more or less involved depending on the culture, socioeconomic factors of the family or couple, or because it is not the parents' financial responsibility to pay for the ceremony in some cultures. Ask the examinee to recall anecdotal stories about the home they established together and experiences they shared. The concrete documents or pictures the examinee provide are a good cue to evoke emotions and thoughts around those memories. Recalling this information through a guided interview can help the examiner develop an opinion regarding the examinee's expectations, beliefs, and intentions regarding the marriage. These are the central evidentiary requirements under immigration law that must be proven by an applicant.

It can also be helpful to demonstrate how heartfelt the examinee's efforts were and what her or his commitment was to make the marriage work before and when the marital problems began. This information helps provide strong evidence that the marriage was in good faith. The interview can also determine, on the basis of the information gathered, whether the abuse was the more heartbreaking, because it constituted a betrayal of the victim's dreams and expectations, if that was the case.

VAWA applications require a great deal of detail-oriented attention from the examiner, but luckily this type of immigration relief has been around for many years and the legal guidance for these applications is extensive.

Chapter 6

Relief from Victimization
U Visa and T Visa

The U visa and T visa were both created in 2000 when the Victims of Trafficking and Violence Protection Act (VTVPA) was passed by Congress. This law creates non-immigrant forms of admission that provide temporary status to individuals in the U.S. who are or have been victims of a severe form of trafficking or who have suffered substantial physical or mental abuse as victims of criminal activity. The intention of the law is to combat trafficking of persons, especially into the sex trade, slavery, and involuntary servitude, and to reauthorize certain Federal programs to prevent violence against immigrant women and children. However, only specific crimes will allow victims to qualify, with some overlapping with other immigration relief forms. For instance, U and T visas both include human trafficking as a qualifying crime, but U visas and T visas each have different requirements. Depending on the case, one of these visas may be a better option over the other.

U Visa or Relief for Victims of Criminal Activity

The requirements for the U visa include that the applicant (any non-citizen who is not a legal permanent resident [LPR]) is an immigrant victim of crime who

> a) has suffered substantial mental or physical abuse as a result of having been a victim of criminal activity, b) has information regarding the criminal activity, and c) has helped, is helping, or is willing to help government officials in the detection, investigation, prosecution, conviction, or sentencing of such criminal activity.
>
> (Federal Register Publications, 2007, p. 53020)

This visa protects victims of domestic violence, sexual assault, human trafficking (DHS, 2015), and also workers from employer retaliation when they are victims or whistleblowers of workplace abuse. The use of this type of immigration relief in connection with abuse in the workplace improves workers' trust and cooperation with labor and civil rights law enforcement agencies (*Garcia v. Audobon Community Mgmt*, 2008).

The statutory provisions have named 28 qualifying criminal activities that fulfill requirements of eligibility for U visa statutory provisions. These qualifying criminal activities are outlined in Table 6.1.

In addition to the qualifying acts themselves, the attempt, conspiracy, or solicitation of these qualifying criminal activities may serve as the basis for U visa eligibility.

Psycholegal Concept

The psycholegal concept that the evaluator needs to address is *substantial mental or physical abuse*, which must be a result of the qualifying criminal activity. In order to qualify for a U visa, the victim must prove as an element of their case that they suffered at least one of the criminal activities, included in the certification they filed, which caused them substantial mental or physical abuse. The definition of substantial physical or mental abuse is more expansive and extensive than extreme cruelty (Cho, Hass, & Salcedo, 2015), because it applies to a broader array of crimes and also because both the abuse and the impact can vary widely. The U visa regulations require that adjudicators must consider:

> The nature of the injury inflicted or suffered, the severity of the perpetrator's conduct, the severity of the harm suffered, the duration of the infliction of the harm, and the extent to which there is permanent or serious harm to the appearance, health, or physical or mental soundness of the victim, including aggravation of pre-existing conditions.
>
> (8 C.F.R. §214. 14 (b) (1))

Table 6.1 Qualifying Crimes for a U Visa

• Abduction	• Hostage	• Sexual assault
• Abusive sexual contact	• Incest	• Sexual exploitation
• Blackmail	• Involuntary servitude	• Slave trade
• Domestic violence	• Kidnapping	• Stalking
• Extortion	• Manslaughter	• Torture
• False imprisonment	• Murder	• Trafficking
• Female genital mutilation	• Obstruction of justice	• Witness tampering
	• Peonage	• Unlawful criminal restraint
• Felonious assault	• Perjury	
• Fraud in foreign labor contracting	• Prostitution	• Other related crimes*†
	• Rape	

Source: US Citizenship and Immigration Services. Victims of Criminal Activity U-Non-Immigrant Status. Qualifying criminal activities. Retrieved April 3, 2017 from www.uscis.gov/human itarian/victims-human-trafficking-other-crimes/victims-criminal-activity-u-nonimmigrant-status/victims-criminal-activity-u-nonimmigrant-status#Qualifying%20Criminal%20Activities.

Notes
* Includes any similar activity where the elements of the crime are substantially similar.
† Also includes attempt, conspiracy, or solicitation to commit any of the above and other related crimes.

The U visa standards contain some nuance in the determination of substantial mental or physical abuse. These standards indicate that the conduct of the perpetrator may be so severe that evidence of that conduct on its own could, in some cases, be considered substantial abuse. However, the regulations caution against relying upon assumptions that equate one or more of the abusive actions as automatically determining that the abuse was substantial. The standards also recognize that, even when the abusive incidents viewed in isolation do not appear sufficiently severe, a series of abusive acts taken together within certain contexts may be considered substantial physical or mental abuse.

Substantial Mental Abuse

For the purposes of evaluating substantial mental or physical abuse, the following types of abuse can be assessed by the examiner: physical violence, sexual violence, psychological abuse (including bullying), immigration, and economic abuse. Negligence can also be assessed. Unfortunately, there is no available mental health research into the forms of abuse that occur in some of the categories covered by this law, such as the case for workplace abuse beyond bullying (Cho et al., 2015). The above-mentioned assessment categories were established in the literature of domestic violence and have been adapted and expanded to the U visa context by Cho and colleagues to cover those criminal activities included in the U visa legislation that do not occur within an intimate relationship. From the comprehensive assessment of abuse, the forensic examiner can identify the qualifying criminal activities, which in his or her opinion may be all, none, or different than what the attorney referring the case mentioned.

Approximately 75 percent of the U visa cases filed nationally include one of the following criminal activities: domestic violence, sexual assault, or human trafficking (Orloff & Feldman, 2011). These criminal activities may have been committed within families, among acquaintances, in schools, in the workplace, or in the community. Although there are different types of abusive behaviors, legally there are only two kinds of injuries possible: An injury may be a physical injury or a mental injury. Also, an injury may be an actual injury, a threatened injury, or an injury that occurs as the result of an attempted criminal activity. The U visa may be filed at any point in time after the victimization, because there is no statute of limitations (DHS, 2015).

This chapter will not review in detail all the different psychological evaluations connected to the different criminal activities under the U visa standards. U visa applications on account of domestic violence will require a psychological evaluation that is similar to the one conducted in a VAWA or asylum case where the underlying criminal activity was intimate partner violence. Under U.S. immigration laws, a domestic violence victim will qualify for a U visa rather than a VAWA case when the victim is not married or when the abuser is not the victim's citizen or LPR spouse or parent. On those cases, the evaluation of emotional injury parallels the assessment for a VAWA applicant as reviewed in Chapter 5. The reader is referred to Chapter 5 for guidance regarding the assessment of the nature and impact of the intimate partner abuse. A victim of female genital mutilation (FGM) or torture perpetrated in the U.S. may not qualify for asylum on the basis of gender violence or persecution, but could qualify to file a U visa application. In these cases, the evaluation of emotional injury parallels the one conducted for cases of asylum on these bases. Readers can refer to Chapter 2 for guidance on evaluating the nature and impact of FGM and Chapter 4 for torture. In cases of victims of human trafficking that apply for the U visa instead of the T visa, the examiner should follow the guidelines provided in the second part of this chapter, which covers T visa applications. In all these cases, the examiner needs to be careful about assessing the direct connection of the psychological impact to the qualifying criminal activity and that the impact is considered 'substantial' (implying functional impairment). The examiner should be careful to use this psycholegal concept and make the link of qualifying crime and impact very clear in the report.

The evaluation of psychological injury when the victim was assaulted, raped, abused, or subjected to any other qualifying criminal activity on the street, in the workplace, or in the community in general, and perpetrated by a stranger or an acquaintance means that the substantial mental abuse is assessed with the requirement that harm was caused from intentional or negligent conduct by someone who does not have a significant relationship with the victim. In these cases, the examiner conducts a comprehensive examination of the victim to determine the nature of the criminal activity and its meaning to the victim as well as whether there is clinical evidence of psychological injury. Additionally, the examiner must assess the data that link or refute that the mental problems of the victim were caused by the criminal activity. The examiner also assesses the credibility of the evidence regarding the alleged criminal activity through the victim's account, police records, and any other collateral materials provided by the victim's attorney.

As in all the U visa, T visa, and VAWA evaluations, this assessment needs to cover the immigrant respondent's functioning across four periods of time: before, during, and immediately following the abusive event, as well as the longer-term impact of the victimization in order to determine the development or aggravation (in the case of preexisting conditions) of symptoms caused by the victimization, which is what is considered the direct impact.

The model of psychological harm developed by the personal injury and tort field provides a useful framework for U visa assessments. That model is helpful in that it examines three types of relationships between the criminal activity and the consequences: (1) physical trauma causing mental injury; (2) mental stimulus causing physical injury; and (3) mental stimulus causing mental injury (Melton, Petrila, Poythress, & Slobogin, 2007).

The first category, physical trauma caused by the criminal activity causing mental injury, provides the most direct link of causation (Melton et al., 2007).

For instance, emotional trauma caused by being assaulted and hurt physically with a weapon when a victim was mugged on the street provides the cause–effect relationship that, with the help of assessment measures and techniques, can provide credible evidence of substantial mental abuse. Examiners need to assess carefully for physical abuse and injury in all U visa cases, because if there is a link to the substantial mental injury, this will make the case stronger.

The second category of mental aspects of the criminal activity that cause a physical injury refers to those qualifying criminal activities that, as a consequence of the victimization, lead the victim to suffer medical problems (Melton et al., 2007). For instance, a pregnant woman who is present at the scene of a shooting suffers a miscarriage. Medical and physical problems caused by non-physical criminal activity may qualify for this category and constitute the second level in terms of strength of evidence. Examiners need to pay attention to the respondent's medical records and track the emergence and aggravation of the medical problems with the start and aggravation of the criminal activity.

The third category, a mental criminal activity causing mental injury, refers to situations in which the victim suffered a psychological assault that led to mental health problems. For instance, an immigrant who became the victim of unwarranted enraged persecution by a store security guard who illegally acted on racial profiling. This situation triggered a panic attack that reoccurred when the immigrant had to enter any store. In these cases, the examiner looks at the non-physical criminal activity and the psychological impact of the criminal activity. These cases are more challenging, because there are other intervening variables to assess and link, such as the fact that the intensity of the trauma is related to the appraisal of the victim, which is then related to his or her resilience, background, vulnerabilities, expectations, preparation, and other factors.

As with the other forms of immigration relief for crime victims, preexisting conditions that were aggravated or accelerated due to the new victimization should be taken into consideration as much as the index offense and trauma. These preexisting conditions need to be assessed in detail and their progress should be explained in the report.

Criminal Activities Perpetrated in the Workplace

The U visa legislation goes to great lengths to cover work-related criminal activities for which immigrants are particularly vulnerable victims. This has led to the successful application of the U visa to workplace abuse. It is important to note that most of the following discussion on workplace-based criminal activities is applicable to cases where the abuse occurs in other contexts in which the perpetrator of the criminal activity is in a position of authority over the victim, but the relationship is not intimate, such as in schools, universities, coaches of athletic teams, clergy, and doctor–patient relationships.

Abusive Actions in the Workplace

Many of the U visa listed criminal activities are forms of abuse that are committed by employers and supervisors against employees. In each U visa case, the forensic evaluation can be extremely useful in providing evidence that helps immigrant victims prove that the harms they suffered as a result of workplace abuse amounted to substantial physical or emotional abuse. To determine substantial harm in the workplace, it is important to understand the type of abuse, as well as its severity, duration, and persistence, in order to distinguish 'substantial' emotional or physical abuse from merely stressful working situations.

One of the areas in which U visa immigration relief is particularly helpful is in low-wage industries where employment sometimes includes a wide array of U visa listed criminal activities perpetrated against low-wage workers. Low-wage, low-skill industries can sometimes have deplorable working conditions that include work environments in which criminal activities directed against workers are rampant. In these environments, undocumented immigrant workers experience exceptionally high rates of basic labor law violations, abuse, and work-related injuries. Therefore, understanding the typical working conditions in the victim's job is essential to determining when certain actions became abusive, exploitive, and may constitute criminal activities.

In spite of the appallingly poor working conditions and lack of labor standards in some industries, the typical conditions of the job usually do not qualify as specific criminal activities necessary to obtain a U visa. The examiner needs to differentiate them from the qualifying criminal activities the immigrant victim suffered and make sure they are not used to support the substantial abuse criteria.

In addition to the criminal activities in which the employer directly abuses, exploits, or manipulates the employees, negligence is also a source of some qualifying criminal activities. Although these jobs are hazardous and stressful, the employer has the responsibility of providing safety. The U.S. Department of Labor's Occupational Safety and Health Administration (OSHA), which is responsible for enforcing the Occupational Safety and Health Act of 1970, requires employers to 'furnish to each of his employees, employment and a place of employment which are free from recognized hazards that are causing or are likely to cause death or serious physical harm to the employees' (Federal OSHA; 29 U.S.C. § 654, 5(a)1). Some cases in which the employer was neglectful regarding safety for the employees can meet criteria for a qualifying criminal activity. Moreover, there are listed criminal activities (e.g., obstruction of justice, witness tampering) where these qualifying criminal activities are committed by some employers as part of retaliation, and which can occur after the worker files a claim with a law enforcement agency. In these cases, the criminal activity is the product of the employer's attempts to prevent or interfere with the investigation.

When interviewing a victim of workplace abuse, the examiner is encouraged to use the structured interview shown in Table 6.2. This interview outline

Table 6.2 List of Workplace Abuse[1]

The following are examples of potential situations to guide the semi-structured interview in U visa cases of workplace abuse, but it is not an exclusive list.

Ask the client: *What was your relationship with the abuser? When and how did your abuser start mistreating you? I am going to go over some ways in which he or she may have mistreated you. Tell me which of these happened. [For each one, ask the client: How often did your abuser do this? Did your abuser do it in front of others? Who? How did it make you feel? What thoughts crossed your mind when this was going on? How did you react? Did you ever tell anyone? Did this change things in your life or the way you feel or behave?]*

Physical Abuse in the Workplace

Throw something	Burning, scalding	Restrict from taking medication
Push, grab, shove	Using or threatening with a weapon	Physically restraining, locking the person in an enclosed space
Scratch, pinch, hair pulling	Use of restraints, holding down	Use car to create a dangerous situation (e.g., driving or forcing person out of the car)
Wrestle, twist arm or bend hand	Bang head against an object	Use a machine to intimidate or threaten (pushing you towards a machine or assigning you to a broken or dangerous machine without having trained you)
Slap, spank, slam	Smother, strangle, choke, hang	Expose to dangerous substances
Kick, hit, beat, drag, pull	Shaking	Fail to seek out medical treatment when the employee is ill and asked for help
Bit	Pulled hair	Force or threat to force taking drugs or alcohol
Hit with something	Force or threat to restrict from eating or drinking	Force or threat to restrict from attending to hygiene
Damage employee's property	Deprive of food and shelter	Endangerment

Sexual Abuse in the Workplace

Direct sexual abuse	Indirect	Creating a sexualized environment (not directed to anyone in particular)	Sexual discrimination
Increasingly aggressive harassment.	Required to wear provocative clothes or cleavage.	Sexual innuendo and giving sexual meaning to regular speech (double entendres).	Discrimination to women who are pregnant or who are assumed to become pregnant.
Attempted or completed rape vaginally or anally by physical force, threat, or blackmail.	Make the worker flirt with a client to attract business. Unwanted indecent advances. Sexual innuendo.	Talk or make allusions to sexual activity or preferences.	To establish a requirement or practice that is the same for everyone but has an unfair effect on pregnant women.
Forcing a person to perform sexual favors other than intercourse by force, threat, or blackmail.	Indiscreet glances. Mentioning intimate themes (such as menstrual cycle, etc).	General use of obscene language or gestures. Sharing sexually inappropriate images or videos, such as pornography, with co-workers.	Treat a woman worker less favorably because she is breastfeeding or needs to breastfeed over a period of time.
Forced nudity or forced to undress.	Asking sexual questions, such as questions about a person's sexual history or their sexual orientation.	Telling lewd jokes, or sharing sexual anecdotes.	Establish a requirement or practice that is the same for everyone but disadvantages women who are breastfeeding.
Unnecessarily rubbing against or getting too close physically while working.	Sending suggestive letters, notes, texts, or e-mails.	Making inappropriate sexual gestures.	
Touch, pinch, patting, or brushing up directly or through clothing any sexual area.	Indecent proposals such as asking for sex or other sex-linked behavior in exchange for a benefit or reward.	Making sexual comments about appearance, clothing, or body parts.	Discrimination to older women workers.
Gross sexual imposition (such as forceful touching, feeling, grabbing, unwanted caresses, groping, or fondling).	Use of sexually denigrating terms to offend a worker. Denying benefits to a worker who did not respond to sexual advances.	Making offensive comments about someone's sexual orientation or gender identity. Calling people sex-specific derogatory names.	Treat a woman less favorably because she has family responsibilities such as caring for or supporting a dependent child or a member of the immediate family

continued

Table 6.2 Continued

Blackmail/threats to force victim to engage or accept unwanted sexual abuse (threats of punishment can include negative performance evaluations, withholding of promotions, threat of termination).
Unwanted hugging and kissing.
Staring in a sexually suggestive or offensive manner, or whistling.
Stalking a worker with a sexual connotation inside or outside the workplace.
Exploitation by requiring sexual favors in exchange for work related benefits.
Voyeurism of female employees, including peeping or using technology to see her in private situations.
Flashing a female worker in a sexualized manner.

Unwanted, inappropriate, and offensive sexual advances. Examples include repeated unwanted sexual invitations, insistent requests for dinner, drinks, or dates, persistent letters, phone calls, and other invitations.
Spreading rumors of the person's sexual preferences or sexual habits.
Threaten to out an LGBTQ worker.
Using ethnic words or cultural values to denigrate sexually.
Aftermath of rape or sexual abuse that includes: denigrating the victim, blaming the victim, making fun of the abuse, telling other workers about the rape, instilling fear in workers that it will or could happen to them.

Saying or doing something about persons who do not conform to sex-role stereotypes.
Posting or sharing pornography, sexual pictures, or cartoons, sexually explicit graffiti, or other sexual images or obscene materials (including online).
Bragging about sexual prowess.

Preference of male workers over females in promotions, training, transfers, terms or conditions, or any other employment-related benefit.
Disparaging comments or biased treatment to a worker who has childcare demands.
Failure to discipline or enforce rules against sexual harassment or assault by supervisors, co-workers or clients.
Having rules for everyone the same when it affects women the most.
Giving women less money for same work or harder work for same pay.

Psychological Abuse in the Workplace

Verbal abuse	Emotional abuse	Intimidation	Manipulation
Yelling, screaming	Blaming	Coercion/control	Making it seem a worker in crazy (gaslighting)
Name-calling	Shaming	Intense surveillance, monitoring, or micromanaging	Turning other people against the worker
Insulting	Isolation	Making fun of the worker	Blackmailing
Using racial or cultural derogatory terms	Threats	Making threatening faces or gestures	Using other people to pressure the worker into something
Putting down the worker's family, race, place of origin, or culture	Doing something to spite the worker	Making the worker do humiliating or demeaning activities	Discriminating against a worker
Belittling of the worker's ideas, feelings, perceptions, physical or personality characteristics	Demanding obedience to whims	Monitoring the worker's personal time (their phone calls, use of the bathroom, lunch breaks)	Shifting from a nurturing to a punishing stance without provocation
	Sulking and refusing to talk to the worker or stamping out of the room	Hitting or kicking walls, doors, furniture, or machines	Playing good cop–bad cop with other superiors against workers
	Getting angry when duties are not completed perfectly		Threatening the worker with punishment
	Acting indifferently to the worker's pressing needs (including liming bathroom breaks, and a worker's ability to respond to emergencies with sick children)		Force participation in criminal activity (including obstruction of justice and witness tampering)

continued

Table 6.2 Continued

Immigration Abuse in the Workplace

Make the worker purchase illegal documents	Force the worker to use false documents	Pretend that they are filing for immigration relief for the worker or his or her family
Take the worker's passport, ID, or social security card	Threaten deportation	Smuggled the worker into the U.S.
Threat to report the worker to immigration authorities	Pretend that they have an arrangement with immigration authorities and only working there would they be safe	Use information regarding the worker's entrance to the country or use of illegal documents to blackmail the worker
Threat to report to local authorities		

Economic Abuse in the Workplace

Charging for things the worker has a right to (use of bathroom, a change of shift, a work uniform)	Decreasing worker's breaks	Forcing the worker to make purchases they would otherwise would not do
Taking away money with lies (payment to immigration authorities, inspectors, etc.)	Punishing the worker with lack of work or payment when they displeased the supervisor	Coercing or forcing the worker to accept unfair working conditions (longer hours, no vacation, etc.)
Not paying for hours worked or not paying overtime	Stealing or destroying the worker's personal possessions	Interfere with work performance (forcing worker to share tools with a new worker, etc.)
Decreasing working hours		
Taking away worker's tips from clients or forcing him or her to share them with him or her		

Note
1. Some of these items are adapted from Dutton (1992).

includes abusive actions very specific to the workplace environment. The examples in the structured interview are not an exhaustive list of the different abusive situations the examiner may encounter, but are a starting point to continue the conversation with the applicant. As further discussed in Chapter 9, structured interviews are important, because they help elicit information that, if not specifically asked, victims may not spontaneously reveal, because they may not think of them as being abusive, they may feel ashamed, they may be afraid of retaliation, or they may not have the words in their language to describe the abuse effectively.

It is important to consider cultural aspects impacting different types of abuse. For instance, in the area of sexual abuse some male employers may argue that men's sexual banter directed at women is sanctioned in some cultures and use this excuse to act in a sexually predatory manner with female employees. To import negative attitudes from cultures where women had lower social status does not minimize the impact of sexual harassment, which may be multiplied by the fact that the victim was not expecting this behavior in what she thought was a more egalitarian society. Similarly, psychological abuse may include strategies that become meaningful due to the cultural background of the employee. For instance, verbally abusive behavior from a superior that includes ridicule, insults, or demeaning comments in front of peers can be of greater emotional distress to workers whose cultures incline them to see feedback from authority figures as private and who feel excessive respect toward authority figures. Some abusive employers or superiors dominate the employee's personal decision-making by telling the employees where they should live, with whom they should socialize, as well as to pressure them to buy a car, rent a place, etc. Sometimes the employer benefits economically from the employee's 'choices' in these matters. This is coercive behavior as these decisions are not the employer's to make. Some employers use coercion, threats, and intimidation to obtain compliance, silence, and collaboration in unlawful activities such as violations of labor laws, workplace safety regulations, fraud in labor contracting, or obstruction of justice, taking advantage of the employee's ignorance of labor laws in the U.S. Sometimes, employers or superiors isolate workers from their family by limiting their ability to communicate with them, interfering with the worker's ability to befriend coworkers, or controlling the worker's whereabouts and their transportation. This isolation is all the more damaging, because immigrants are already socially alienated and may have limited social networks. Abuse can interact with gender, age, and other characteristics as well. For instance, employers that forbid older employees' use of compensation devices due to decline in certain capacities (e.g., seating due to an inability to stand for a long time) or who force minors to work during the time they should be at school. Examiners need to pay attention to these types of interactions that may aggravate the psychological injury.

Physical, sexual, and psychological abuse need to be evaluated in the manner described in the earlier VAWA chapter, paying particular attention to the mental health consequences of each of the criminal activities committed against the employees. Although there is not a relationship of intimacy between workers and employers, an employer's unequal level of power with employees provides the backdrop for abuses to occur based on control and coercion. Dependence on the employment for economic support of the victim and often her or his family, usually with very limited alternative job options for undocumented immigrant workers, amplifies the psychological impact of the abuse perpetrated and traps victims in abusive employment.

A form of workplace psychological abuse is bullying, described as a systematic, gradual, and prolonged process of perpetrating indirect and subtle forms of psychological violence against the victim (Einarsen, Hoel, Zapf, & Cooper, 2011).

> The types of psychologically violent actions that are considered in this category include: unreasonable deadlines, unmanageable workload, excessive monitoring, withholding of crucial information, sabotage, work devaluation, and also interpersonal behaviors such as gossip, insulting remarks, scolding, threats, excessive teasing, social exclusion and persistent criticism.
> (Giorgio, Ando, Arenas, Shoss, & Leon-Perez, 2013, p. 186)

While bullying, rudeness, vulgarity, and conflict in the workplace are not *per se* qualifying criminal activities, they are microaggressions that can be highly stressful, produce a toxic working environment, and set the stage for the subsequent criminal activities to have greater psychological impact.

Immigration-related abuse occurs when employers or supervisors threaten to report the worker to the Department of Homeland Security (DHS) if workers report abuse or attempt to quit. Employers/supervisors may tell employees that the DHS could show up in town and only in this job would they be safe. Employers and supervisors may arrange for the worker to purchase an illegal social security number. Immigration-related abuse also occurs when the employer files or pretends to file for a work-based immigration visa for the worker and uses this to blackmail, exploit, and lock the worker into abusive working conditions. Another immigration-related type of abuse specific to the workplace is when the employer or supervisor takes and holds the worker's passport, implying that they control the worker's presence in this country.

The task for the examiner is to evaluate all abusive actions, including the qualifying criminal activities, malicious actions, and microaggressions. When criminal activities occur in the workforce, the minor forms of abusive behaviors are part of the totality of the circumstances that create vulnerability, induce dependency, silence victims from seeking help and amplify the impact of the criminal activities perpetrated by employers and supervisors. The forensic examination plays an important role in demonstrating how these other actions are related to and are also a significant part of the qualifying criminal activities perpetrated.

Coercion in U Visa Cases

Some of the qualifying criminal activities for the U visa do not have clear-cut social science evidence of its psychological impact. For instance, whereas there is plenty of research demonstrating the psychological impact of sexual abuse in many settings including the workplace, there is much less research regarding the deleterious impact of blackmail, extortion, fraud in foreign labor contracting, obstruction of justice, witness tampering, and perjury. In particular, it may be hard to assess and understand the psychological impact of attempts, conspiracy, or solicitation of those types of criminal activities, based on available research.

However, in addition to being criminal under state laws, Federal laws, or both, these criminal activities have in common two important issues: (1) they were typically conducted through coercion, intimidation, or threats; and (2) they force the individual to betray his or her own moral values and integrity. Both of these issues produce negative psychological consequences. The forensic assessment in these cases includes evaluating the psychological impact around the link between these two prongs, the criminal activity perpetrated and the impact on the victim (Figure 6.1).

The demand or expectation, the consequences if the demand is met or not, and the surveillance to make sure that the victim complies with the demand are key to the definition of coercion as explained earlier in the VAWA chapter. It is important to assess all of these aspects of the coercive behaviors that the perpetrator utilized in order to understand and explain in the report its psychological impact on the victim and how abusers exploited the victim's vulnerabilities. Perpetrators of coercion intimidate victims by creating fears, credible to the victim,

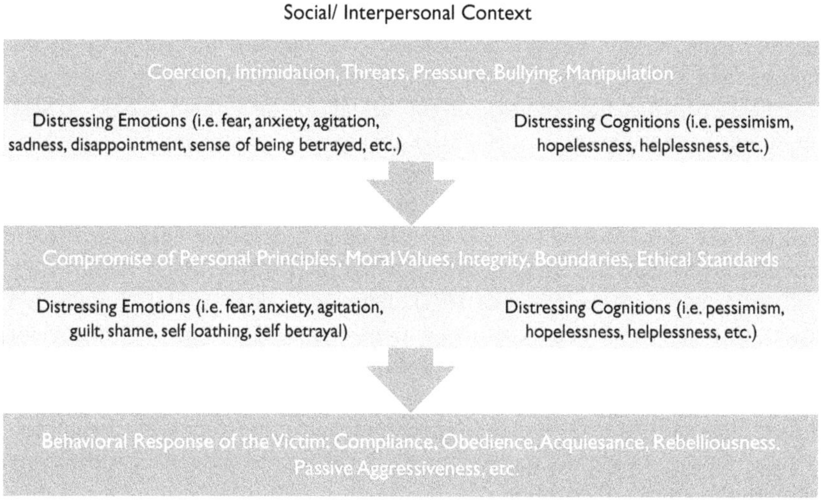

Social/ Interpersonal Context

Coercion, Intimidation, Threats, Pressure, Bullying, Manipulation

Distressing Emotions (i.e. fear, anxiety, agitation, sadness, disappointment, sense of being betrayed, etc.)

Distressing Cognitions (i.e. pessimism, hopelessness, helplessness, etc.)

Compromise of Personal Principles, Moral Values, Integrity, Boundaries, Ethical Standards

Distressing Emotions (i.e. fear, anxiety, agitation, guilt, shame, self loathing, self betrayal)

Distressing Cognitions (i.e. pessimism, hopelessness, helplessness, etc.)

Behavioral Response of the Victim: Compliance, Obedience, Acquiesance, Rebelliousness, Passive Aggressiveness, etc.

Figure 6.1 Psychological Aspects of Coercion in the U Visa.

of disastrous consequences if they do not obey. This threat creates a great deal of anxiety and anguish for the victim.

Moreover, being intimidated, forced, or coerced to betray one's honesty, integrity, and moral values can be extremely distressing and even life-altering. Victims of forced self-betrayal may feel guilty, angry, self-doubting, grieving, and self-loathing. In particular, when the perpetrator turns the victim's vulnerabilities against them and exploits their fears, helplessness, and dependency, the victim may feel psychologically incapacitated and subjugated. Forced self-betrayal involves being dishonest and disloyal with one's own sense of integrity and for many violating this boundary changes them into seeing themselves as persons they despise. For instance, Sussman (2005) characterizes self-betrayal as one of the most harmful consequences of torture, because it alters the sense of self through a perversion of our dignity and sense of being one's own self-governing agent. Assessing these issues through a careful interview is especially important when the immigrant has experienced qualifying criminal activities that are more psychological than physical in nature, including, but not limited to, blackmail, extortion, fraud in foreign labor contracting, obstruction of justice, witness tampering, and perjury.

It is important to assess the social context of the coercion. Attitudes and behaviors of others in the workplace may exacerbate or minimize the effects of the victimization. For instance, social pressure may incline a victim to submit or to resist the abuse. In certain social contexts, shame and social ostracism may become indirect psychological consequences of the criminal activities. Social context also plays a role in that employers expect that immigrant workers will be hard workers, accommodating and subservient, not only because usually immigrants need the job and need to preserve it, but also because of cultural characteristics in many countries and cultures of origin that incline immigrants to be amicable, friendly, and helpful. In fact, in some cultures the authority of the employers and gaining their acceptance is exceedingly important in an employee's life, especially when the employer is the bridge to the foreign society. These same strengths of the immigrant character are stereotyped and exploited, because some employers may think that these employees are more willing to accept the employer's controlling tactics (Bronfenbrenner, 2009). Actually, it has been found that the lack of work authorization is often a desirable characteristic for some employers because, due to their immigration status, these workers are afraid to resist coercive demands (Waldinger & Lichter, 2003). Employer's threats, retaliation, and other coercive actions can be extremely distressing for workers, because they may fear that, if they disobey, they would lose the job which is an essential resource sustaining the lives of these workers and their families. The particular differential power and status, together with the numerous disadvantages of immigrant workers vis-à-vis their employers or supervisors multiplies the impact of coercion.

Severity of Harm of Workplace Abuse

Although both immigrant and non-immigrant workers can be subjected to crim-inal activities and workplace violence, employers who abuse immigrant workers have additional tools in their arsenal. Employers and supervisors can more effectively control immigrant workers by using their position of greater power, status, knowledge, and acculturation. Employers usually have knowledge of the worker's vulnerabilities, including their financial situation and the fact that they may be unauthorized to be in the country and may not have permission to work lawfully in the U.S. Financial concerns are a major issue for undocumented immigrants who depend on their hard work to survive financially and who have responsibilities to provide support to family members both in the U.S. and in their native country. Immigrant workers may fear that they cannot find another job, which, combined with their lack of social networks in the U.S., their limited English-language skills, and insufficient tangible resources like transportation, makes it difficult to enable them to work somewhere else. Together these factors can force a worker into staying in working places where they are being abused and economically exploited. When an employer or supervisor inflicts economic abuse, their goal is to exploit the worker and force them into an economic dependence that locks them into the job and the resulting abuse.

Forensic mental health examiners need to especially assess the psychological impact of threats of deportation. The threat of deportation can be particularly stressful for immigrant workers, because being sent back to their country may engender life-threatening consequences. Immigrant workers who fled countries with civil strife, conditions of intense deprivation, family violence, or sexual assault face risk to their safety if they were to be forcefully returned. In other cases, being deported would cause shame to them, their family, and ancestors, because it can be perceived as a testament that they are a failure. This stigmati-zation makes it harder for victims to seek new employment and rebuild their life back in their home country. In some cultures, respect, honoring one's word, and good work ethic are precious moral values, and when one's reputation is lost because of being fired or failing to pay debts due to unemployment, it can be shameful, demoralizing, and cause social ostracism. This context aggravates the psychological impact of abuse for the worker and locks them further into abusive working conditions. While factors such as fear of deportation, economic depri-vation, and social stigma or ostracism will not by themselves be sufficient to demonstrate substantial physical or emotional abuse in a U visa case, these factors can become an important part of the totality of the circumstances con-sidered in proving substantial abuse, particularly with evidence that the abuser was aware of and used these vulnerabilities. In evaluating the substantial abuse suffered, it is important to consider the victim's vulnerabilities and their contri-bution to the impact of the criminal activities and the contextual consequences, which often go beyond the individual and also impact his or her family and community.

The key issue for the examiner is to determine whether the victim's psychological functioning provides evidence that he or she suffered substantial physical or emotional abuse as a result of the criminal activity the law contemplates, when both the severity of the perpetrator's conduct and effect of the criminal activity on the victim are taken into consideration. The U visa regulations note that several acts taken together can be considered substantial physical or mental abuse even where no single act alone rises to that level. Therefore, it is important to assess also seemingly minor microaggressions and threats of abuse and retaliation. These ostensibly minor actions, which the assessee may neglect to report unless asked, take on a different meaning when viewed in the larger context of the employee's life. These include the employee's vulnerabilities; the risks and limitations to escaping the abuse, seeking help or calling the police to report the abuse; the social context; the preexisting conditions, and the consequences of resisting or rebelling (Ammar, Orloff, Dutton & Hass, 2005).

Preexisting Conditions

While mental health examiners routinely assess and integrate preexisting conditions when assessing and diagnosing someone, the U visa specifically includes this issue as a key factor in the evaluation of substantial physical or mental abuse as a consideration that is directly affected by the impact of the abusive criminal activities on the victim. This enlightened perspective acknowledges the series of factors that impact the way a person may experience and manage victimization. The following areas of inquiry are recommended when looking at preexisting conditions.

Prior History of Abuse, Loss, and Deprivation

Immigrants not only often come from countries ravaged by violence, crime, poverty, violence against women and children, or natural disasters, but also often suffer from traumatic experiences during the journey to the U.S. There is ample literature noting that trauma is cumulative and causes greater vulnerability for the victim by limiting her or his ability to cope and recover.

Mental Health Disorders

Previously diagnosed or comorbid mental health problems also create vulnerabilities that modify the way the new trauma is expressed and managed. Issues such as intellectual deficits, developmental disorders, mood disorders, anxiety disorders, and psychotic disorders engender psychological liabilities that may impair a person's ability to deal with new stressors and cope with challenging situations.

Other Types of Highly Stressful Environmental Factors

Exposure to violence, gender-based violence, natural or man-made disasters in the community, social discrimination and abuse, domestic violence, child abuse, indirect exposure to traumatic events, recurring traumatic events occurring in another or the same setting (e.g., home, school, workplace), and other traumatic experiences may leave emotional scars that become vulnerabilities and impediments to effectively addressing new traumatic experiences.

Helpfulness to Government Officials

It is helpful to explore and report the victim's desire and attempts to be of help to law enforcement, prosecutors, government agency staff (e.g., EEOC, Labor Departments, child or elder abuse workers) or to the courts in criminal, civil, or protection order cases, whether they were successful or not. It is important to note in the evaluation if the victim called the police, participated in investigative interviews with police, prosecutors, or other government agency staff. The victim's entire experience with law enforcement and investigators needs to be explored, including her or his intentions and efforts to provide information and evidence. Ask your assessee to describe the experience with the police, prosecutors, and other government agency staff in order to understand whether they captured accurately the elements of the criminal activity and the victim's efforts to offer help to government officials (Dutton et al., 2013).

Assess whether there were charges brought against the perpetrator and if these were congruent with the victim's experience. Ask questions to understand the victim's role and whether the victim was interviewed, asked to provide a report, had to testify in court or provide deposition, or if he or she was asked to attend a court hearing but not called as a witness (Dutton et al., 2013). There are times when the good intentions of the victim to cooperate are curtailed by factors outside of the victim's control, such as police's lack of receptivity and sensitivity. In some cases, the victim was not given an opportunity to help, because investigators did not speak her language, could not deal effectively with the victim's emotional trauma, did not accurately obtain her story, or already had enough evidence. Since U visa laws require victims to be helpful or willing to offer future helpfulness, it is important to document the victim's efforts, intentions, and external obstacles in this regard.

The U visa requires that victims be willing to offer continued cooperation to government officials both while their U visa case is pending and after receiving the U visa. Victims, however, can continue to receive a U visa and can obtain lawful permanent residency based on a U visa as long as the victim did not unreasonably refuse to cooperate with reasonable requests for cooperation. Whether a particular victim's non-cooperation is unreasonable depends on the totality of the facts of the case, preexisting conditions, ongoing abuse and threats, and the victim's history, traumatic experiences, vulnerabilities, and expectations about the danger that justice system interventions may pose. The types of factors that typically contribute to showing that failure to cooperate was not unreasonable include: threats from the abuser; the abuser controlling or monitoring the victim's activities; fear of the abuser's retaliatory actions including deportation; ongoing physical and emotional harm; or coercion perpetrated against the victim, the victim's children, or the victim's family members in the U.S. or abroad. The forensic examiner can play an important role in documenting the abusers' control, threats, and coercion and the impact on the victim. The Threat Appraisal Scale (Dutton, 2013) can be a particularly effective method for this purpose.

The examiner can also document the role that a victim's previous negative experiences with law enforcement, whether in the U.S. or in his or her native country, may play in the victim's ability to trust and provide ongoing cooperation to law enforcement. Perpetrators may effectively use knowledge of these fears to manipulate victims into ceasing cooperation and not continuing to trust police and other government officials. Victims' limited or lack of cooperation may be related to having been told repeatedly by the perpetrator that contact with law enforcement will trigger an investigation regarding the victim's immigration status. In many situations, victims are afraid that contacting the police or making reports of abuse will lead the perpetrator to retaliate against themselves or their relatives. Moreover, in some cases perpetrators may use victims' fears about the shame and ostracism they could be subjected to if members of their family or cultural or religious community learn about the abuse they suffered (e.g., sexual assault, domestic violence) to silence the victim and keep him or her from providing any additional help to governmental officials. Assessing and documenting these issues and explaining their complexity, cultural context, and the psychological reality and reasonableness of the victim's fears can be very helpful to the victim's U visa case.

T Visa or Relief for Victims of Trafficking

Under Federal immigration laws, severe forms of human trafficking are defined as

> '1) sex trafficking in which a commercial sex act is induced by force, fraud or coercion, or in which the person induced to perform such an act has not attained 18 years of age; or 2) labor trafficking through the recruitment, harboring, transportation, provision, or obtaining of a person for labor or services, through the use of force, fraud, or coercion for the purpose of subjection to involuntary servitude, peonage, debt bondage, or slavery.
>
> (TVPA§ 103(8): 22 USC§ 7102(8))

To obtain a T visa, the victim must prove the following four requirements (Trafficking Victims Protection Act of 2000; USCIS, n.d.). The applicant:

1. is or has been the victim of a severe form of human trafficking;
2. is in the U.S., American Samoa, or at a port-of-entry to the U.S. or American Samoa on account of human trafficking; and
3. Satisfies one of the following three conditions:
   a. The victim has cooperated and is willing to cooperate with reasonable requests for assistance by federal, state, or local law enforcement in investigating or prosecuting crimes related to human trafficking; or
   b. The victim is excused by the Attorney General from failing to cooperate with reasonable requests for assistance by federal, state, or local law enforcement in investigating or prosecuting crimes related to human trafficking because of physical or psychological trauma; or
   c. The victim is under 18 years of age.
4. Demonstrate that he or she would suffer extreme hardship involving unusual and severe harm if he or she were removed from the U.S.

Trafficking victims must provide evidence of the qualifying elements in order to be granted continued presence or a T visa form of immigration relief designed to help victims of severe forms of human trafficking as defined in the Victims of Trafficking and Violence Protection Act (TVPA §103(80): 22 USC§ 7102(8)).

Victims of human trafficking are among the most vulnerable undocumented immigrants, because traffickers exploit their lack of a social safety net, limited English proficiency, fear of the trafficker and of deportation, and the hardships that made them want to leave their country, such as economic hardship, political instability, gender-based violence, natural disasters, or other causes, to lock them into inhuman and slave-like conditions. Human trafficking is tied either directly or loosely to organized crime networks, mostly because it is considered highly profitable and low-risk. Organized crime has the networks and sophistication to handle the many steps needed to smuggle, kidnap, and enslave victims (U.S. Department of State, 2017). Traffickers include recruiters, transporters, document forgers, fake employment agencies, pimps, and employers, and are unbelievable crafty, devious, and callous in the ways they procure their victims and maintain control and exploit them. In some cases, organized crime is engaged in corruption and complicity with law enforcement, immigration officials, and border patrol agents (Tiefenbrun, 2002a), or make their victims believe they are, which serves as another deterrent for victims who wish to seek help to escape. There have been cases in which victims seek help from local authorities and instead are either ignored or arrested and ultimately deported, which further reinforces victims' fears.

Psycholegal Concepts

Under the T visa legislation, *psychological coercion* includes:

a) threats of serious harm to or physical restraint against any person, b) any scheme, plan, or pattern intended to cause a person to believe that failure to perform an act would result in serious harm to or physical restraint against the person, and c) the abuse or threatened abuse of the legal process.

(TVPA §103(2) C; 22USC §7102(2)(C))

T visa regulations also state that psychological coercion includes psychological threats that are meaningful to the person, as defined by the patterns or schemes that would make a person feel like they may be harmed if they fail to perform the act demanded of them (TVPA, 28 CFR §1100). The assessment of coercion for victims of trafficking should follow the steps delineated earlier in this document both for VAWA and U visa victims. The T visa also requires that the victim provide evidence that he or she would suffer extreme hardship involving *unusual and severe harm* if removed from the U.S. This is a very high standard. The assessment of extreme hardship is addressed in Chapter 7.

The psychological evaluation in IC may support the victim's experience of the psychological harm they suffered as trafficking victims, and helps provide evidence that force, fraud, or coercion were involved in making the victim come to the U.S., and trapping the victim in a human trafficking situation in the U.S. The forensic evaluation also sheds light on whether or not the human trafficker was involved in the victim's entry into the U.S.; in procuring the victim's work; engaging the victim in behavior they would not have chosen to do otherwise or would not have agreed to; or if they knew what they were actually going to be required to do. Issues that can differentiate a victim of trafficking from a victim of another labor exploitation crime are:

1. Working under the total or near-total control of another person or organization (slavery or involuntary servitude).
2. Being forced to pay off a loan by working instead of paying money, for an agreed-upon or unclear period of time (debt bondage) or without an agreement as to the timeframe (peonage) (U.S. Customs and Border Protection, 2015).

Psychological Impact of Trafficking

When interviewing a victim of human trafficking, forensic mental health examiners may want to have information about the common issues and patterns that human traffickers employ to help the examiner facilitate the narration of the many delicate subjects to be addressed in the interview. Knowledge about the typical experiences of human trafficking victims allows examiners to be alert to important signs of human trafficking when gathering the victim's story and assists in ensuring that the examiner is asking detailed questions that elicit important details from the victim. In addition, having knowledge about the trafficking industry limits the extent to which the examiner is dependent upon the victim's understanding of and ability to articulate the human trafficking they experienced. Knowledge about human trafficking also prepares examiners to not be shocked and emotionally overwhelmed by what they are going to hear to the point that they become compromised in their ability to conduct a thorough interview. When interviewing a victim of human trafficking about the aspects of their ordeal, examiners need to pay attention to the verbal and non-verbal signs of the victim's emotional and cognitive state, both when talking about the time the human trafficking occurred and also about the victim's emotional state at the time of the interview. This information helps the examiner build the picture of psychological harm and make decisions about the empirically validated measures to use in order to test the clinical hypotheses regarding the impact that the human trafficking had on the victim.

The T visa is based on the concept of slavery type of exploitation and does not require crossing borders or being transported. However, many cases of T visa applicants experience two aspects to the crimes committed against them. Both of these issues need to be separately assessed regarding the psychological impact to the victim, because they may have been traumatic. These two aspects are trafficking and enslaving.

Trafficking and Alien Smuggling

Human trafficking and smuggling are distinctly different crimes. Smuggling is a financial transaction for the purpose of obtaining illegal entry into a country. Human trafficking may include the fact that the trafficker uses coercion, fraud, or force to control the victims and make them migrate in order to exploit them through slavery, involuntary servitude, peonage, debt bondage, or commercial sex work (Cooper, 2002).

Victims of human trafficking may have been kidnapped or taken off the streets in the victim's home country or after they have already entered the U.S. In some cases, family members sell the victim to traffickers. Women may be kidnapped or purchased to be brought into a brothel or club where she becomes a sex worker. Children may be kidnapped or purchased to be sold to adoption agencies, adoption applicants, or sexual or labor slavery. For these victims, it is very hard to escape because they disappear and nobody is trying to find them. Also, child victims are unable to escape, because they are too young and disoriented; possibly drugged during the capture or smuggling; are under intense surveillance; or are moved from one place to another by traffickers.

In many human trafficking cases, the coercion takes the form of manipulation and scheming based on false promises of the American Dream. The situation is often one of 'bait and switch,' as victims are initially lured by promises and later locked into the horrible conditions of abuse by threats, abuse, or coercion. Traffickers usually lure individuals in developing countries through deception and transport them to wealthier countries under the false pretense that a better job awaits. Once the victims are in the receiving country, they find slave-like conditions that they did not anticipate and would not have agreed to endure (Tiefenbrun, 2002a). Some of the countries targeted for trafficking victims include Asia, Latin America, and Central and Eastern Europe (O'Neil Richard, 2000).

Traffickers travel to or reside in developing or transitional countries where the living conditions are very difficult and people are motivated to make sacrifices in order to have a better future. However, U.S. human trafficking laws also provide protection to trafficking victims in cases that started as smuggling cases. These became human trafficking cases once the individual enters the U.S. and is forced or coerced into a situation of labor or sexual exploitation (Office for Victims of Crime, n.d.).

When asking victims about the situation that motivated them to accept the migration proposal, if it was seemingly voluntary, it is important not to assume that all human trafficking victims come from countries or lived in conditions of extreme poverty. Sometimes there are other social or individual issues that force a person to separate from their family in search of better conditions abroad, such as domestic violence, sexual assault, gender-based violence, natural disasters, war, and other such critical situations. There may be victims escaping from physical or sexual abuse because they have been persecuted on account of their sexual orientation or gender identity, or from crime, poverty, persecution, or culturally sanctioned traditions that they could not tolerate. While some of the victims who were duped into migrating for better conditions had few or no work prospects in their country of origin, others could be teachers, nurses, and other professionals who had high levels of education and social standing. For instance, there was a case in which at least 347 Pilipino teachers were asked to pay exorbitant fees to be brought to the U.S. under the disguise that they had a contract to work as teachers in Louisiana; they were then placed as caregivers earning minimal wages (*Mairi Nunag Tanedo* et al. *v. Charlotte D. Placide* et al., 2015).

Examiners should ask about the circumstances by which the victims became aware of the overseas employment option. Sometimes victims learn through newspapers or television ads, posters, online messages, and even word of mouth. Sometimes they are deceived with offerings of a different job than the one they end up doing. At other times the offer is accurate about the job, whether working in agriculture, the food industry, manufacturing, sweatshops, domestic work, or babysitting, but not about the conditions of the employment. Sometimes victims are directly propositioned to do sex work including prostitution, stripping, and pornography. The fact that a person accepts to travel to another country to do a job, including sex work, and that this is what they end up doing after migrating does not necessarily disqualify them for the T visa. A person could have agreed to work in a garment factory, meat-packing plant, or a bar, but was fraudulently induced into slave-like conditions.

Once the victim has been procured by force, fraud, or coercion, human traffickers use different methods to transport them to the U.S. Being smuggled by air requires visas and passports. The easiest way is to obtain a visa for the victim, which would allow the victim to legally enter the U.S., and then traffickers make the victim stay after the visa expires. There are cases in which a person is deceived into coming to the U.S. under a special visa, such as a fiancée or visitor's visa, and then is forced or coerced into labor or sexual exploitation. A fiancée visa may have been obtained without the intention of following through with the marriage. In other cases, traffickers procure visas such as student or entertainment visas. In cases of fraudulently obtained visas, traffickers prepare the victims for the immigration interview to obtain the visa and even give them false evidence (O'Neil Richard, 2000). Victims are provided false documentation and, after gaining entrance, traffickers move the victim to locations where their presence becomes untraceable. For this, they may switch boarding passes among victims inside the boarding area to board with a different identity, or they are moved to a different city than what they declared in customs. Human traffickers provide them with a different identity and then recycle or destroy the false documents (Shannon, 1999).

Another means of gaining entry to the U.S. is through sea travel in cargo containers. This method is cheap. Hundreds can be moved at once, no documents are involved, and bribing officials in the ports is considered easy. Because the victim does not have a role in convincing a border patrol or visa issuer, victims who did not consent can be transported to their destination by the traffickers. This is a deadly method as it may include starvation, disease, and death (Beare, 1999).

Victims can also be transported by land, with the most likely port of entry to the U.S. being through the border with Mexico. This journey is also perilous and the dangers are many. Victims are transported in cars, trucks, trains, containers, buses, and even mopeds, and they may have to walk through forests or deserts and cross dangerous bridges and rivers. Because the physical demands are very high, victims considered weak, such as some women and children, may be drugged by the smugglers to help them withstand the journey. The danger to traffickers of crossing the border on foot is that victims may get caught by border patrols and the trafficking business is exposed. Traffickers also use methods such as passing the victims through tunnels used for drug smuggling, inside cargo containers, or in trunks of cars, so that victims who do not cooperate can be brought to the U.S.

When the victim of trafficking is in the U.S., traffickers make sure to enslave them by stripping away their freedom. Any documents, whether provided by the traffickers or not, are confiscated. Victims are housed in communal places where they may need to sleep on the floor or live in precarious conditions, because they are not given enough resources or provisions. If the victims have been conned into believing they will obtain legitimate employment, the traffickers often continue the ruse by lying about the employers changing their mind, selling the contract, or having a disaster happen and not being able to employ them at this time. Other women are just thrown into brothels or other settings without much explanation; virgins are not raped until their virginity is sold at a higher price (Gardiner & Mohan, 2001).

Usually traffickers require the victims to pay exorbitant recruitment and smuggling fees, 'loan' those fees to the victims, or require them to work off their debt (Raymond & Hughes, 2001). Victims are told that they need to start paying the debt of the passage. Victims have to find the money for recruitment and journey by using their savings, selling their possessions, and borrowing from family and friends. Those situations create an enormous sense of responsibility with the lenders, and economic dependence on the traffickers. Usually victims who were kidnapped and enslaved do not have the means to pay and must try to work their way out (Nelson, 2002).

This is a debt that is rarely paid off, because traffickers make sure to place as many obstacles in the way of repayment as they can. Interest accrues and any costs associated with food, boarding, and essentials increase the debt. Because victims are not paid as promised, there is little they can spare to pay their debt, especially if they need to send money to their relatives in their country of origin. Some traffickers sell alcohol or drugs to the victims in order to help them get numbed through their hellish lives, and this also increases the debt. In sex trafficking rings, victims are charged by the number of customers they need to 'serve,' but this arrangement is also used to manipulate them and the traffickers continuously change the rules or re-sell them, preventing them from ever paying off their debt (Raymond & Hughes, 2001).

When evaluating victims who were aware and consented to the perils of the journey and the high fees, it is important for the examiner to ask about their understanding of the type of work they were going to be doing, the often-desperate motivations they had to agree to such conditions, and if they were fraudulently trapped in the job once they were in the U.S. Proof of force, fraud, or coercion is required for adult victims to qualify for T visas. While some people may judge these victims as not having been coerced into the job and the migration, the law acknowledges that some victims may have originally agreed to participate, but may not have agreed to the abusive and slave-like working conditions (Doezema, 2000). An initial agreement to travel or to perform work does not mean the employer is later allowed to restrict a victim's freedom or use force or threats to obtain repayment. Documenting the types of force, fraud, or coercion the traffickers used with the victim is essential to the success of a trafficking victim's T visa case, and the forensic evaluation can provide evidence important to the success of the case.

Abuse and Slave-Like Conditions in the Host Country

Once human trafficking victims arrive in the U.S., they are forced, coerced, manipulated, extorted, and fraudulently engaged in labor. Trafficking victims find themselves stripped of documentation, disoriented in a foreign environment and a strange culture, often without knowing the language, and without a social network. Because of their undocumented status, their financial need, and an assortment of hoaxes by the traffickers to keep them locked in the situation, victims are prey to the whims of their abusers and the abuse and exploitation of others. For instance, victims of sex trafficking are not only forced to serve customers, but often are raped by the traffickers or the guards employed to supervise them (Gardiner & Mohan, 2001).

Like victims of labor exploitation that qualifies for the U visa, victims of labor trafficking may not believe they have bad working conditions and may be unaware of the criminal nature of their situation. Domestic workers whose employment forces them to live and work at all times in the employer's home, and are not allowed any freedom, may wrongly believe that it is a cultural practice or the nature of the job. Examiners may want to look into the following considerations to assess the lack of freedom that characterizes trafficking victims once they reach their destination job.

Behavior or Physical State

*   Does the victim act fearful, anxious, depressed, submissive, tense, or nervous/paranoid?
*   Does the victim defer to another person to speak for him or her?
*   Does the victim show signs of physical and/or sexual abuse, physical restraint, confinement, or torture?
*   Has the victim been harmed or deprived of food, water, sleep, medical care, or other life necessities?
*   Does the victim have few or no personal possessions?

Social Behavior

*   Can the victim freely contact friends or family?
*   Is the victim allowed to socialize or attend religious services?
*   Does the victim have freedom of movement?
*   Has the victim or family been threatened with harm if the victim attempts to escape?

Work Conditions and Immigration Status

*   Does the victim work excessively long and/or unusual hours?
*   Is the victim a juvenile engaged in commercial sex work?
*   Was the victim recruited for one purpose and forced to engage in some other job?
*   Is the victim's salary being taken to pay off a smuggling fee?
    (Paying off a smuggling fee alone is not considered trafficking.)
*   Has the victim been forced to perform sexual acts?
*   Has the victim been threatened with deportation or law enforcement action? Is the victim in possession of identification and travel documents? If not, who has control of the documents?

Minor Victims

*   Is the victim a juvenile engaged in commercial sex work?

Forced, Fraud, and Coercion in T Visa Cases

Force, fraud, and coercion include situations in which individuals are forced, either physically, indirectly, or psychologically, to do something against their wishes through coercion, compulsion, constraint, or restraint, or where they are tricked through truth distortion or suppression to do something (U.S. ICE, n.d.).

As reviewed earlier, coercion includes threats that imply that if the victim does not comply with the request, it will result in harm to herself or someone else. Fraud refers to intentionally distorting the truth in order to get someone else (who relies on that version of the truth) to surrender a legal right or give up something valuable that belongs to them. (U.S. CBP, 2015)

Victims are kept under the control of the traffickers through threats. In addition to the threats against the person's life or integrity, and other factors reviewed in the VAWA section, some traffickers maintain ties to the victim's country of origin and threaten to hurt the victim's relatives (Raymond & Hughes, 2001) or smear her reputation in her country of origin. Victims of trafficking who are procured in their home countries may be wrongly told that they are participants in the crime and, if they report the crimes committed against them, they will be jailed and deported.

Traffickers also use psychological maneuvers to eliminate any thoughts of or attempts to escape. Traffickers may go to great lengths to make the victims believe that eventually they are still going to have a better life and that they are arranging official papers for them. Traffickers also may take the money that victims were saving for a future education or to live on in the future. Victims are told that whatever work they are doing is a step toward better, legitimate, well-paid jobs, or that many better opportunities await if only they withstand the poor conditions now. Sometimes they promise love and attention to victims who are psychologically vulnerable and lost, such as children who have left homes due to abuse or neglect.

Traffickers also use strategies such as isolation, moving victims from one town to another to keep them disoriented and from making friends, or making sure that the victims do not fraternize with each other. In fact, many times they force victims to punish each other or pit them against each other with gossip and competition. Victims often become so debilitated emotionally that they are unable to escape or report the abuse and have nobody to trust, not even the other victims sharing their plight.

In the forensic evaluations, each of these issues need to be assessed in detail and placed within the context of the victim's culture, trauma history, and vulnerabilities, resulting in a clear picture of the victim's fragile mental state. The examiner needs to make the point that, in addition to the debt, abuse, and exploitation, threats to self and family, and imprisonment-like conditions in which victims of trafficking are kept, victims often do not speak English, are disoriented in a foreign place and culture, lack a social network, lack economic and logistical resources, and lack knowledge of U.S. laws and systems of protection in U.S. society in order to escape. These are extremely hard obstacles to overcome, leading to helplessness and aggravating the psychological impact of the criminal activity.

Psychological Impact of Human Trafficking

In light of the nature and conditions of human trafficking examined above, forensic evaluators can expect that victims of human trafficking will often be greatly harmed psychologically and extremely weakened emotionally. They will have difficulty recounting their experience because they will often utilize dissociation, alcohol, drugs, or other forms of numbing to get through their torment. Their level of shame and self-recrimination is indescribable and often related to both having been captured or conned, not trying or having been unsuccessful in escaping, and even not trying or having been unsuccessful in committing suicide. Their self-esteem is very low, while their sense of helplessness and hopelessness very high. In addition to the physical deterioration caused by the work, the abuse, the lack of medical attention, and the lack of self-awareness of their physical and bodily wellbeing, many victims may suffer from psychosomatic problems that are often culturally accepted ways of channeling distress. Spiritual conflict is not unusual, as victims have to grapple with the fact that they were abandoned to their terrible fate and nobody helped them when they needed it the most.

When victims are duped and deceived based on their own dreams of a better life and ambition to escape from poverty, their shame and self-recrimination is very intense. Similarly, the opinions others have of them can be harsh and add to their self-deprecation. It is not unusual to find people who erroneously think that the victims put themselves in the position of being exploited due to greed, naiveté, or stupidity (Halperin, 2011); typically, victims think this of themselves also. Victims blame themselves and feel so guilty and ashamed that it makes it harder to seek help, which submerges them deeper into depression and self-hatred. While most victims of interpersonal crimes tend to become mistrustful of others, victims of trafficking also learn to distrust themselves, which is devastating to a person's self-esteem, sense of personal value, and feeling safe in the world.

Examiners need to carefully assess these issues through an artful interview and performance-based and self-report measures, and integrate this information as part of the psychological impact of the criminal activity. Documenting the psychological impact of human trafficking is very important for trafficking victims applying for T visas. This same documentation can also help human trafficking victims who may qualify for a U visa instead of a T visa. Some victims will initially apply for a U visa based on sexual assault or workplace-based criminal activities; later it is determined that they are eligible for a T visa because what they have suffered meets the Federal definition of human trafficking. In other cases, victims of human trafficking will need to pursue U visas rather than

T visas because they cannot meet the high burden of proving extreme hardship involving unusual and severe harm if they were removed from the U.S. When human trafficking victims apply for U visas, the information gathered by the forensic examiner discussed in the context of the T visa can help prove substantial physical or emotional abuse for the U visa case.

Cooperation with Law Enforcement

The T visa holder must be willing to cooperate with a law enforcement investigation or prosecution against the trafficker. The evaluation of cooperation with law enforcement is assessed following the model noted in the U visa. However, it is important to remember that trafficking victims whose physical or psychological trauma impedes their ability to cooperate with law enforcement are allowed to seek a waiver of the cooperation requirement of the T visa (VAWA, 2006).

Examiners have an important role in helping the victim justify the need for a waiver. Fear of retaliation may be realistic and well-founded, and an assessment of this risk factor is part of the waiver evaluation. Traffickers may have ties to organized crime and have agents or recruiters in the community of origin of the victim who know about her relatives and community ties. Additionally, victims usually are in very precarious psychological states and seeking justice or revenge is not their priority. Having to cooperate in an investigation that may take one or two years will force a victim to remember hideous experiences, and this is re-traumatizing. Further, they may not be emotionally able to submit themselves to the humiliation and indignity of being cross-examined and questioned in detail about their traumatic experience. Many victims may be unable to cooperate even if they want to, because they cannot remember the details of their experience due to the psychological strategies they used to endure the suffering (Sadruddin, Walter, & Hidalgo, 2005) or neuropsychological damage caused by the violence.

In addition, victims need help to overcome their own prejudices, fears, and internalized shame and guilt in order to recall the ordeal in all its details and dynamics. A key symptom of trauma is avoidance of triggers and memories related to the traumatic experience. Finally, forensic examiners need to consider that human trafficking victims lived in an underground community at the margins of society, and it is very difficult for them to provide evidence of their situation. The forensic examination provides important evidence in helping uncover the details and dynamics of the *force, fraud, or coercion* suffered.

In cases where human trafficking victims were identified in a raid, the assumption of many uninformed law enforcement officials (as other T and U visa certifiers may have been) is that the victims were just undocumented workers or prostitutes, or even accomplices. These views by government officials cast doubt about victimization from the beginning of the investigation and it requires greater effort to dispel those assumptions. When there is no concrete evidence of the victim's ordeal, the psychological exam can become the strongest tool to support the victim's case.

Extreme Hardship

The T visa also requires that the victim provides evidence that he or she would suffer extreme hardship involving *unusual and severe harm* if removed from the U.S. This assessment of extreme hardship is covered in detail in Chapter 8.

Inadmissibility

Psychologists may be asked to opine regarding grounds of inadmissibility that may need to be waived for the victim of human trafficking to qualify for the T visa. If the victim merits a waiver of inadmissibility due to the extreme circumstances surrounding the criminal activity, forensic examiners are often in a very good position to evaluate and document how and why the victim deserves a waiver. For instance, victims who have engaged in prostitution separately from the coercion by the traffickers are not admissible (Hartsough, 2002). Sometimes that was the only way they could obtain money for their own escape plan. With good forensic evidence, such victims may be able to obtain an inadmissibility waiver in a T visa case. Good documentation of the history of traumas the victim has suffered, combined with active participation in the trafficking prosecution, could lead DHS adjudicators in a compelling case to grant an inadmissibility waiver despite the victim's prior non-coerced involvement in prostitution or other inadmissibility grounds.

In every VAWA, T visa, or U visa case, at some point in the application process or in VAWA cases where the victim applies for legal permanent residency, the victim will be required to submit fingerprints. DHS adjudicators will therefore have all of the criminal information that exists in the victim's criminal history. Forensic examiners assessing and documenting inadmissibility need to consider the words of advice published along with the U visa regulations (USCIS, 2007b, p. 4):

> It's better to acknowledge and explain as much as possible to not appear evasive. It's better to include and explain as much as possible upfront so your client will appear more credible. Err on the side of caution and disclose up front.

The implications for forensic examiners are to present coherently and clearly the victim's actions for which the assessee is seeking inadmissibility waivers and to present also an understanding of any mitigating facts or factors that may have played a role in the action or any criminal offense committed by the victim. The forensic mental health examination provides an important opportunity to provide documentation that considers the totality of the victim's circumstance, history, and traumatic experiences, including any objectionable actions or offenses and the role that cultural barriers, limited English proficiency, fear of law enforcement, and victimization may have played.

Chapter 7

Forensic Psychological Assessment of Extreme Hardship

An extreme hardship waiver in IC essentially allows an immigration judge (IJ) or other U.S. Citizenship and Immigration Service (USCIS) adjudicator the discretion to suspend removal (i.e., stop deportation) of an immigrant respondent who otherwise would be deported for a violation of immigration law. The basis for this legal action can include the adversity it would cause to U.S. citizen or legal permanent resident (i.e., qualifying) spouse, children, or parents. As will be discussed below, immigration law in this area is complex and there are no absolute guidelines. As such, working closely with the referring immigration attorney to understand the law and how it fits into psycholegal questions is essential.

Among the factors considered in these removal proceeding are extreme hardships to qualifying spouse, children, or parents. In some circumstances, extreme hardship can be considered under asylum law to an individual facing deportation. Forensic psychological assessment of immigrants in deportation proceedings can help establish psychological, development, educational, and other hardships that qualifying family members would experience because of the devastating loss of their immigrant family member. The purpose of this chapter will be to provide an overview of legal concepts in extreme hardship, with emphasis on psycholegal questions that can be addressed in forensic psychological assessment as well as a recommended methodology for conducting such assessments.

Legal Concepts

Deportation of non-citizens violating U.S. criminal law is a basic part of every country's enforcement of its immigration laws. Immigrants who are violent, dangerous, and recidivistic criminal offenders are rightly subject to deportation to their native countries for the protection of citizens. On the other hand, many immigrants with families and a long history of responsible behavior in the U.S are also subject to deportation, even when they committed relatively minor and non-dangerous misdemeanor offenses, if they served a short sentence with a perfect record of good conduct, or even when the entire sentence was suspended. Not infrequently such immigrants plea to crimes (perhaps without an adequate defense) at the advice of attorneys, only to later find out the dire consequences with the USCIS of doing so.

In cases of crimes of 'moral turpitude' (see Chapter 8), before 1996 IJs had relatively broad discretion to weigh desirable factors such as humanitarian, family unity preservation, or public interest considerations balanced against the seriousness of the immigrant's criminal offense and the degree of rehabilitation showed by the immigrant. Extreme hardship and its variants to affected families were an important aspect of establishing a desirable factor. As a result, so-called 'family impact statements' provided powerful evidence of the hardships that would be suffered by the family due to the removal of the immigrant. Since 1996, many petitions for extreme hardship waivers are adjudicated directly by the USCIS, placing even greater importance on a compelling evidentiary application.

When considering the concept of extreme hardship, it is critical to remember that evidence of the hardship to the qualifying spouse, parent, or child must be substantially beyond what ordinarily would be expected from the immigrant's deportation, that is 'extreme' or 'exceptional and highly unusual.' The USCIS (1998) issued a statement titled 'What factors are considered in evaluating extreme hardship?':

> An applicant for suspension of deportation under former section 244(a)(1) of the Act, as in effect prior to April 1, 1997, or special rule cancellation of removal under section 309(f)(1)(A) of IIRIRA, as amended by section 203 of NACARA, must establish that his or her deportation or removal would result in extreme hardship to the applicant, or to a parent, child or spouse who is a United States citizen or lawful permanent resident alien. In adopting the same standards for special rule cancellation of removal as were required for suspension of deportation under former section 244(a)(1) of the Act, prior to amendments by IIRIRA, Congress appears to have intended the same standard for extreme hardship to apply to both forms of relief. The phrase 'extreme hardship' is not defined in the Act, and NACARA provides no additional guidelines for interpretation of this requirement. Instead, 'extreme hardship' has acquired specific legal meaning through interpretation by the Board and Federal courts.
>
> (USCIS, 1998)

This guidance further notes that extreme hardship 'is not a definable term of fixed and inflexible content or meaning. It necessarily depends upon the facts and circumstances peculiar to each case.' Relevant factors specifically mentioned by the USCIS include:

1. the immigrant's age at the time of entry to the U.S. and at the time of application for suspension of deportation;
2. the age, number, and immigration status of affected children and their ability to adjust to life in another country, including their ability speak its native language;

3. the immigrant's health condition as well as that of his or her child, spouse, or parent, including the availability of any required medical treatment in the returning country;
4. the immigrant's ability to obtain employment where she or he would be returned;
5. the immigrant's length of residence in the United States;
6. other extended family members legally residing in the United States;
7. the financial impact of departure;
8. the disruption of educational opportunities;
9. the psychological impact of deportation or removal;
10. the current political and economic country conditions in the country where he or she would be returned;
11. family and other ties to the country of origin;
12. contributions to and ties to a community in the United States, including the degree of integration into society;
13. immigration history, including authorized residence in the United States; and
14. the availability of other means of adjusting to permanent resident status.

The concept of the extreme hardship waiver is found in numerous areas of immigration law. Hake's (1994) comprehensive review of extreme hardship in immigration law remains an essential legal reference and points out that the term 'hardship' in immigration law carries a variety of qualifiers that can vary from exceptional to extreme to extremely unusual. He noted that the criteria for hardship are not well defined by immigration law and subsequent IC decisions, and the USCIS law qualifier terms such as 'extreme hardship' and 'exceptionally and highly unusual hardship' are basically interchangeable pragmatically. Emphasizing that no one extreme hardship is sufficient with regard to specific factors in family impact statements, Hake and Banks (2005) developed the Hake Hardship Scale, a weighted measure covering six major areas for extreme hardship to the spouse, child, or parent of the individual in deportation proceeding. These are:

1. medical hardships;
2. psychological hardships,
3. career or educational disruptions;
4. very serious financial hardships;
5. sociocultural hardships upon relocation to the home; and
6. significant risk of physical harm upon relocation due to political or sectarian violence.

As a result, throughout this chapter, we use the general term 'extreme hardship' to discuss this area of forensic practice, though caution is given to use the specific legally sufficient and accurate term when writing reports or presenting testimony.

Forensic psychologists and other mental health professionals can be of considerable value in certain immigration cases by providing information that can flesh out psychological and psychosocial hardships to individuals and families. The most obvious area for psychologists in helping to establish extreme hardship would involve demonstrating that either an affected family member, or even the immigrant, is suffering from a mental disorder (such as depression or schizophrenia) or mental deficiency (such as an intellectual disability). Additionally, it would need to also be shown that deportation would significantly worsen the individual's condition or that appropriate and necessary treatment would not be reasonably available in the destination country.

While a well-qualified IC forensic mental health assessor can readily assess psychological hardship due to a mental disorder, she or he also has relevant evidence-based knowledge to assess additional relevant hardship areas. For example, there is a large and valuable empirical literature on the psychosocial impacts of deportation on the members of the family – for example, the psychological impact of parental loss; severe financial and educational hardship on child development; and impact of career disruption on the psychological condition of a relocated spouse.

Impact of Separation through Deportation on Families

In recent years the damaging impact of separation through deportation on immigrant families has received increasing attention in the professional literature (see Brabeck & Xu, 2010; Cavazos-Rehg, Zayas, & Sptiznagel, 2007; Cervantes, Mejía, & Guerrero Mena, 2010). Policy initiatives from organizations such as Human Rights Watch (2007) provide a chilling report of the pervasively damaging impact of deportation on immigrants' families as the result of harsh post-1996 immigration law. For example, they report that, according to the 2000 US Census estimate, over 1.5 million spouses and children living in the U.S. were separated from their parent, husband, or wife because of deportations. This disquieting reality has led to an immigration rights movement to lobby Congress to revise immigration laws to ensure access to a hearing before an impartial adjudicator for all non-citizens. This advocacy is aimed at balancing the value of families for an immigrant in removal proceeding to remain in the U.S against the understandable U.S. interest in deporting dangerous, recidivistic criminal non-citizens.

While separation through deportation of immigrant families is a significant social concern that grows more important as USCIS policy toughens, it is important for forensic mental health evaluators to move beyond broad social concerns to provide specific assessment responsive to psycholegal questions. An application of forensic psychology to extreme hardship waivers is the 'family impact statement,' which provides evidence establishing the specific impact of loss through deportation of a parent, child, or spouse on his or her family. While we could find limited specific empirical psychological research on the impact of deportation on affected spouses and children, there is more than ample psychological literature to illustrate the deleterious psychological impact of loss of a parent.

For example, Rojas-Flores, Clements, Hwang Koo, and London (2017) recently examined the impact of potential forced parent–child separation and parental loss in children whose immigrant parent was in detention awaiting deportation. They found that such loss was best considered as a potentially traumatic event with adverse effects on children's mental health in terms of increased PTSD symptoms. Cavazos-Rehg, Zayas, and Spitznagel (2007) studied the impact of worries about deportation on families with a deportable member, finding that affected Latino immigrants were at significantly increased risk of experiencing negative emotional and health outcomes. Additionally, the psychological literature strongly indicates the short-term and long-term damaging impact of the loss of a parent on children through death (see Cerel, Fristad, Verducci, Weller, & Weller, 2006; Kaffman & Elizur, 1984; Lehman, Lang, Wortman, & Sorenson, 1989; Sossin, Bromberg, & Haddad, 2014), divorce (e.g., Amato & Keith, 1991; Wallerstein & Kelly, 1980; Wolchik & Karoly, 1988), and all forms of parental absence (Amato 1991). Children facing loss of a parent through deportation will likely experience depression, anxiety, or other mental disorders, and children with prior mental disorders can suffer an exacerbation of the disorder because of the loss. Further considerations include the psychological impact of removing the child to a different culture with a different language and, a critical factor often overlooked, the psychological impact of the extreme loss of financial resources (i.e., poverty) on affected children's subsequent development (see Brooks-Gunn & Duncan, 1997) and children's health (Aber, Bennett, Conley, & Li, 1997).

Similarly, psychological assessment can also evaluate the U.S. citizen spouse or elderly parent for mental disorder, either caused or exacerbated by loss (see Carnelley, Wortman, & Kessler, 1999; Maciejewski, Prigerson, & Mazure, 2001), for the impact of loss on health (see Martikainen & Valkonen, 1996), and for vulnerability to suicide after profound and sudden loss (see de Vries, Davis, Wortman & Lehman, 1997; Li, 1995). Finally, consistent with Horowitz's (1993) research on stress response syndromes, social disruption of the family arising from the deportation of a spouse or parent can also trigger powerful stress responses similar to posttraumatic stress disorder. More specifically, as Lin (1986) has noted, the social disruption experienced by refugees commonly results in powerful emotional and behavioral manifestations of distress, including depression, anxiety, dissociation, and even reactive psychosis. The loss of a family member to deportation can activate a similar process.

While the psychological literature clearly supports likely extreme hardship to affected spouse, children, or parent, only through a careful psychological assessment can individual and family impact be reasonably determined for the particular individuals involved. This is to say that, even though severe psychological impacts are likely for qualified family members, it is also possible that the deportation of a non-citizen can be a neutral, or even a positive, event for a qualified family member.

Assessing Extreme Hardship on a Spouse

As noted above, the forced loss of, and permanent separation from, a spouse can be overwhelming and even traumatic, especially when the U.S. citizen or permanent resident spouse suffers from a mental disorder or otherwise has significant psychological vulnerability to separation. As stated above, the most obvious area in establishing extreme hardship would involve demonstrating that an individual is suffering from a mental disorder (such as depression or schizophrenia) or mental deficiency (such as intellectual disability), that deportation of the immigrant spouse would significantly worsen the individual's condition, and that appropriate treatment would not be available in the destination country.

It is our strong opinion, backed by considerable experience providing IC forensic assessments, that a comprehensive, multi-method assessment must include four elements to be optimally helpful to the IC judge or USCIS adjudicator. First, no forensic assessment method ever takes the place of an in-depth clinical interview, which best provides the psychosocial context of the affected individual, as well gauging the nature of the relationship of the affected U.S. citizen with the immigrant in deportation proceedings. Second, to be comprehensive and neutral, the forensic examiner must: (1) obtain collateral materials to support or challenge the claim of the individual; and (2) conduct a formal assessment of malingering and deception. These latter two methods are critical, as the credibility of the individual evaluated must never be taken for granted, no matter how compelling their story, especially given the deep concerns about credibility in IC (Evans, 2000). Third, wherever feasible, an appropriate psychological test battery tailored to the psycholegal questions allows for a deeper understanding of the individual than the interview alone, as well as serving as an empirical check and balance on the examiner's perceptions and biases. Naturally, such psychological testing must be sensitive to cultural issues and be appropriate for international adaptation (see Okawa, 2008; Pope, 2013). Fourth, all forensic assessments need to be sensitive to issues of credibility. Forensic mental health evaluators must formally and systematically address issues of possible false imputation, deceptive reporting, feigning, and malingering (see Melton, Petrila, Poythress, & Slobogin, 2007).

Clinical Interview

The comprehensive clinical interview is the core of forensic psychological assessment in IC. While there is no prescription for the interview protocol, there is critical information that should be gathered. Using interviews, the forensic assessor gathers information on the evaluee's reported life problems (e.g., possible deportation of spouse), subjective reactions to these problems, symptoms (including mental status examination), diagnosis of mental disorder(s), and proximate cause of these symptoms to life events. The goal of the interview is to develop a thorough narrative of the evaluee's life story including: family history, including attachment; marriage and dating relationships (especially with the immigrant in deportation proceedings); current and past psychological trauma; history of mental disorder and treatment, including substance abuse; medical problems; work and educational endeavors; and legal problems.

Using interviews, the forensic assessor forms an initial opinion on the client's problems, subjective reactions to these problems, symptoms, diagnosis of mental disorder(s), and proximate cause of these symptoms to life events. An important consideration is whether the forensic assessor uses a completely open-ended interview approach or some combination of open-ended questions and semi-structured interview format. One recommended approach is to develop a consistent interview format that the forensic mental health examiner uses as a methodology common to all forensic assessments. A systematic approach that is replicated across all assessments can provide extra evidence of neutrality that is welcomed by the court (see Chapter 9).

Another consideration during the clinical interview is whether or not to incorporate evidence-based structured interviews such as the Structured Clinical Interview for DSM-5 (First, Williams, Karg, & Spitzer, 2015) for assessment of specific symptoms and disorders. As Rogers (2001) pointed out, inter-rater reliability between different mental health examiners using an open format methodology to determine a specific diagnosis is strikingly poor. While this may be adequate, or at least normative, for clinical practice, the scientific integrity of reliable diagnosis is critical in forensic assessment settings. Examiner bias in arriving at a forensic mental health opinion is always at issue before the IC and other courts (see Hagen, 1997), and using methodology that reduces bias addresses this legitimate concern for IC judges and adjudicators. To emphasize what we have reiterated throughout this book, a comprehensive interview of the affected individual alone is a critical, but never sufficient, element of forensic mental health assessment for IC.

Couple's Interview and Observation

Another central part of the forensic psychological assessment of extreme hardship to a U.S. citizen or permanent resident spouse is a careful review of their marital relationship. In our view, it is insufficient to depend on the affected spouse's information without showing a strong attempt to gain corroborating evidence of the nature of her or his relationship with the immigrant. In fact, an important concept in immigration law is evidence of '*bona fide*' marriage versus 'sham' or 'fraudulent' marriage. Uncovering sham marriages is a central priority of USCIS, which believes that a high number of the marriage-based green card applications are fraudulent. USCIS is quite aware that some U.S. citizens accept money or other advantages to marry a foreign-born individual and even that organized illegal services exist to arrange marriages between U.S. citizens and permanent-residence-seeking foreign nationals. While this is especially a concern for USCIS whenever a U.S. citizens petition for their immigrant spouse to get permanent resident status, evidence of a *bona fide* valued by USCIS can provide important guidance in establishing the strength of a marriage in extreme hardship matters as well. Because the burden of proof in IC is always on the immigrant, careful psychological assessment can be especially useful in helping address this critical question of the importance of the marriage in an affected individual's life.

As part of the forensic assessment of extreme hardship, a core element of the clinical interview will include detailed questions on the nature of the relationship between the affected individual and her or his immigrant spouse. As such, an interview with the immigrant spouse in deportation proceedings is also essential. Following the guidance of the USCIS, questions commonly found in the 'Stokes' interview (also known as the 'marriage fraud' interview) (*Stokes v. INS*, 1976) can be especially valuable to the IC judge or adjudicator because of its basis in immigration law. In addition to broader questions, examples of detailed Stokes questions to be asked of each spouse are:

- Where and how did you meet? Where did you go on dates? Who knew about your dating relationship?
- How many people attended your wedding? What did you serve at your wedding (to eat or drink)?
- Do you have a pet? If so, who feeds it, what food, and when?
- Do you use contraception (birth control)? If so, what form?
- Who goes to work every day, and when?
- Do the two of you attend regular religious services? Where and when?
- Where did you go on your last vacation together?

Further, issues that often raise questions for the USCIS include the following, which should be reviewed and understood by the forensic mental health assessor, when they occur:

- large disparity in age;
- inability of petitioner and beneficiary to speak each other's language;
- vast difference in cultural and ethnic background;
- family and/or friends unaware of the marriage;
- marriage arranged by a third party;
- marriage contracted immediately following the beneficiary's apprehension or receipt of notification to depart the U.S. or in advance of a visa expiration;
- discrepancies in statements on questions for which a husband and wife should have common knowledge;
- no cohabitation since marriage (although there can be valid reasons);
- beneficiary is a friend of the family;
- petitioner has filed previous petitions in behalf of aliens, especially prior alien spouses.

Naturally, in addition to specific questions to spouses in separate interviews, the forensic mental health assessor should conduct a couples' interview as well. The focus of this interview will be to observe the nature of the couple's relationship as well as to assess the immigrant spouse's behaviors and attitudes toward the affected spouse's psychological vulnerabilities. Carefully documented observation of the verbal and non-verbal behavior within the spousal relationship can provide narrative in the psychological report that is likely to be welcomed by IC judges and other adjudicators. Additionally, there are psychological tests that address the strength and health of a marital relationship. Among those are: the Dyadic Adjustment Scale (Spanier, 1976); Family Assessment Measure-III-Dyadic Scale (Skinner, Steinhauer, & Santa-Barbara, 1995), and the Marital Satisfaction Inventory-Revised (Snyder, 1997).

Third-Party Information

It is axiomatic in forensic mental health assessment that corroboration of information provided by individuals in extreme hardship evaluations provides important evidence to move beyond hearsay, 'he said/she said' communications found in interview-only assessments. Indeed, the value-gathering of third-party information is codified in *Specialty Guidelines for Forensic Psychology* (American Psychological Association, 2013). It is standard practice within forensic psychology to oblige attorneys or courts retaining experts to provide a complete case file (not selected or 'cherry picked' by the attorney) of evidence in the case, including all relevant legal documents. Additional information not necessarily found in files commonly requested by forensic assessors includes mental health records, medical records, educational records, and employment records. In immigration matters, important information includes detailed documentation of country conditions of the immigrant's home country relevant to the psycholegal questions, such as safety, availability of medical and mental health services, and employment opportunities.

Additionally, in assessments of extreme hardship to a qualified U.S. citizen or permanent resident spouse, it can be useful to request specific third-party information focused on whether the marriage can be readily established as *bona fide* under USCIS rules. Such information to be requested from the respondents' attorney in advance of interviews includes evidence of specific steps the couple have taken to join their lives, such as making the partner the beneficiary on the affected individual's retirement account; health insurance policy; deed, mortgage, or apartment lease in both spouses' names; utility bills; joint bank and credit card accounts; proof of joint automobile ownership; and joint income tax returns. Further documentation demonstrating a committed relationship can include receipts from trips, such as for airplane tickets or hotel bills; copies of phone records showing calls made to each other; photos of the wedding and other family events; and birth certificates of children or a doctor's report verifying pregnancy, or a fertility specialist's report indicating that the couple are trying to have a child together.

Throughout the course of the various interviews, the forensic assessor develops and re-assesses initial hypotheses about reported signs and symptoms and their causes and, in turn, alters the assessment accordingly. Additionally, during the interview, the forensic assessor will compile a list of sources of information from third-party verification, such as collateral interviews and documentation in addition to the original file given to the assessor. The assessor must insist of receiving this additional information or the probative value of the overall psychological report can be weakened.

Psychological Testing

As will be discussed in more depth in Chapters 9 and 10, psychological testing can be of considerable value in forensic psychological assessment in IC and, because of its scientific grounding, can provide useful empirical (i.e., fact-based) evidence. Psychological testing fits well into issues involving extreme hardship as it can demonstrate and corroborate mental disorder and other special vulnerabilities to separation. In some instances, psychological testing, especially performance-based measures, can provide a 'voice' for the U.S. spouse when psychological issues are hard to articulate. Two examples of how the Rorschach test can provide evidence beyond interviews and self-report measures like the MMPI-2 or PAI in forensic assessment of extreme hardship can be found in Evans (2004) and Hopwood and Evans (2017).

The ability of psychological testing to validate an affected U.S. citizen's claim of extreme hardship is especially useful for individuals who otherwise appear to be highly successful, as is often the case of exceptional and highly unusual hardships in physicians' J-1 waiver claims.

KH was seen for a forensic evaluation involving exceptional and highly unusual hardship related to his wife's visa requirement to return to Saudi Arabia. He was a 44-year-old naturalized U.S. citizen, having emigrated from Iran as teenager and worked as a tenured university professor. He described a history of pervasive childhood bullying due to a physical deformity and was happy when his parents left Iran for the U.S. He threw himself into school work and excelled academically, quickly receiving bachelor's and Master's degrees and his PhD by the time he was in his late twenties. He quickly got a faculty position and received tenure in his mid-thirties because of his scholarly excellence and high publication rate. He did not date until his early forties, when he met and soon married his wife, who was a student at his university. When he applied to receive permanent resident status for his wife, they found out that she did not have a regular student visa, but a more highly restrictive one that required a return to her country of origin for two years before she could apply to return to the U.S.

When asked about the impact of this enforced separation, KH related that his relationship with his wife was the first truly secure, stable relationship he had ever experienced and the first where he did not constantly feel vulnerable and unsafe. He stated that he could not bear the thought of being separated from her for the minimum two-year requirement. Yet, he had no history of mental health treatment and, on self-report testing, indicated no mental disorder, though a careful analysis of his validity scales revealed an exceptional ability to disguise severe psychological difficulties. On the other hand, results of the Rorschach suggested that he had a chronic vulnerability to becoming clinically depressed and was experiencing considerable emotional distress that interfered substantially with his life. His otherwise good ability to see reality accurately became compromised when he was overwhelmed with worries about loss. He exhibited a hypervigilant cautious, suspicious, and self-protective personality style, and saw his interpersonal world as dangerous. Not surprisingly, he was a socially withdrawn and interpersonally isolated individual with significant limitations on his ability to form close attachments, even though he deeply longed for closeness. The psychological test findings validated KH's at times inchoate dread of being separated from his wife. The results of the psychological evaluation were noted as helpful in the INS adjudicator's decision to grant a waiver and allow his wife to remain with him in the U.S.

Assessment of Credibility

Because substantial concerns about credibility in the IC context, a critical dimension of forensic psychological evaluation is the assessment of false imputation, deceptive reporting, feigning, and malingering. Because IC requires affirmative evidence to overcome the presumption of deportation, the burden of proof rests with the immigrant respondent and her or his legal representative. As such, providing fact-based evidence of credible reporting is a key feature of all forensic mental health assessment in IC. Clearly, forensic mental health professionals are well equipped to provide such information. Because of the considerable secondary gain to the respondent of feigning mental disorder, assessors must formally assess malingering and deception beyond the simple reports of the affected citizen and respondent in deportation proceedings. The formal assessment of malingering and deception (see Rogers, 2008) can also address issues involving credibility of a claim of extreme psychological hardship (Evans, 2000; Frumkind & Friedland, 1995), as research indicates clinical judgment based on interview alone is not sufficiently accurate to merit scientific support (see Bourg, Conner, & Landis, 1995; Garb 1998). This assessment is accomplished using a variety of methods. Perhaps the most valued method by IC judges is the use of information corroborating the self-reported claim of the respondent, which is why we emphasize the use of third-party information in our approach to forensic mental health assessment. Additionally, psychological testing increases the accuracy of clinical decision-making (Garb, 1998) and can provide another level of assessing overreporting or even feigned response styles.

Assessing Extreme Hardship on Children

When an application for waiver of deportation involves an affected U.S. citizen or permanent resident child or children, the forensic mental health assessor can provide useful psycholegal evidence by conducting a forensic psychological assessment of the child and her or his relationship to the immigrant. Allen, Cisneros, and Tellez (2015) found that children with a deported parent were more likely to demonstrate elevated levels of psychological and behavioral problems than children without a deported parent. An evaluation of children whose parent or parents are in deportation proceedings takes this research into account, but further explores specific vulnerabilities of affected children as well as the children's particular relationship to the immigrant parent. This is achieved through utilizing four methods: (1) developmental and family history interview; (2) parent–child observation; (3) psychological testing of the children; and (4) review of collateral sources. If a child does not have a good bond, or even has a traumatic relationship, with the parent, his or her psychological state may not be affected, or may even be improved, by the deportation of the parent.

> LM was a 35-year-old female from a South American country in deportation proceedings. As part of her legal representation, her attorney requested an assessment of the extreme hardship LM's five-year-old daughter would experience if her mother were deported. It became clear from the interview that LM was highly invested in her work, left the child with the nanny most of the time during the day, and spent very little time with her daughter. LM worked or went out most evenings and left the daughter in the care of her daughter's U.S. citizen father or a babysitter. The child–parent observation revealed that the daughter was poorly bonded with LM. Psychological testing provided evidence of LM's low empathy and relative disinterest in close relationships. The evaluator shared these findings with the referring attorney, who opted not to have a report of the evaluation results written.

Comprehensive Child Development and Family History

Depending on the age of the child, a detailed child development and family history is gathered by an interview with the parent, supplemented as appropriate by individual interviews with the child or children. As stated above, there is considerable value in developing a systematic interview involving open-ended questions, semi-structured interviewing, and occasionally structured interviews. Areas to be covered include developmental milestones, children's activities and school performance, peer relations, family relations, self-perceptions, feelings, and parent-/teacher-reported problems (see McConaughy, 2013 for a compendium of child history measures). When considering a comprehensive standardized interview for children ages 6–18, McConaughy and Achenbach's (2001)

Semi-structured Clinical Interview for Children and Adolescents provides a flexible protocol with a substantial normative sample that has both parent observation and child self-report rating forms. Further, it works well in concert with the Child Behavior Checklists (CBCL; Achenbach & Recorla, 2000, 2001) in identifying emotional and behavioral disorders (McConaughy & Achenbach, 1996). These instruments are of particular value because of the broad number of translations available and their multicultural research (Achenbach & Rescorla, 2007, 2010).

Parent–Child Interaction Observation

Of special importance is each child's particular relationship with both parents, as the nature and quality of the child's relationship to the respondent parent will be particularly valuable for the trier of fact. It our strong belief that Bowlby's (2008) understanding and classification of parent–child inner working models of attachment (Attachment Theory) provides a critical knowledge base for structuring observations of, and making assessments about, the impact of child–parent separation through deportation from an immigrant parent. In some cases the U.S. citizen child may have a better relationship with this parent than with his or her U.S. citizen parent. Substantial research indicates powerful relationships between attachment processes, psychological adaptation, and psychopathology (Cassidy & Shaver, 2008; Mikulincer & Shaver, 2015). The Circle of Security model (Marvin, Cooper, Hoffman, & Powell, 2002) provides a 'user-friendly' description of Attachment Theory that is very useful in organizing parent–child attachment observations and for describing these observations in reports and to IJ judges and adjudicators.

Observations should be structured so that the forensic mental health assessor can see interactions between the child and both parents together, the child with each individual parent separately, and, when age and circumstances permit, the child with the assessor alone, such as in the 'Strange Situation' (Ainsworth, Blehar, Waters, & Wall, 1978). A combination of open-structured observation, structured play interactions, direction/teaching activities, and separation and reunion can provide valuable information about the parent–child bond. The assessor may provide age-appropriate play tasks as well as teaching tasks to structure the observation. When observing parent–child interactions and behaviors, the assessor may focus on questions such as:

- Does the child seem to feel safe, secure, and comfortable?
- What does the caregiver do to help the child become comfortable?
- Can the child explore and play with toys? Can the child play independently?
- Does the child 'check in' the parent?
- Do the child and the caregiver share enjoyment in their relationship and activities?
- Does the dyad seem familiar with play and having fun together?
- How does the parent redirect the child in potentially harmful situations?

- How does the child respond when the parent sets limits?
- Does the parent provide scaffolding to learn something new or complete a given task?
- How does the child relate to the examiner?

Observations should be recorded as much as possible *in vivo* or, when not possible, immediately following the child–parent observations sessions. Often, these clinical notes provide rich performance-based descriptions of the child–parent relationship, which is frequently among the most compelling information for the triers of fact (see Krauss & Sales, 2001). Immigration examiners will benefit from receiving training in these methods of assessment of the parent–child relationship, because interpreting non-verbal interactive behavior is a skill that needs to be formally developed and is rarely part of the graduate curriculum of mental health providers. In spite of this, these observations will not be a measure of attachment pattern, but of the parent–child relationship.

Assessors should not use the concept of attachment pattern unless it was formally assessed because it is the type of attachment pattern by itself that is predictive of the health of the relationship and child development. Formal methodologies for assessing child attachment, such as the Strange Situation or the Child Attachment Interview (Shmueli-Goetz, Target, Fonagy & Datta, 2008; Target, Fonagy & Shmueli-Goetz, 2003), are available but they require extensive training, are very time-intensive to code, and, while useful, they may be only useful in cases in which the forensic mental health assessor finds it difficult to make a determination about the health of the relationship between parent and child.

Psychological Testing of the Child

Where psychological disorders and problems are suspected for an affected child of a parent in deportation, psychological testing can be of further help for the IC judge or adjudicator to understand the special needs of the child and the impact of the loss of the immigrant parent on the child. Chapter 10 outlines a number of performance-based measures, such as the Rorschach and Thematic Apperception Test (Murray, 1943), which offer empirically grounded findings with considerable cross-cultural use and research. In terms of self-report and observational methods, the Child Behavior Checklist (CBCL; Achenbach & Rescorla, 2000, 2001) is especially useful in forensic mental health assessment in IC. Besides being well researched and empirically studied, the CBCL data are gathered using multiple informants such as parents and teachers, with a broad range of multicultural translations available (see www.aseba.org/ordering/translations.html.)

Third-Party Information

Third-party information corroborating claims made by the parents of children impacted by the potential deportation of an immigrant parent provides important substantiation of these claims. In order to provide evidence of credibility so centrally important to IC judges and adjudicators, forensic mental health assessors are strongly encouraged to make a clear written agreement with the referring attorney that the assessor must have access to requested corroborating information about the child's functioning. In fact, our initial contract with attorneys indicates that failure to provide requested information to the forensic assessor can be grounds for the assessor to unilaterally withdraw from the forensic assessment. We recommend that the following information be available before the assessors meet with parents and children: educational records (including verification of special educational needs); mental health records; relevant medical records; and country conditions, especially availability of meeting education, mental health, and medical needs of the child. Further, as becomes necessary, the forensic assessor may wish to have interviews with collateral sources, including the child's teachers, mental health therapists, and other family members. Together, the child development interview, observation of child–parent interaction, relevant psychological testing, and third-party information provide elements of the narrative mosaic of the affected child and the impact of deportation of a parent on the child.

Chapter 8

Other Areas of Forensic Assessment in Immigration Court

The last chapter of this part of the book focuses on forensic assessment of criminal matters in Immigration Court (IC); competency to represent oneself in IC; and Special Juvenile Status, where immigrant children can obtain permanent residence when they are unable to safely reunify with their parents. These diverse areas have limited exposure in the forensic assessment professional literature and it is our intent to introduce these practices in the hope that we spur future writing and research on these topics.

Criminal Matters in Immigration Court

We address the psychological assessment in three major criminal IC areas: suspension of deportation for crimes of moral turpitude; parole from indefinite detention; and relief under the *Adam Walsh Child Protection and Safety Act* (2006) for U.S. citizens convicted of sexual crimes. Underlying all of these areas are concerns regarding potential recidivism and dangerousness, as well as support for rehabilitation. Providing evidence-based assessment of dangerousness, an area well represented in the criminal forensic assessment literature (see Hilton, Harris, & Rice, 2010; Otto & Douglas 2010), is essential in consideration of release from imprisonment from indefinite detention or while individuals are awaiting adjudication when seeking asylum or relief under the Convention Against Torture (United Nations General Assembly, 1984). We will start with a general discussion of the forensic mental health assessment of violence risk, sexual offense risk, and recidivism, and then review how these assessments are useful in criminal immigration matters.

Assessment of Dangerousness and Recidivism

Central to all forms of relief for immigrants who committed crimes of moral turpitude or for U.S. citizens who committed a sexual offense is the clear demonstration that these individuals are unlikely to be dangerous or to have a risk of recidivism. The carefully crafted forensic psychological evaluation must provide a coherent and defensible method for the assessment of risk of recidivism and risk of dangerousness (Evans, 2000). When used in a manner consistent with sound forensic practice, the forensic evaluation provides a systematic method for gathering, organizing, and quantifying certain clinical, historical, and dispositional variables (see Monahan & Steadman, 1994) shown to have empirical relevance. Such methods include traditional clinical interviewing and personality testing (such as the Rorschach, MMPI-2, PAI, MCMI-III), a thorough review of pertinent collateral and third-party data (such as arrest records, Department of Parole and Probation presentence evaluations, prison records, and collateral interviews with significant individuals), and administration of the Hare Psychopathy Checklist – Revised, 2nd Edition (PCL-R: 2nd ed.) or Hare Psychopathy Checklist – Screening Version (PCL-SV), an abbreviated screening version (Hart, Cox, & Hare, 1995).

The PCL-R is a 20-item scale used to measure psychopathy in forensic and research settings. It is administered and scored by a qualified examiner based on a semi-structured interview and record review (including substantiation through corroborative sources). Inherent to the method, PCL-R findings can only be reliable and valid when, (1) there is enough substantiated, collateral data to ensure factual scoring, and (2) the examiner is well-versed in PCL-R interviewing. Scores above 20 (out of a possible 40) are of concern for chronic criminality, while scores above 30 indicate the high likelihood of severe psychopathic style and represent a very high risk for future dangerousness and recidivism. The PCL-R has strong normative data that allow comparison of the individual to antisocial and psychopathic individuals found in minimum to maximum security prisons and forensic hospitals, as well as non-criminal/non-psychiatric college undergraduate control samples. Additionally, the PCL-R provides additional information because of its two-factor structure. Factor 1 taps interpersonal and affective features of psychopathy, such as selfish, callous, and remorseless use of others (Hare, 2003), while Factor 2 measures 'chronically unstable and antisocial lifestyle' (Hare, 2003) and contains behavioral/historical items that assess irresponsible, impulsive, sensation-seeking behavior patterns. Factor 2 correlates with criminal and antisocial behavior, while Factor 1 correlates most highly with both violent and non-violent recidivism.

The PCL-R is perhaps the single most useful assessment method in this area of forensic assessment because of the substantial empirical work establishing the PCL-R's role as the most important component in a comprehensive dangerousness risk assessment (Quinsey, Harris, Rice, & Cormier, 1998; Webster, Douglass, Eaves, & Hart, 1997) and recidivism (Walters, 2003). During its brief history, a wealth of research on the PCL-R has consistently demonstrated that high PCL-R scores have been associated with various important outcome variables such as violent and non-violent recidivism. In almost every study, regardless of race, gender, or presence or absence of a major mental illness, individuals who score high on the PCL-R demonstrate more problematic behaviors than those with low scores (see Gacono, Loving, Evans, & Jumes [2002] for a review of relevant literature and legal admissibility of the PCL-R). Of particular note is the replication of PCL-R findings in international settings (Hare, Clark, Grann, & Thornton, 2000), making the instrument even more valuable in Immigration Court matters.

In addition to the PCL-R, there are formal risk assessment models measuring the potential for violence and dangerousness (see Monahan & Steadman, 1994; Webster, Douglas, Eaves, & Hart, 1997), as well as for potential sex reoffending (see Douglas & Otto, 2010; Rettenberger, Boer, & Eher, 2011). For example, the HCR-20, Version 3 (HCR-20: V3: Douglas, Hart, Webster, & Belfrage, 2013) provides an empirically based guide to the assessment of risk of future violence. It consists of 20 items (ten historical, five clinical, and five risk management items), which are intended to increase the accuracy of predicting future risk of violence, including instances of serious previous violence, major mental illness, and psychopathy (as measured by the PCL-R). Because the individual factors should never be taken in isolation of each other when arriving at a decision, the HCR-20 weights the 20 factors in order to arrive at an overall risk judgment.

Where sexual re-offense risk assessment is at issue in IC, such as in Adam Walsh Act cases, the similarly structured Sexual Violence Risk-20 (SVR-20: Boer et al., 1997) provides an evidence-based scheme of structured professional judgment guidelines for conducting sexual violence risk assessments in forensic contexts. Like the HCR-20, the SVR-20 is not a quantitative test that yields specific norm-referenced or criterion-referenced scores. Rather, it was developed as systematic approach to risk assessment of individuals who have committed an act of sexual violence. The SVR-20 is not limited to likelihood of a new offense (recidivism), but also assesses other aspects of risk, such as level of victim harm, victim specificity, frequency, and imminence of previous sexual offenses.

It is important to remember that any single psychological instrument, inventory, or risk assessment scheme is only part of a comprehensive multi-method assessment approach necessary in evaluating complex psycholegal questions. Forensic mental health assessors interested in the complex and compelling world of criminal forensic issues will necessarily need to become well-versed in the literature of criminal violence and its psychological assessment. For those interested in forensic psychological assessment of recidivism and dangerousness in immigration adjudications, please see Rosenberg and Evans (2003).

Suspension of Deportation for Crimes of Moral Turpitude

Non-citizens, even those who have lived in the country legally for decades, are always vulnerable to deportation, especially if they have been convicted of a crime. Under immigration law, immigrants convicted of crimes of 'moral turpitude' are deportable. Non-citizens were subject to deportation for crimes of moral turpitude committed within five years after the date of entry and with a sentence of at least one year, whether or not the sentence was suspended. Non-citizens are also subject to deportation for violating a controlled substance law or for unlawful possession of an automatic weapon. It is not uncommon for many individuals in deportation proceedings for criminal matters to have little or no risk of recidivism and to be of no danger to society. The burden of proof is on the immigrant to demonstrate clearly and compellingly that he or she has rehabilitated following conviction and possible imprisonment and that society is not endangered by his or her being out of detention or remaining in the U.S. Information provided by a forensic psychological evaluation can be of significant value in helping the immigrant meet this burden.

Until 1996 under Waiver of Deportation (212(c)), IC judges were allowed to waive deportation of legal permanent residents based on the balance of positive factors versus negative factors. Positive or appealing factors include family ties within the U.S., duration of residence in the U.S. (especially if this began at a young age), hardship to family if deportation occurred, service in the U.S. Armed Forces, history of stable employment, and other evidence attesting to the non-citizen's good character, including genuine rehabilitation. Adverse factors included the nature and seriousness of the crime and whether the individual had a record of immigration or additional criminal offenses, especially aggravated felonies with five or more years of incarceration. There are two prongs in the determination of a waiver of removal of an aggravated felon (i.e., a person convicted of a felony carrying a sentence of greater than one year). The first prong is whether or not the individual has rehabilitated him/herself, including future risk of dangerousness to the community and recidivism. The second prong involves extreme hardship to a qualifying U.S. citizen or legal permanent resident spouse, child, or parent (this forensic assessment area was addressed in Chapter 7). While, after 1996, changes in immigration law removed this discretion from IC judges, there are still occasionally cases in deportation proceedings related to a guilty plea to the crime prior to April 1, 1997.

At the heart of this matter is the demonstration that the immigrant respondent has been 'rehabilitated' and is no longer a significant threat to society (see Rosenberg & Evans, 2003). Often representation of these individuals is immensely complicated by what Maruna (2001) calls the myth of the 'bogeyman' – i.e., the powerful tendency to label such individuals as immutably flawed. As Maruna (2001, p. 5) stated, 'Once a person finds him- or herself on the wrong side of that line, the bogeyman stigma is likely to persist even when deviant behaviors do not.' Zamble and Quinsey's (1997) landmark study on the assessment of criminal recidivism also noted a significant overreliance on historical factors in developing risk assessment models predicting future criminal behavior. Such an overreliance on past behaviors creates what they call 'tombstone markers,' that is, assessment based on acts in an individual's distant past, which will never change regardless of the degree of rehabilitation. Such factors do not take into account dynamic elements such as personal change and choice of better environmental influences, leaving the former criminal with high risk factor scores after even 20 years of crime-free behavior. A carefully crafted forensic psychological evaluation can be of considerable value in both demonstrating rehabilitation and clarifying misconceptions regarding the myth of the bogeyman.

Naturally, an understanding of the criminal recidivism literature supports the entire assessment strategy. Again, it is important to consider the pervasive influence of the myth of the bogeyman and to provide the empirical data necessary to meet the objective standards of the court. As stated above, Zamble and Quinsey's (1997) caution about 'tombstone markers' on recidivism assessment models (with PCL-R having some potential vulnerability to overinterpretation) and suggest the importance of community support and favorable environmental circumstances. It is important to consider also the compelling research of Maruna (2001, p. 26), which focused on the factors that he terms *desistence* – i.e., 'the long-term abstinence from crime by individuals who had previously engaged in a persistent pattern of criminal offending' – or the process of 'making good.'

The following case illustrates a forensic mental health assessment involving suspension of deportation for crimes of moral turpitude.

MS was a 31-year-old man who was a legal permanent resident, having emigrated to the U.S. with his mother as an adolescent from a dangerous Central American country. The index crime for which he was in deportation proceedings was a guilty plea to the charge of one count of statutory rape. Specifically, at age 19, he became sexually involved with a 12-year-old girl who became pregnant with his child. Mr. S stated that he pled guilty to the charge on the advice of his criminal attorney, because his attorney told him that he risked a greater penalty if he took the case to court. Mr. S believed accepting the guilty plea was a safer decision and, after giving a guilty plea, he was released on probation with time served. He stated that he had no idea about immigration consequences of his decision and was not informed of them by his attorney. FBE was asked to conduct a comprehensive forensic psychological evaluation of Mr. S to determine his risk of dangerousness and recidivism.

When asked about the offense, Mr. S reported that he did not realize that what he was doing was illegal until after his arrest. He himself became sexually active when he was 12 years old, reportedly a common pattern among fellow countrymen. An independent interview with his mother revealed that she had her first child at the age of 12. A cross-cultural psychology expert independently corroborated this pattern of early sexual relationships in his home country.

A review of collateral records indicated that Mr. S's extensive criminal background check revealed no previous or subsequent arrests or convictions. His presentencing evaluation indicated strong family bonds and no major violence risk factors and his parole officer indicated that Mr. S had cooperated with all aspects of supervision. Mr. S had consistently held responsible jobs, and had no mental health treatment. He provided regular and uninterrupted financial support of his child and visited the child regularly.

The results of Mr. S's forensic psychological testing revealed an open and non-defensive approach with no indication of significant psychological difficulties. His score on the Hare Psychopathy Checklist-Screening Version (PCL-SV) revealed that his very low score is far more similar to the non-criminal control sample than to criminal or forensic psychiatric samples. His assessment of dangerousness and recidivism using the HCR-20 showed no definite risk factors, including no serious previous violence, major mental illness, or psychopathy. In conclusion, it was FBE's opinion that Mr. S posed a very low, if any, risk to the community statistically regarding the possibility of future dangerousness or reoffending. Based on exceptionally good legal representation and good facts including the forensic psychological evaluation, the IC judge subsequently granted suspension of deportation for Mr. S's crime of moral turpitude.

Assessments Related to Parole from Indefinite Detention, Custody, and Bond

Every year, hundreds of thousands of immigrants are held in detention centers across the country. These individuals are subjected to protracted periods of imprisonment, called indefinite detention, in a complex network of prisons and jails with little or no government supervision to ensure that conditions are humane and their detention is not indiscriminate. Over the past several years, Immigration and Customs Enforcement (ICE), has increased their use of detention, creating massive backlogs in IC, resulting in ever-longer periods of detention. In many cases, immigrants are held for months or years before their first appearance before a court. Immigration attorneys and others have worked diligently to challenge indefinite detention and to increase immigrants' access to bond hearings. Many immigrants in indefinite detention are seeking asylum and have been detained awaiting their IC, while still others already have asylum or refugee protection, but are held indefinitely after the commission of a crime of moral turpitude.

Forensic examiners may be called on to conduct risk assessments in relation to cases in which a release from detention pending immigration proceedings is sought. The legal representative of the detained immigrants may use this risk assessment as supporting evidence for a request for bond or alternatives to detention, such as ankle bracelets. In these cases, the scope of the evaluation is the issue of the respondent's danger to the community as well as the flight risk.

The forensic examiner assesses the respondent and collects evidence regarding the issues at stake. Unless the individual has been in the U.S. for some time, it may be hard to obtain evidence of fixed address, employment, criminal history, family and community ties in the U.S. that would support the prediction that they are not dangerous and are not going to avoid the proceedings. Psychological testing may become key evidence regarding the individual personality and antisocial inclinations if the findings are favorable. Because the determination to release from detention is discretionary, the examiner is, to a certain extent, free to develop arguments that look at the favorable facts and circumstances that outweigh the precaution of detention, and which merits a favorable decision. The standard in these cases is the preponderance of the evidence.

Another role for forensic mental health assessors in IC involves expert evaluation and testimony on issues regarding the parole of individuals in indefinite detention. There are two primary areas in which expert opinion may be useful. The first involves parole for 'emergent reasons' of aliens who are detained after arrival in the U.S without proper documentation. Such emergent reasons include serious medical conditions, including severe mental disorder. Appropriate psychological assessment can help establish the presence and credibility of a mental disorder. As Frumkind and Friedland (1995) point out, the psychologist expert can also consider the psychological impact of detention and imprisonment (see Haney & Zimbardo, 1998). This assessment, combined with an assessment of potential dangerousness (see Monahan & Steadman 1996; Webster, Douglas, Eaves, & Hart, 1997), can help establish whether or not continued confinement is in the best interest of the public. The use of such expert assessment and testimony was important in establishing the deleterious effects of incarceration in the case of Fauziya Kassindja (see Kassindja & Miller, 1998; Musalo, 1998).

An additional area for psychological expertise involves parole from indefinite detention of undeportable aliens who are incarcerated for aggravated felonies. The use of Rorschach, along with powerful psychological tools such as the Hare Psychopathy Checklist-Revised (Hare 1993, 2003; Gacono, Loving, Evans, & Jumes, 2002) and the HCR-20: V3 (Douglas, Hart, Webster, & Belfrage, 2013), can provide attorneys with valuable information regarding violent recidivism and the potential danger to the public of parole of an incarcerated alien. The same methodology is used as crucial evidence for parole from indefinite detention as in petitioning the USCIS for exceptions to mandatory deportation for aggravated felony, especially concerning the rehabilitation and future recidivism risk as described by Rosenberg and Evans (2003). The following case illustrates the use of this approach.

Mr. M, a refugee from Afghanistan since his early childhood and permanent resident alien, was in proceedings with the USCIS to determine whether his release from indefinite detention would present a significant risk to the community. FBE was requested to evaluate Mr. M's psychological risk of dangerousness. On the advice of his criminal attorney to avoid the risk of jail time, Mr. M decided not to pursue a self-defense claim and pled guilty to the charge of malicious wounding. There was no indication that the attorney discussed potential IC ramifications of pleading guilty to an aggravated felony. He was physically threatened by a much larger adolescent over a disagreement involving his former girlfriend, and hit him in the face with brass knuckles. A small young man, Mr. M obtained the brass knuckles after being menaced by the much larger boy in school and hearing from friends that the other boy had vowed to beat him up.

Subsequent to his criminal plea and receipt of a suspended sentence with no jail time, Mr. M was detained by the then INS and placed in indefinite detention in a private prison a considerable distance from his home. Because of his refugee status, Mr. M could not be deported to his country of origin and was therefore held in INS detention indefinitely. FBE conducted the forensic psychological evaluation in the prison and reviewed prison records and interviewed prison staff during the visit. The results of the psychological testing showed indications of hypervigilance, helplessness, and fearfulness consistent with an individual whose life had been threatened in Afghanistan while this family attempted to flee the country during the government overthrow by the Taliban. His father, who was a strong supporter of the U.S., and his family were granted refugee status after finally escaping the country through the mountains in winter.

A careful review of collateral data was conducted, including a criminal background check, prison records and behavior during incarceration, and educational and employment history. His PCL-R results were well below the lowest cut-off point for concern and statistically lower than inmate scores commonly found in prison settings. Based on the results of the assessment, the examiner opined that Mr. M. was far more similar to the non-criminal/non-psychiatric college undergraduate control sample than any criminal or psychiatric samples and Mr. M was unlikely to be a danger to the community. Subsequently, an IC judge granted Mr. M parole from indefinite detention including the requirement for regular in-person reporting to the INS about his progress.

Relief Under the Adam Walsh Child Protection and Safety Act (2006)

The Adam Walsh Child Protection and Safety Act, also known as the Sex Offender Registration and Notification Act, is a commendable Federal statute that was signed into law in 2006. The Act was designed to protect children from sexual predators, particularly protecting children from sexual exploitation, preventing child abuse and child pornography, and promoting internet safety (Silver, 2015). The following is a non-exhaustive list of offenses against a minor that could trigger a visa petition to be denied based on the Adam Walsh Act: kidnapping or false imprisonment (unless committed by a parent); sexual solicitation; solicitation to engage in acts of prostitution; video voyeurism; offenses involving child pornography; certain instances of statutory rape; or anything else that is determined to be an offense involving sexual conduct against a minor (Silver, 2015, p. 294). The Act's provisions include a revised sex offender registration system; child- and sex-related amendments to Federal criminal procedure; child protective grant programs; and other initiatives designed to prevent and punish sex offenders and those who victimize children. One of these last initiatives imposes immigration penalties on U.S. citizens who are convicted of certain sexual crimes against minors.

Such an individual who is convicted of a 'specified offense against a minor' may be prevented from filing a visa petition on behalf of a close family member, such as an immigrant spouse or child. Under amended Section 204(a)(1)(i) of the Immigration and Nationality Act, the statute governing the petitioning procedure for immediate relatives, U.S. citizens who have been convicted of any 'specified offense against a minor' are prohibited from filing a family-based immigrant petition on behalf of any beneficiary. The law provides an exception only if the Secretary of the Department of Homeland Security (DHS) or his or her designate makes a sole and unreviewable discretionary decision that the U.S. citizen petitioner poses no risk to the petitioned relative despite the conviction. Unlike many legal decisions, the DHS's decision is not subject to appeal or review. It should be noted that, if the petitioner were a U.S. legal permanent resident rather than a U.S. citizen, the person would be referred to removal proceedings for probable deportation for committing a crime of moral turpitude.

As such, this area of forensic immigration assessment primarily involves a U.S. citizen and his or her foreign-born spouse and/or children. The law sets an extremely high bar with the concept of 'no risk,' unlike other U.S. laws where all evidentiary bars are probabilistic, e.g., preponderance, clear and convincing, or beyond a reasonable doubt. While court decisions in the future are likely to better define, or even challenge the legality of, this evidentiary standard, the law currently stands and forensic mental health assessors can be called upon to provide evidence in support of such a petition for exception.

Much like the other forensic mental health assessments in other criminal IC cases, the question of risk and dangerousness is central to the legal question at issue. With regard to Adam Walsh Act cases, there are several distinct features to be emphasized. The first involves the nature of the risk assessed, which here focuses on sexual risk and recidivism. As a result, knowledge of both static and dynamic risk factors for sexual re-offense form the underlying necessary expertise (see Craig, Browne, & Beech, 2008; Phenix & Hoberman, 2016) as well as appropriate assessment methods (Otto & Douglas, 2010; Rettenberger, Boer & Eher, 2011) and risk assessment guides (e.g., Sexual Violence Risk-20 (SVR-20); Boer et al., 1997). Second, the interview should include highly detailed description of the index sexual crime or crimes and a thorough history, including sexual history. Naturally, comprehensive third-party and collateral sources should be obtained and reviewed to corroborate this history. Third, it is important to place these data into the specific context of the risk of sexual offense to the immigrant spouse, as well as any children of this spouse. Fourth, given the very high evidentiary bar set in Adam Walsh Act cases, it is necessary to include a discussion of the legal concept of 'no risk' in the context of psychological assessment and sexual risk assessment, which by their nature are probabilistic. The following case illustrates a successful Adam Walsh Act assessment.

TT is a 63-year-old U.S. citizen who married a 55-year-old woman who was a citizen of Thailand. They met through a mutual friend, while TT was doing business in Thailand and TT applied to the USCIS to sponsor his wife to come to the U.S. as a legal permanent resident. She had two adult children, a son and a daughter, who would remain in Thailand if their mother moved to the U.S. This marriage was the third for TT and the second for his current wife.

Thirty years prior, TT was convicted for the index crime of unlawful sexual intercourse with a minor, a 17-year-old girl originally placed by the DSS for Emergency Shelter care with TT and his first wife, and who subsequently became a babysitter for the family. TT indicated that he had sex several times with the minor, which ended when she reported to the DSS that she was pregnant by him. He reported this occurred during a period of marital conflict and compulsive sexual behavior by him. After he was arrested and released, TT made a suicide attempt and was hospitalized psychiatrically for a month.

TT subsequently pleaded guilty, served three months in jail and paid a large restitution to the minor. He was placed on the national sex offender registry (pre-Adam Walsh Act). His wife divorced him and he got supervised visitation with his two young female children. He underwent extensive mental health treatment for sexual abuse and maintained continued contact with his psychotherapist for 30 years.

TT reported a family history of benign emotional neglect by his otherwise successful and accomplished professional parents. He was not sexually active until the age of 20, but became very sexually active with his first wife who was compliant with his desire for daily sex. Not many years after marrying, he began a series of casual sexual encounters with coworkers and occasionally streetwalkers, leading to regular affairs and additional encounters with prostitutes. Before his index crime, he was arrested for sexual solicitation in a police sting operation. He reported no other arrests, no mental health treatment, and a history of successful educational and vocational achievement. He was working in a highly skilled position at the time of the interview.

The forensic mental health assessment included a comprehensive interview with TT; collateral interviews with his ex-wife, current wife, therapist, and coworker friends, and extensive review of criminal proceedings and mental health records. Psychological assessment was conducted with the PCL-R; HCR-20: V3; SVR-20; Personality Assessment Inventory (PAI); and the Rorschach inkblot method. Results indicated a low score on the PCL-R and low risk of violence on the HCR-20: V3. There were no definite current risk factors on the SVR-20, with a literature review indicating probabilities of re-offense after 15 years being extremely low, as well as also dropping dramatically at the age of 60. PAI and Rorschach results did not show severe psychopathology.

FBE opined that the results of the assessment suggested that TT posed essentially no threat to his wife or her adult children. In the face of nearly 100 percent rejection by DHS administrative review of similar waivers from Adam Walsh Act immigration bars, TT's case was granted on an affirmative basis. In the DHS administrator's written opinion, the forensic mental health assessment was mentioned as an important factor of the decision.

Competency to Represent Self in Immigration Court

Jose Antonio Franco-Gonzalez and Guillermo Gomez-Sanchez were two immigrants with mental disabilities who were detained in immigration jail for years, because they were mentally incompetent to represent themselves in their immigration proceedings (Kowalski, 2015). They were the identified respondents in a class action suit filed on behalf of the many immigrants who were detained or even deported without having the ability to fairly present their cases in Immigration Court. Some immigrants arrive to the U.S. suffering from intellectual delays, traumatic brain injuries, cognitive or emotional impairments caused in their home country and which may be related to the reason why they left, or caused by traumatic experiences during the journey or after arriving in the U.S. There are immigrants who present with serious psychiatric disorders such as schizophrenia, bipolar disorder, and posttraumatic stress disorder that are often made worse as they sit in detention without medical or mental health care. There are accounts of individuals representing themselves in removal proceedings who were hallucinating in court, suffered from amnesia, were disoriented, could not even state their name or nationality, and did not understand the notion of deportation (Marouf, 2014). These immigrants may have good cause to receive immigration relief but were too incapacitated to present their case.

After more than five years of litigation, *Franco-Gonzalez v. Holder* was won and became a landmark ruling. The suit attempted to dispel the myth that immigration applicants are always mentally competent to meaningfully participate in their immigration cases (Buys, 2013). The outcome of the suit was the court order that immigrants with serious mental disabilities have a right to legal representation. A subsequent implementation order required the Federal government to establish comprehensive screening and competency determinations. This law provides enhanced protections to immigrant respondents with mental illnesses or developmental disabilities, and it involves a judicial duty to identify relief and develop a record, together with some ability to appoint legal representation for those who need it.

The process may start at the respondent's intake conducted by the DHS, which includes an initial screening review to determine a serious mental condition or disorder. If the competency of an applicant is in doubt, a judicial inquiry is open.

The judge has several options at that time about how to handle the case. It is essential that the competency process be tailored to the individual facts and unique circumstances of the respondent (*Matter of M-A-M*). The immigration judge may: (1) pose questions to the respondent to assess his or her state of mind and understanding; (2) allow a family member or close friend to provide information; (3) continue the proceedings so that further evidence can be gathered; (4) manage the case so the respondent can obtain mental health care or legal representation; (5) continue the proceedings so that an assessment of mental state changes over time can be conducted (Capital Area Immigrant's Rights Coalition, (CAIR), 2013, p. 46).

Another option the judge has, and which is relevant to this section, is to refer the case to a forensic examiner for a competency evaluation. Ultimately, during a competency review, the judge will make the decision about the competency of the petitioner to proceed (BIA, 2011), but forensic examiners are tasked with conducting competency evaluations that can aid the trier of fact.

As a model to conduct these evaluations, the IC decided to adapt *Dusky* (*Dusky v. United States*, 1960), which is the standard of competence in criminal proceedings. The basis of the standard is that the respondent is assessed in relation to two capacities: the information he or she must possess (adjudicative competence) and the ability to act on that knowledge (decisional competence) (Dawes, Palmer, & Jeste, 2008). Therefore, lack of competency is not based on the respondent's lack of knowledge, but on the inability to act on that knowledge. For Immigration Court, the key is the connection of these aspects with the ability to meaningfully participate and represent oneself. There are three prongs that will need to be assessed by the forensic examiner (Korngold, Ochoa, Inlender, McNiel, & Binder, 2015):

1. knowledge of the nature and object of the proceedings;
2. understanding, exercising, and waiving rights;
3. performing functions necessary to self-representation, including: responding to allegations and charges, presenting information and evidence on relief eligibility, and following instructions.

In contrast, a respondent is considered competent to represent himself or herself in an immigration proceeding if he or she has (Weil, 2015, p. 20):

1. rational and factual understanding of:
   a. the nature and object of the proceedings
   b. the privilege of representation by counsel
   c. the right to present, examine, and object to evidence
   d. the right to cross-examine witnesses, and
   e. the right to appeal;
2. sufficient present ability to:
   a. exercise the rights listed above

b. make informed decisions about whether to waive the rights listed above
c. respond to the allegations and charges in the proceedings
d. present information and evidence relevant to eligibility for relief
e. act upon instructions and information presented by the immigration judge or government counsel.

It is important that forensic examiners conducting this type of competence are trained in order to properly interpret these psycholegal concepts in practice. Dawes et al. (2008) noted that without consensus guidelines and without specialized assessment instruments, psychologists and psychiatrists conducting competency assessment show significant inconsistency in their application of the standards.

The assessor must evaluate for a significant impairment of the cognitive, emotional, or behavioral functioning of a person (Weil, 2015). This does not mean that any diagnosable mental disorder will qualify, as the standard requires that the mental disorder is meaningful only if it causes functional impairment in the respondent's performance around his or her role in Immigration Court. The intellectual, cognitive, neuropsychological, emotional, and personality functioning of the examinee as revealed in the psychological assessment do not determine in and of themselves the capacity of the examinee. Rather, it is the link between the impairments created by those disorders vis-à-vis the demands of the capacity which is of interest.

Therefore, the forensic evaluation includes the respondent's rational and factual understanding of: (1) the nature and object of the proceeding, including its adversarial nature; (2) the allegations and the charges; (3) possible outcomes of the proceeding; (4) the roles of the participants in the proceeding. In addition, the forensic examiner needs to evaluate the respondent's rational and factual understanding of: (1) privilege of representation by counsel; (2) right to present, examine, and object to evidence; (3) right to cross-examine witnesses; (4) and right to appeal. Similarly, the forensic examiner assesses the examinee's ability to: (1) make decisions about exercising and waiving rights; (2) respond to the allegations and charge(s) in the proceedings; (3) present information (e.g., respond to questions) and evidence relevant to eligibility for relief; and (4) act upon instructions and information presented by the judge and government counsel (Weil, 2015, p. 27). Examiners are also free to assess other relevant factors to the competency, such as the capacity to conduct oneself appropriately in court proceedings.

The forensic examiner needs to consider several important factors when conducting this evaluation. First, competency is a fluid state of mind and it can change from one moment to another. Similarly, a respondent may have some capacities but not others. Thus, the competence evaluation has a date of expiration and may need to be repeated if the legal process is delayed. Second, there are cultural factors that need to be taken into consideration. For instance, delusional thinking or hallucinations have a strong cultural component to the point that in certain cultural contexts they are not considered abnormal. In some cultures, the individual is expected to defer major decisions, such as those related to their immigration case, to elders or other relatives (Kim, 2007). Both verbal and non-verbal cultural behavior may be confused with signs of psychopathology when they are not observed through cultural lenses. Third, using interpreters in this context has to proceed with extreme caution, given the weight of the findings. Cultural knowledge is important to determine the motivation for certain behaviors, expression of mental disorders, and ability to communicate one's own mental state. Fourth, the attorney representing the respondent is not permitted to speak with the forensic examiner who assessed the client at the government's request (American Bar Association, 2015). However, the attorney can access the report directly from the court after it was filed.

Ultimately, the forensic assessor pulls all this information together to opine whether the respondent:

1. has the abilities and there is no impairment;
2. has sufficient present ability despite some level of impairment; or
3. there is significant impairment with inadequate ability (Weil, 2016).

It is the judge's responsibility to make the decision regarding competence considering the totality of the record and rule whether the respondent is:

1. competent (no *bona fide* doubt);
2. incompetent (by preponderance of the evidence); or
3. insufficient evidence (reasonable cause) (Weil, 2016).

Judge Weil (2016) in his competency trainings has advised that the report needs to be succinct and without irrelevant information, while at the same time it needs to be precise and note the specific grounds for the opinion. Further, it is considered essential to note in the report any alterations in response style, meaning whether the examinee minimizes or dramatizes their presentation in order to obtain secondary benefits. The examiner also needs to provide a hypothesis regarding the reasons for such biased presentation. Just as in criminal competency examinations, when the examiner recommends an adjudication of incompetence, there is a need to clearly identify in the report the impairments and mental disorders that are the cause of incompetence, and clearly describe the respondent's ability to make a rational decision about being represented by and assist his or her counsel.

Special Immigrant Juvenile Status

The Special Immigrant Juvenile Status (SIJ) was created by the Immigration and Nationality Act of 1990 to provide immigration relief to children and youth who have been abused, abandoned, or neglected. SIJ applies to undocumented immigrant children in foster care or the juvenile court system, but it also applies to recent young immigrants who were abused, abandoned, or neglected by at least one parent in the child's home country and are not in the foster care system. Congress passed this law based on the documentation of the vulnerability of immigrant children who live in the U.S. and have been subjected to child abuse, incest, sexual assault, child exploitation, abandonment, and/or neglect by their parents, step-parents, or adoptive parents, whether in the U.S. or in their home countries.

Children may encounter traumatic experiences by a parent before migration, during migration, or after migration to the U.S. Many children escape from horrific conditions of abuse and neglect perpetrated by one or both parents. Children are at risk of suffering victimization during the journey by one or both parents, a step-parent, or adoptive parent they are traveling with. Given the dangers and arduousness of the journey, a child is expected to be on his or her best behavior, and could be harshly punished if he or she disobeys, or punished and even be blamed for not preventing accidents or abuse from others. Children may suffer abuse after arriving in the U.S. when they come to join one or both parents who have migrated earlier, and in the process, encounter a different configuration of their family in which they need to renegotiate their place. There may be step-parents, half-siblings, step-siblings, and other family members or in-laws. These children have to deal with both the acculturation to a new society and adjustment to a new family with whom they may have limited bonding ties. These children are at great risk of abuse, and in many situations of domestic violence their non-abusive parent may also be abused. This law intends to provide protection to these children so that they can heal and grow up in a safer environment (Fitzpatrick & Orloff, 2016).

The SIJ application requires an order from the state court judge with jurisdiction on the case dependency, including: (1) findings of the abuse, abandonment, or neglect; (2) the lack of viability of the reunification with the parent who victimized the child; and (3) that deportation to the home country would not serve the best interests of the child.

For SIJ, the applicant must be younger than 21 or whatever the age of majority for his or her state, live in the U.S., and be unmarried at the time of the application. SIJ should not be confused with the Deferred Action for Childhood Arrivals (DACA), which provides protection from deportation for immigrants who came to the U.S. as children. DACA is not related to victimization of the minor by their parents. In addition, when the victimization of the minor was perpetrated by others, there are different forms of immigration relief that may apply, such as U visa, T visa, or VAWA.

Forensic evaluations that help these children with the evidence they need regarding their background of abuse, abandonment, or neglect by one or both parents may come from different public sources or may be contracted privately. Because many of these children are in state child protective programs, they receive ordinary psychosocial evaluations by government examiners in order to plan for the permanency of their situation. In other cases, such as children in

Federal custody, the government hires examiners to conduct evaluations to determine dangerousness and placement planning. These forensic examiners may not be directly focusing on the requirements for immigration relief that may come later in the case, but their reports may become key to those applications and it is important that they are aware of the relevant issues for SIJ, be thorough in the evaluations, and follow the outline provided next. Other children are in the community, living with the non-abusive parent, relatives, or strangers. They may find evaluators to help their cases through their attorney or through non-profit organizations. In any of these cases, these forensic evaluations can contribute greatly to the SIJ application.

The scope of the mental health evaluation for SIJ includes: (1) a comprehensive description of the abuse, neglect, or abandonment and its psychological impact; (2) issues that interfere with the minor's ability to reunite with one or both of his or her parents, due to the abuse, abandonment, or neglect; and (3) reasons why it is not in the minor's best interest to be returned to the country of origin, and staying in the U.S. ensures their continued safety. Ultimately, the forensic evaluation in these cases provides information to pursue the intention of the law of removing fear of deportation, promoting stability, and facilitating access to nurturing family relationships, stable school environments, mentors, role models, and community support (Fitzpatrick & Orloff, 2016).

There is a provision for government officials working with SIJ children, which it will be wise for forensic examiners to also follow, regarding not contacting or pressuring the child to contact the abusive parent or family members of the abusive parent (VAWA, 2005 amended §287 of the INA). Contact with a perpetrator is emotionally harmful to the child and gives information to the abuser that can be used against the child or the case. Similarly, it is understood that children who obtain this form of immigration relief cannot use their legal residency to provide immigration status to their abusive parent. However, the law allows children applying for SIJ immigration relief to continue living with a protective non-abusive parent, other relative, or a guardian (Fitzpatrick & Orloff, 2016).

Part III

Methodology

Diagnostic Interviewing and Trauma-Specific Instruments in Immigration Evaluations

The purpose of this chapter is to introduce a wide variety of available clinical psychological assessment methods that can aid the forensic mental health assessor in understanding the experience of the adult trauma victim. This chapter will review diagnostic interviewing methods, trauma-specific psychological assessment instruments, and generic psychological tests with an eye toward the application of these instruments in forensic assessment in Immigration Court (IC), especially in the cross-cultural use of these instruments.

Why Use Psychological Assessment Methods in Immigration Court Evaluations?

For the purposes of the next three chapters, psychological assessment refers to the use of psychological tests and interviews (structured or unstructured) to measure personality attributes, psychological symptoms, or cognitive functions in developing hypotheses and predictions about the respondent's psychological symptoms, inner experience, and interpersonal behavior. There are considerable advantages for assessors to incorporate psychological assessment into forensic evaluations, either through consultation with an assessment professional or receiving the education and training on how to administer, score, and interpret psychological assessment in a professionally ethical manner. Perhaps the major advantage is that psychological assessment is empirically grounded (see Kubiszyn et al., 2000; Meyer et al., 2001), providing objective information that considerably enhances the accuracy of clinical judgment (see Garb, 1998). Additionally, psychological assessment makes considerably more information available about the examinee's psychological functioning than the forensic assessor gains from unstructured clinical interviews alone. Last, because of the psycholegal context of the assessment, unstructured interviews alone are unlikely to move much beyond being considered as hearsay evidence and be accorded less probative weight by the IC judge or USCIS administrator weighing the evidence.

Psychological assessment instruments include clinical interviews, symptom-specific tests, and comprehensive personality tests. *Clinical interviews* are naturally at the heart of all mental health practice. They provide forensic assessors with a powerful way to understand their client's history, interpersonal relationships, personal experience, and subjective reactions to these experiences and relationships. However, relying on unstructured clinical interviews alone has some important disadvantages, the first of which is that it runs the risk of missing important information. Additionally, as noted by Garb (1998) and Rogers (2001), all mental health professionals have their set of biases, based on their own experience, education, and values. Structured interviews (as well as psychological testing in general) improve accuracy and reliability of clinical judgments and reduce bias. Interviews can be seen on a continuum from a completely unstructured interview all the way to carefully constructed and highly structured interviews. Harry Stack Sullivan's (1954) classic work, *The Psychiatric Interview*, skillfully introduced the idea of increasing reliability through a standard interview. With the advent of the *Structured Clinical Interview for DSM III-R* (Spitzer, Williams, Gibbon, & First 1990), the structured interview has become increasingly a gold standard for the most reliable diagnosis of mental disorder for research and clinical purposes.

Symptom-specific tests are psychological assessment instruments, which includes straightforward, face-valid instruments measuring a particular disorder or clinical phenomenon. They range from highly specific instruments for depression and anxiety (e.g., Beck Depression Inventory II [BDI II; Beck, Ward, Mendelson, Mock, & Erbaugh, 1961] and the Beck Anxiety Inventory [BAI; Beck, Epstein, Brown, & Steer, 1988]) to comprehensive assessment measures for psychological trauma such as Biere's excellent Trauma Symptom Inventory-2 [TSI-2; Briere, 2010]).

Among the most useful psychological assessment instruments are *personality assessment tests*, which are designed to comprehensively assess cognitions, attitudes, emotions, and psychological symptoms, as well as behavioral predispositions and inner experience. As will be discussed in this chapter, omnibus personality tests include *self-report tests*, i.e., inventory-type, question-and-response tests, such as the Minnesota Multiphasic Personality Inventory-2 (MMPI-2; Butcher, Dahlstrom, Graham, Tellegen, & Kaemmer, 1989) and the Personality Assessment Inventory (PAI; Morey, 1991). In Chapter 10 we will discuss *performance-based tests* such as the Rorschach inkblot method (see Exner, 2003; Weiner, 2003) and storytelling tests (see Teglasi, 2010), such as the Thematic Apperception Test (TAT) (Murray, 1943). The value of these comprehensive personality assessment measures is that they assess a wide variety of psychological states, allowing the forensic assessor to better understand comorbid mental disorders and underlying personality issues as well as posttraumatic states (Evans, 2012).

Why Conduct Psychological Assessment for Posttraumatic States?

When a forensic assessor first sees a person with possible psychological trauma, she or he is faced with a complex and daunting task. What is the nature of her or his trauma and how severe is it? Who was the perpetrator, a stranger or someone the trauma victim counted on for protection? How long ago did it occur? Was the trauma a single episode or a series of repeated events over an extended period of time? What are the trauma victim's vulnerabilities and strengths? How has the inner experience and outer behavior manifested both in terms of symptoms of psychopathology and disturbed interpersonal relations? These are but a few of the many issues and concerns that confront us when we enter the lives of individuals facing the impact of overwhelming, terrifying, horrific, and often incomprehensible life experiences. Psychological trauma is so profoundly destabilizing that it may be hard to imagine mistaking, over-diagnosing, or entirely ignoring it. Yet trauma disorders present in different and confusing ways, often with symptoms similar to other mental disorders, creating complex diagnostic and treatment challenges. Naturally, as in all forensic psychological assessments, the issue of secondary gain through malingering or dissembling must be directly assessed to address the critical issue of credibility in IC. To provide some groundwork for understanding the complexity of assessing psychological trauma, a brief description of trauma theory will be presented along with implications for trauma assessment.

Prevalence studies of psychiatric patients show rates of trauma exposure that range from 60 percent to over 80 percent (Bryer, Nelson, Miller, & Kroll, 1987). Carlson's (1997) review concludes that forensic assessors can expect at least 15 percent of their adult assessees to have current or past trauma symptoms. As will be stated below, presentations of psychological trauma will range from straightforward and clear to complex and disguised. As such, it is likely that forensic assessors will be challenged with understanding examinees with a wide variety of psychological trauma presentations. Therefore, forensic assessors who become acquainted with a range of psychological assessment tools will increase their ability to understand and treat a wide range of trauma responses. When faced with this daunting task, psychological assessment methods can help quickly and reliably provide a comprehensive view of the person and their struggles.

In particular, as noted earlier in this book, there are numerous circumstances under which traumatized people come to the attention of forensic assessors for assessment in IC. First, immigrants may be referred following a clearly identified trauma such as torture, domestic violence, assault, rape, or life-threatening accidents, illness, or injury. In these instances, the presenting psychological trauma is overt. Yet, posttraumatic stress disorder (PTSD) is only one of many possible ways in which traumatic experience presents itself (van der Kolk & McFarlane, 1996), and it not infrequently presents with comorbid mental disorders such as depression (Kessler, Sonnega, Bromet, Hughes, & Nelson, 1995). Further, the examinee may have past traumatic experiences that are activated by the current traumatic event. Using assessment methods, the forensic assessor can better address the complexities of different trauma presentations in terms of symptoms, diagnosis, and, most importantly, effective treatment.

Secondly, forensic assessors will also see individuals with past psychological trauma where their trauma presentation is less obvious. In this instance, the trauma victim may be unaware of the link between past traumatic experiences and their current suffering and symptoms and may not even see such experiences as relevant. For adult examinees with past chronic fear and persecution, traumatic dissociation may be used to survive the ordeal, which can limit clear memory of traumatic events and make it difficult for such individuals to reveal their experience in a coherent fashion. In such instances, psychological assessment, especially performance-based measures such as the Rorschach or AAP (see Chapter 10), can provide the forensic assessor with a clearer indication of such buried trouble.

What are the Faces of Psychological Trauma?

The word 'trauma' is misused increasingly in the common parlance as a word to indicate an unpleasant event, e.g., 'my girlfriend is giving me a lot of trauma these days about going out with the guys.' Therefore, a more precise definition of psychological trauma is important. Unlike a distressing experience, the trauma response involves specific psychophysiological responses that are more extreme and enduring than the psychophysiology of distress (see Southwick, Rasmusson, Barron, & Arnsten, 2005). Such traumatic physiological reactions underlie the biphasic psychological response to trauma, which is the phasic alternation between intrusive and avoidance/numbing symptoms (van der Kolk, 1994). Assessing the biphasic trauma response is critical in determining how to approach the client in treatment.

The best-known definition of the traumatic stressor is the stressor criteria used for PTSD described by DSM-5 (American Psychiatric Association, 2013). Criterion A-1 PTSD stressor criterion describes trauma exposure as

> was exposed to: death, threatened death, actual or threatened serious injury, or actual or threatened sexual violence, as follows:
>
> 1. Direct exposure.
> 2. Witnessing, in person.
> 3. Indirectly, by learning that a close relative or close friend was exposed to trauma. If the event involved actual or threatened death, it must have been violent or accidental.
> 4. Repeated or extreme indirect exposure to aversive details of the event(s), usually in the course of professional duties (e.g., first responders, collecting body parts; professionals repeatedly exposed to details of child abuse). This does not include indirect non-professional exposure through electronic media, television, movies, or pictures.
>
> (American Psychiatric Association, 2013, p. 467)

Following these criteria are four symptom clusters: intrusion; avoidance; negative alterations in cognitions and mood; and alterations in arousal and reactivity, which must cause distress and social and emotional impairment. The advantage of this definition is that it is relatively easy to quantify and therefore provides criteria that are reliable and researchable. The disadvantage is that it focuses on symptoms rather than experience and does not capture the terrible reality of protracted traumatic experience, such as torture, domestic violence, and systematic mistreatment, where understanding the impact of captivity, degradation, and emotional abuse is critical.

A second, more inclusive, and perhaps more satisfactory, definition is the ICD-10 (World Health Organization, 1992), which defines PTSD as

> a delayed and/or protracted response to a stressful event or situation (either short- or long-lasting) of an exceptionally threatening or catastrophic nature, which is likely to cause pervasive distress in almost anyone (e.g. natural or man-made disaster, combat, serious accident, witnessing the violent death of others, or being the victim of torture, terrorism, rape, or other crime).
>
> (p. 147)

The three symptom clusters are largely similar to those in the DSM-4, but not the new four symptom clusters model for DSM-5. This ICD-10 stressor was rejected for a more narrow definition in DSM-4, because it was harder to quantify. The emphasis on a stressor that would cause pervasive distress in almost everyone provides a broader understanding of the power of events that are not strictly life-threatening or integrity threatening.

A third definition arises from the work of Herman (1997), whose work indicated that current PTSD diagnosis frequently does not capture the severe psychological harm from prolonged, repeated trauma, and suggested a new diagnosis, *complex PTSD* or *disorders of extreme stress not otherwise specified* (DESNOS) to describe the pervasive psychological and physiological effects of long-term trauma. The stressor criterion for diagnosis of complex PTSD is that the individual experienced a prolonged period (months to years) of total control by another. Six clusters of symptoms have been suggested for diagnosis of complex PTSD:

1. alterations in regulation of affect and impulses;
2. alterations in attention or consciousness;
3. alterations in self-perception;
4. alterations in relations with others;
5. somatization; and
6. alterations in systems of meaning (Pelcovitz et al., 1997).

Because of the different and more severe symptom pattern, assessment of complex PTSD is important in forensic assessment in IC where psychological trauma is at issue before the IC for determining sequelae from extreme and repeated trauma, such as rape and torture, and trauma in captivity such as imprisonment. See Herman (1992a), Courtois and Ford (2009), and Resick et al. (2012)

for a more comprehensive discussion of the etiology, clinical phenomena, and treatment approaches of complex PTSD.

In addition to these three specific diagnostic presentations of PTSD, other symptoms commonly found in individuals experiencing trauma include somatization, panic reactions, emotional lability, anxiety, agitation, depression, hopelessness, loss of life purpose, inability to self-soothe, and disturbances in thinking and reality testing. Physiological dysregulation in chronic trauma can mask accurate diagnosis, because it resembles many other psychological disorders, such as bipolar disorder, panic disorder, and borderline personality disorder (see Pope, 2013). Affective dysregulation can increase cognitive confusion, intrusions can be experienced on a cognitive level as hallucinatory flashbacks, and psychotic-like thinking has been observed in traumatized people who were previously clinically normal (Weisath, 1989), giving the impression of a psychotic disorder. Efforts to avoid re-experiencing traumatic memories may make traumatized clients appear withdrawn, uncooperative, and exhausted, causing difficulties connecting with them and complicating forensic assessors' efforts to understand their experiences.

It is important to remember that not all individuals experiencing trauma show clinical signs and symptoms. There is no one-to-one relationship between an external trauma and the person's psychological response. Researchers estimate that only 9–30 percent of those exposed to trauma develop PTSD (Breslau et al., 1998; Ozer, Best, Lipsey, & Weiss, 2003; Wisco et al., 2014), though risk rates vary depending on the kinds of stressors such as combat, rape, childhood abuse, or assault with a weapon. The studies indicate that women consistently show higher risk rates than men. However, many people spontaneously resolve the trauma and, in the process, may even develop greater coping skills (Solomon, Mikulincer, & Avitzur, 1988). Such findings underscore the importance of assessing individuals' strengths as well as vulnerabilities (Sullivan, 1954), further complicating the forensic assessor's task.

Psychological Assessment Methods

Clinical Interviews

The clinical interview is the most common psychological assessment strategy used by forensic assessors – psychologists, psychiatrists, counselors, and social workers alike. Using interviews, the forensic assessor forms an initial opinion on client's problems, subjective reactions to these problems, symptoms, diagnosis of mental disorder(s), and proximate cause of these symptoms to life events. Throughout the course of a forensic assessment, the forensic assessor re-assesses initial hypotheses about reported signs and symptoms and their causes and, in turn, alters the assessment methods accordingly. While the clinical interview is the core tool used for assessing and understanding the forensic evaluee, all forensic assessors are vulnerable to their biases and the limitations of understanding from a single or selective source of data. George Miller's classic (1956) article on the limits of our capacity to process information indicates that at any one time we can hold seven pieces of information, plus or minus two. The implication for this psychological reality is that, in order to deal with the complexity of psychological trauma, the forensic assessor does well to operate from multiple information sources beyond an unstructured clinical interview, which is in turn a requirement of competent forensic psychological assessment (see American Psychological Association, 2013).

Interviewing in forensic psychological assessment settings frequently range from unstructured, free-form methods to carefully designed, validated, and researched structured interviews. The value of more open-ended interview methods is the flexibility for the assessor and respondent to explore important issues and the absence of leading questions. When working with trauma victims, this more open format can cause on the examinee considerable anxiety and even trigger feelings of being interrogated, especially if done in a 'neutral,' skeptical manner (see Evans, 2005, 2016). Additionally, because of the IC trier of fact's concerns about unexamined bias central to forensic psychological testimony, a methodology common to all forensic assessments may provide extra evidence of neutrality that is welcomed by the court. Semi-structured interviews such as the Evans Evaluation of Difficulties Interview (EEDI; Evans, 2002) have a long history (see Sullivan, 1954) within mental health. They are a good compromise between the value of open-ended and structured approaches and can provide needed structure to demonstrate replicability across forensic psychological assessments.

Structured Interviews

The assessment of symptoms and reactions to psychological trauma is aided by additional methods, such as structured interviews. For arriving at a valid and reliable assessment of psychological trauma signs and symptoms and other diagnostic phenomena, structured diagnostic interviews are more accurate than unstructured interviews (see Rogers, 2001). Using evidence-based, objective methodology dovetails well with the IC interest in factual evidence and serves to overcome concerns about hearsay evidence when assessors rely solely on unstructured interview. Two major structured interviews for the assessment of psychological trauma and PTSD in IC are described below. Although there are many others, it is beyond the scope of this chapter to be exhaustive. Additionally, given the importance of assessing traumatic stressors, two questionnaires about traumatic exposure to be used in concert with these interviews are described as well.

When the presenting problem includes a clear description of a traumatic stressor, structured interviews of posttraumatic stress employing dimensional rather than categorical (presence/absence) rating scales can be invaluable in arriving at an accurate diagnosis and more deeply understanding the severity and nature of

PTSD symptoms. Two examples of such interviews include the gold standard Clinician-Administered PTSD Scale for DSM-5 (CAPS-5; Weathers et al., 2013; for CAPS development see Blake et al., 1995) and the PTSD Symptom Scale-Interview Version (PSS-I; Foa, Riggs, Dancu, & Rothbaum, 1993).

Of all the structured interviews for PTSD, the CAPS-5 is the most comprehensive for assessing core and associated symptoms of PTSD and is frequently referred to as the gold standard for interview assessment of PTSD. Weathers, Keane, and Davidson (2001) review the literature on the CAPS, which includes over 200 studies indicating impressive evidence of its reliability and validity. Several advantages of the CAPS over other structured interviews for PTSD is that it assesses the frequency and intensity of each symptom, has excellent prompt questions to elicit clinical examples, assesses both current and lifetime PTSD symptoms, and provides explicit, behaviorally anchored rating scales. The CAPS can be scored, providing both continuous and dichotomous scores with a number of scoring rules to assist the forensic assessor (Weathers, Ruscio, & Keane, 1999), and CAPS-5 is updated to directly assess the new DSM-5 criteria for PTSD symptoms. The CAPS-5 is available for free from the National Center for PTSD and a training course to achieve proficiency in the measure is also available at www. ptsd.va.gov/professional/continuing_ed/caps5_clinician_training.asp. The CAPS's primary disadvantages are its long assessment time of about 50–60 minutes and the lack of systematic research with immigrant populations.

Returning to structured interviews for trauma assessment, the PSS-I can have important adaptations to assessment of traumatized immigrants seeking relief in the IC. When time is at a premium, the PSS-I may be a reasonable alternative to the CAPS. Studies indicate that the PSS-I is reliable and valid in civilian trauma survivors (Foa et al., 1993), making it a good instrument for many evaluees' forensic assessment for the IC. In a comparison study with the CAPS (Foa & Tolin, 2000), the PSS-I performed about equally well in arriving at a diagnosis of PTSD, decreasing assessment time without sacrificing reliability or validity. On the other hand, what is gained in timesaving is lost in providing a detailed, rich description of the examinee's past and present psychological trauma. An extra value of the PSS-I is that it is face-valid and less complex when the forensic interview is conducted in translation into a language where no normed structured interviews are available.

Naturally, such use should be approached with caution, given Pope's (2013) concerns regarding use of tests in which the standardization, norms, validity, reliability, specificity, sensitivity, and similar measures are not specific to the individual's cultural group. Such 'off brand use' should be weighed carefully regarding potential probative value and specifically noted in the report. The forensic assessor should be prepared to defend his or her decision to use the test in this manner. Unfortunately, unlike the CAPS, the PSS-I has not been updated at present to meet DSM-5 new PTSD diagnostic symptoms and clusters.

Systematically assessing trauma exposure is of great evidentiary importance in presenting psychological assessment evidence in the IC. The IC and USCIS frequently raise questions of proximate cause of psychological trauma and the forensic assessor needs to be prepared to separate legally relevant from irrelevant traumatic exposures. Additionally, research indicates that common stressful life events such as divorce, relational problems, financial difficulties, and serious illness can elicit PTSD-like symptoms (Long et al., 2008; Robinson & Larson, 2010), which is crucial in forming psycholegal opinions of proximate cause between legally pertinent events and signs and symptoms of psychological trauma. While there are numerous trauma exposure measures to consider, two readily obtainable measures stand out. The Life Event's Checklist for DSM-5 (LEC-5; see Gray, Litz, Hsu, & Lombardo, 2004) is a brief, 17-item, self-report measure to screen for potentially traumatic events in a respondent's lifetime. The LEC-5 was developed concurrently with the CAPS-5 and is administered before the CAPS-5. The LEC-5 is available for free from the National Center for PTSD for qualified mental health professionals (www.ptsd.va.gov/professional/ assessment/documents/LEC-5_Extended_Self-report.pdf). Where more in-depth assessment of traumatic exposure is valuable, the Trauma History Screen (THS; Carlson et al., 2011) goes beyond the LEC to ask for a more detailed description of marker traumatic exposure as well as ratings for critical aspects of traumatic events. The THS is also available for free from the National Center for PTSD for qualified mental health professionals (www.ptsd.va.gov/professional/assessment/documents/ THS.pdf). Because it is more comprehensive, the THS is especially useful in forensic settings because of the value the IC places on detail and accuracy.

In many instances of assessment of psychological trauma in the IC, forensic assessors evaluate respondents with histories of multiple traumatic experiences in countries from where they fled, as well as histories of being in captivity in prisons or trapped in abusive relationships from which they feared escape. With the work of Judith Herman (1992a), we have come to understand that such circumstances yield complex psychological sequelae well beyond what is captured in the diagnosis of PTSD. Herman, Perry, and van der Kolk (1989) conducted groundbreaking research finding a strong association between histories of profound and repeated trauma exposure abuse in childhood and pervasive psychological symptoms and impairments, which Herman formerly called DESNOS and now is more commonly called complex PTSD (CPTSD). Adults exposed to chronic interpersonal trauma, such as experienced by torture victims, asylum seekers, and refugees, consistently demonstrate specific psychological disturbances that are not captured in the PTSD diagnosis (van der Kolk, Roth, Pelcovitz, Sunday, & Spinazzola, 2005).

The CPTSD diagnostic entity has received considerable research, including two studies particularly relevant to the IC, which point out the value of assessing CPTSD. Kissane, Szymanski, Upthegrove, and Katona (2014) studied asylum seekers who have experienced major human rights violations and found that extensive CPTSD symptoms were common in all participants, regardless of the type of trauma experienced. Palic et al. (2016) also showed validity in a cross-cultural setting for CPTSD. Their research included a sample of refugees and ex-prisoners of war – i.e., adulthood trauma of severe interpersonal intensity – and demonstrated CPTSD was not exclusively associated with childhood abuse, but also with exposure to adulthood trauma of severe interpersonal intensity. It also demonstrated that CPTSD links with the highest frequency of work-related functional impairment, as well as the severity of prolonged trauma exposure with the level of ongoing posttraumatic symptoms.

As part of the field trials for DSM-4 (Roth et al., 1997), this research team developed the Structured Interview for Disorders of Extreme Stress (SIDES, Pelcovitz et al., 1997), a validated structured interview assessment for CPTSD, which subsequently was found to have considerable clinical utility (van der Kolk & Pelcovitz, 1999). The SIDES is a 48-item structured interview that consists of seven subscales measuring the seven complex PTSD symptom clusters: regulation of affect and impulses; attention in consciousness; self-perception; perception of the perpetrator; relations with others; somatization; and systems of meaning. Like the CAPS, the SIDES measures current and lifetime presence of complex posttraumatic stress symptoms as well as symptom severity. The SIDES was used successfully in both the Palic et al. (2016) and Kissane et al. (2014) studies, and offers an additional way for forensic assessors to accurately measure and describe psychological difficulties arising from the kinds of extreme and chronic traumatic exposures experienced by many immigrants seeking relief in the IC.

Finally, dissociative responses and disorders (formerly called multiple personality disorder) are another clinical phenomenon closely associated with especially severe psychological trauma. Dissociation is a state of fragmented consciousness involving amnesia, a sense of unreality and feeling, and of being disconnected from oneself or one's environment. While dissociation is a psychological process common to everyone, in the extreme it can become a severe disorder with fragmented identity states, previously and inaccurately referred to as multiple personalities. Putnam (1997) estimated that most, if not all, dissociative disorders are caused by severe abuse in childhood. Because of the complexity and shifting emotional and identity states in dissociative disorder, comprehensive, multi-method forensic evaluation provides a significant advantage over simple clinical interview.

An excellent method for the comprehensive assessment of dissociative states and disorders is Steinberg's Structured Clinical Interview for DSM-4 Dissociative Disorders-Revised (SCID-D-R; Steinberg, 1994). Rigorously developed through NIMH field trials, the SCID-D-R is a structured diagnostic interview that is specific to the assessment of dissociative disorders. While the diagnostic criteria for dissociative disorders changed in the DSM-5, the SCID-D-R remains the best measure for assessing dissociative disorder symptoms, which can easily be adapted to the new DSM-5 criteria. It provides a careful and detailed decision-tree approach, arriving at an accurate diagnosis of dissociative identity disorder, dissociative amnesia, depersonalization disorder, other specified dissociative disorder, acute stress disorder, and dissociative trance disorder. Perhaps of more importance to forensic assessors, the SCID-D-R assesses a broad variety of post-traumatic dissociative symptoms that examinees may not spontaneously share in unstructured interviews. Many dissociative individuals have long learned that their dissociative experiences are seen by others as strange and bizarre and indeed these individuals often feel this way about themselves as well. As a result, immigrants with dissociative experiences have learned to automatically avoid discussion of these symptoms. Careful and empathic administration of the SCID-D-R can help immigrants with dissociative symptoms more accurately share their experiences and can reveal symptoms and psychological states highly relevant to the IC. Steinberg and Schnall (2001) offer an approachable overview of dissociative disorder and its various manifestations.

Trauma-Specific Scales

The next methods for assessing psychological trauma are the *trauma-specific scales*, a group of self-report instruments that focus specifically on the symptoms and phenomena of PTSD and psychological trauma. They range from highly face-valid instruments – e.g., instruments that directly assess specific symptoms of PTSD – to more subtle instruments, which include associated traumatic symptoms and experiences as well as, in some instances, validity scales that assist in addressing credibility issues. The advantages of trauma-specific scales include: (1) focus on specific psychological trauma symptoms and phenomena; (2) provide ratings of symptom severity and frequency; and (3) allow the forensic assessor to select specific scales that best match specific populations – e.g., sexual assault, torture, or partner or domestic abuse. Such instruments allow the forensic assessors to focus their evaluation on specific symptoms that are most distressing to the immigrant and most probative to the psycholegal questions before the IC.

As mentioned above, there are variations in posttraumatic symptom presentation – i.e., the biphasic response in which the examinee may have predominantly avoidant/numbing presentations, intrusive/flooding presentations, or, in some instances such as with torture victims, alternate between the two. For example, some trauma victims may so repress trauma memories that they do not have current intrusive symptoms and therefore do not meet formal PTSD criteria under DSM-5 or ICD-10. As Foa and Rothbaum (1998) report, rape victims with an avoidant presentation have poorer treatment outcomes generally, and require a very different approach, than victims with active intrusive symptoms. Trauma-specific assessment tools can alert the forensic assessor early on to the immigrant's particular dilemmas, increasing the forensic assessor's accuracy of the psychological impact of psycholegally relevant trauma issues. The three commonly used PTSD-specific scales frequently used in studies of asylum seekers and other immigrant populations relevant to IC are: (1) the clinical version of the PTSD Checklist (PCL; Weathers et al. 1993 – recently updated to the PCL-5 to correspond to changes in the DSM-5); (2) the Posttraumatic Stress Diagnostic

Scale (PDS; Foa, 1995); and (3) perhaps most importantly, the Harvard Trauma Questionnaire (HTQ; Mollica et al., 1992).

The PCL-5 is a brief 20-item self-report measure of the 20 DSM-4 symptoms of PTSD that assesses both symptoms and their severity. The PCL can be used for screening individuals for PTSD, diagnosing PTSD, and assessing symptom change during treatment. Blanchard, Jones-Alexander, Buckley, & Forneris' (1996) study of motor vehicle accident victims and sexual assault victims found a high correlation with the CAPS, concluding that the PCL is effective as a brief screening instrument for core symptoms of PTSD. A problem with the PCL is that it assesses only PTSD symptoms and not the specific trauma or life stress causing the symptoms. Unlike the CAPS, it assesses only severity of symptoms (i.e., 'how much you have been bothered by' each PTSD symptom), but not frequency of symptoms (i.e., how often you have experienced these symptoms). The PCL asks about symptoms in the past month, so lifetime incidence is not assessed. The PCL can even be significant for individuals going through severe life events that do not specifically meet DSM-4 stressor criteria for PTSD (Robinson & Larson, 2010), making it a sensitive, but not specific, PTSD assessment instrument. Indeed, the problem with PCL specificity was addressed by Arbisi et al. (2012), in which the PCL had very high false-positive rates (65–76 percent), and they concluded that the PCL may actually be a measure of general distress rather than specific markers of PTSD alone. The requirement for test specificity is especially important in the forensic assessment context where issues of proximate cause are critical in arriving at well-founded psycholegal expert opinions.

The PDS is a 49-item self-report measure best used when assessing the severity of PTSD symptoms related to a single identified traumatic event. The PDS is one of only two among trauma-specific self-report inventories to specifically assess all of the DSM-4 criteria for PTSD (Criteria A–F), assisting in a clear formal diagnosis, when such a determination is required by an IC judge. Further, it asks about the presence and frequency of symptoms in the past month, although other time frames can be used. Unlike the CAPS and PCL, the PDS does not ask about severity of each PTSD symptom, though it does ask specifically for the marker traumatic event(s), which is an improvement on the PCL. Finally, the PDS currently has not published an update to assess DSM-5 PTSD criteria, though a PDS-5 appears to be in development (see www.adaa.org/sites/default/files/Yusko%20_210.pdf).

Perhaps the most relevant PTSD-specific scale for psychological assessment in IC for immigrants seeking asylum is the HTQ, an instrument developed by Mollica and colleagues (1992). Initially developed to assess psychological trauma for Southeast Asian refugees from Vietnam, Cambodia, and Laos in their native languages, the HTQ is a straightforward checklist measuring psychological trauma, torture events, and trauma-related symptoms, capturing both refugee- and culture-specific symptoms as well as meeting PTSD diagnosis. The HTQ has four parts: Part I assesses 41 different traumatic life events; Part II asks for the most traumatic experience or event the respondent experienced during their immigrant experience; Part III assesses the possibility of traumatic brain injury: and Part IV includes 40 symptoms of trauma, including the 16 DSM-4 PTSD and 24 more items focusing on how these trauma symptoms affect functioning in everyday life. The HTQ exhibits good validity and reliability and is the gold standard for how to develop a psychological test for its purposes. The HTQ has since been translated into many languages, including several using rigorous standards of translation, including Bosnian, Cambodian, Croatian, Japanese, Arabic, and Farsi versions. The test and manual are available through the Harvard Program in Refugee Trauma (*Measuring Trauma, Measuring Torture*; http://hprt-cambridge.org/screening/measuring-trauma-measuring-torture).

While the trauma-specific self-report assessment methods mentioned above can be quite useful, these measures also have several notable disadvantages, which are shared with other self-report assessment measures. Self-report measures depend on the evaluees' ability both to understand themselves sufficiently to respond accurately to the questions and to be willing to report what they experience. In the case of trauma victims who are emotionally shut down, they may not realize and report symptoms that are obvious to others. Alternatively, other examinees may carelessly respond or underreport or overreport symptoms and experiences on self-report measures for a variety of motivations such as secondary gain or concerns about who will see their records if they report fully and honestly. These tendencies are known in assessment circles as response styles – i.e., test-taking approaches that can bias or skew the interpretation of self-report measures. A weakness of trauma-specific measures above is that they do not have scales that assess for response style, a particular concern of IC, where overreporting or even feigning trauma symptoms could occur in the context of a secondary gain, being granted asylum or permanent residence status. IC judges are deeply concerned about issues of credibility of the respondents and the measures above cannot address these concerns directly.

Following the lead of major self-report inventories such as the MMPI-2 and PAI, John Briere has created several excellent, comprehensive trauma-specific self-report inventories, which not only measure traumatic experiences comprehensively, but also assess response style. The most widely used and best researched of his scales are the Detailed Assessment of Posttraumatic Stress (DAPS; Briere, 2001), and the Trauma Symptom Inventory – Second Edition (TSI-2; Briere, 2010), which take about 20–30 minutes to administer and are easily scored. Both of Briere's inventories include validity scales that assess defensiveness (denial of difficulties) and symptom over-endorsement (endorsement of atypical symptoms not common to PTSD). Additionally, the TSI-2, includes a validity scale for inconsistent, random reporting.

The focus of the DAPS, like the PCL-5, is on assessing the severity of PTSD symptoms related to an identified traumatic event, which allows the forensic assessor to establish a reliable DSM diagnosis of PTSD. The DAPS goes beyond other such PTSD instruments in that it comprehensively assesses:

1. the client's history of possible traumatic exposure and identification of a specific current traumatic event;
2. immediate posttraumatic reactions, such as thoughts and feelings about the event as well as peritraumatic dissociation;
3. presence and severity of PTSD symptoms (intrusion, avoidance/numbing, and hyperarousal) and psychosocial impairment in response to the traumatic event;
4. three supplementary scales of frequent comorbid difficulties, including ongoing dissociation, suicidality, and substance abuse (Briere, 2001).

As a result, the DAPS provides the forensic assessor a broader perspective of the client's experience of posttraumatic stress beyond simple diagnosis. It is a more powerful 'empathy magnifier' (Finn & Tonsager, 2002, p. 15), allowing the forensic assessor a more complete understanding of the impact of trauma on the immigrant.

Next, Briere's TSI-2 is based on a well conceptualized and well researched understanding of traumatic phenomena and yields excellent information about the client's experiences and behaviors that are exceptionally useful for framing empathic interventions. It surveys on both acute and chronic posttraumatic symptoms and experiences and has been widely used to assess the effects of sexual assault, domestic partner abuse, physical assault, combat experiences, major accidents, and natural disasters. In particular, the TSI-2 is an excellent instrument to use with adults subjected to domestic abuse, such as in VAWA cases (see http://s1097954.instanturl.net/ for an extensive list of publications). In addition to assessing common PTSD symptoms such as angry/irritable affect, intrusive symptoms, avoidance/numbing, and hyperarousal, the TSI also assesses comorbid symptoms of both mood and cognitive distortions found in trauma-related depression, as well as dissociative symptoms. Further, this measure goes beyond the immediate posttraumatic symptoms and evaluates the long-term self-disturbance and interpersonal difficulties frequently found as part of chronic sequelae of earlier psychological trauma. The Self Scales include sexual concerns (sexual dissatisfaction and distress), dysfunctional sexual behaviors (indiscriminate and self-harming sexual relations), impaired self-reference (identity confusion and poor self-care), and tension-reducing behavior (external ways of reducing inner tension, such as suicidal threats, self-mutilation, and dysregulation of anger).

No survey of trauma-specific measures would be complete without mention of the Dissociative Experiences Scale II (DES-II; Bernstein & Putnam, 1986; Carlson & Putnam, 1993), the widely used screening instrument for the frequency of dissociative experiences. As noted above, severe dissociative reactions are common in adult survivors of severe childhood trauma and identification of these phenomena, such as dissociative identity disorder, can be essential in providing a good description of behavior that may seem inconsistent with what would be expected by IC judges. The DES-II is a briefer screening measure that assesses a continuum of dissociative experiences with normative data for normal, traumatized, and dissociative clients that can indicate the need for a more in-depth assessment of dissociative phenomena. It can be obtained online for free at http://traumadissociation.com/des.

Additionally, as discussed in Chapter 5, special mention should be made of a powerful assessment measure for forensic assessors working with both women and men who are the victims of domestic battery. Often such individuals have extreme difficulty articulating their domestic abuse experience in interviews with even experienced forensic assessors (see Dutton, 2000; Walker, 2000). Mary Ann Dutton's (2000) Abusive Behavior Observation Checklist (ABOC) was developed to document the types and degree of interpersonal violence on domestic abuse, such as physical, sexual, and psychological abuse, as well as victims' behavioral and cognitive adaptation to such abuse. The ABOC provides an exhaustive survey of the ways in which batterers abuse their spouses and spouses' adaptation to these abuses. This instrument can be found at in Dutton's (1992) *Empowering and Healing the Battered Woman*. The Domestic Violence Interview Guide is a semi-structured interview designed by the Battered Women's Justice project and is divided in three areas: (1) The first column seeks information about: (a) personal interactions; (b) access to resources; (c) children and parenting; (d) control of daily life; (e) emotional abuse; (f) physical abuse; and (g) sexual abuse. The second column provides areas to explore in order to identify the nature, context, severity, and implications of domestic violence and coercive controlling behaviors. The third column provides a checklist of key concepts, behaviors, and dynamics to listen for. This instrument can be found at: www.nij.gov/funding/Documents/2013/domestic-violence-interview-guide-form-and-instructions.pdf. Used together the TSI-2, the ABOC, and the Domestic Violence Interview Guide provide an important way for battered spouses to share their traumatic experiences and effects on their functioning and view of themselves.

It should be noted that there are many trauma-specific self-report inventories for psychological trauma, though it is beyond the scope of this chapter to survey most of them. The reader is referred to two excellent books (Briere, 2004; Wilson & Keane, 2004) for a more detailed survey of psychometric issues as well as a wide variety of self-report trauma instruments for both adults and children. Additionally, the assessment link of the remarkable National Center for PTSD is an indispensable resource for anyone with a serious interest in psychological trauma. Copies of some instruments can be obtained for free from the website (www.ptsd.va.gov/professional/pages/assessments/list-adult-self-reports.asp).

Generic Psychological Self-Report Tests

Briere and Scott (2014) have noted that an effective battery to assess trauma should include at least one generic measure in addition to the trauma-specific instruments. There are several generic psychological tests that have been designed to evaluate a person's overall psychological and adaptive functioning.

These tests are useful to identify a comprehensive range of psychopathology, including trauma disorders, nonspecific symptoms, personality patterns, and comorbid disorders, and identify the assessee's response style, which is an important aspect to evaluate in immigration evaluations. Next, we will review the utility of the MMPI and PAI families of tests in immigration evaluations.

It is important that the assessor remember that, in order to utilize a psychological test developed in the U.S. with an immigrant individual, its applicability to the characteristics of the examinee need to be determined. The assessor wants to know:

1.   if the examinee's demographic information fits the normative population for the test normative population;
2.   the level of the examinee's acculturation and its impact on the assessment instrument; and
3.   the impact of acculturation on the assessee's coping and adjustment to their immediate environment (Phinney, Horenczyk, Liebkind, & Vedder, 2001).

Responses to these issues help determine the level of confidence that assessors may have that a standard administration and interpretation will be accurate in its representation of the assessee's functioning. Otherwise, it is more appropriate to find an adaptation of the test conducted in the country, region, or culture of the examinee, because the individual is not like the members of the American sample.

Some tests have been translated but not adapted to the country or culture where this translation is intended to be used. This definitely constitutes a limitation because a translation does not include the processes related to the cultural fit of the instrument which goes beyond the fact that the test-taker is able to read the items (Hambleton, 2005). When an instrument has been adapted, studies among different groups can be conducted to compare the characteristics of individuals in different cultural contexts (Gjersing, Caplehorn, & Clausen, 2010; Hambleton, 2005). When the test has been translated but not adapted, the assessor needs to make a decision as to whether to utilize the instrument for the merits of obtaining standardized information, while risking that this information may be misleading or plainly wrong. If the assessor decides to use the test despite these drawbacks, the interpretation should be cautious and the caveat will be described in the report.

However, as long as the examiner consider the limitations of a lack of adaptation and takes this issue into consideration when interpreting the results, the test can provide important clinical and standardized information. A more serious problem arises when there are no adaptations for the examinee's demographics nor translations. Orally translating the items from a generic psychological test by an interpreter or a computer program is not an acceptable practice. There is no guarantee that the translation is equivalent to the original version and has linguistic, contextual, and cultural accuracy.

However, both the MMPI and the PAI can be adapted to facilitate that some immigrant clients are able to complete them. For instance: (a) examiners can have the client read the instructions and first few items aloud if there are questions regarding comprehension level (Morey, 2003); (b) oral administration is possible with audiotapes that are commercially available by the publisher; (c) the client should hold their own response sheet and mark the responses there; (d) concrete aids can be used to facilitate differentiating the options that can be developed for clients.

Many of the issues that need to be assessed in the different immigration evaluations are included in the data derived from these generic tests. For instance, VAWA, U visa, and T visa assessments benefit from test data that confirm the psychological injury, including its different presentations such as psychotic reactions or dissociative symptoms. These generic tests assist the expert in explaining the psychological processes at play when a respondent cannot fully recollect, testify about, or have a bizarre attitude when testifying about their traumatic experiences. Evaluations of extreme hardship will benefit from the knowledge regarding the assessee's psychological vulnerability, and potential adjustment to a foreign environment. This will help when predicting the outcome for a person whose loved one is deported, either if the person stays in the U.S. without her or his loved one or if he or she leaves the U.S. with the deported individual. Similarly, generic psychological tests illuminate the treatment needs of the examinee, which can help the expert check for availability of needed services in the country for a person being deported. These generic tests may also help the expert provide evidence of good moral character, because they offer data that characterizes a person as not being antisocial, not lacking empathy, or having other traits that are normally associated with deficits in moral values (Butcher & Perry, 2008). Most importantly, generic tests allow for comparison of the examinee's data to thousands of individuals to determine where he or she falls in terms of psychopathology, which helps determine, for example, when a traumatic reaction is 'substantial.'

Minnesota Multiphasic Personality Inventory

The Minnesota Multiphasic Personality Inventory-Second Edition (MMPI-2; Butcher et al., 1989) is appropriate for use with adults (age 18 and over). The MMPI-2 has 567 items, and is designed to require a sixth-grade reading level. There is an abbreviated form of the test that consists of the MMPI-2's first 370 items, but the information available on the shorter version is not as extensive as that available in the full version. The MMPI-2 is the gold standard measure in the assessment of psychopathology. The MMPI-2 is used worldwide and has the largest research databank supporting its applications with adult populations (Greene, 2000). Further, the MMPI-2 has developed significant literature supporting its cross-cultural (Butcher, 1996) and forensic applications (Lally, 2003). The MMPI-2 has been translated into a large number of different languages.

Pearson Assessments (Pearson, n.d.) publishes Spanish, Canadian French, and a Hmong booklet translation, and also a CD in Spanish which can be used for individuals who speak Spanish, but have limited literacy proficiency. The University of Minnesota has endorsed the following translations: Bulgarian, Chinese, Croatian, Czech, Danish, Dutch/Flemish, French Canadian, French, German, Greek, Hebrew, Hmong, Hungarian, Italian, Korean, Norwegian, Polish, Romanian, Spanish for Mexico and Central America, Spanish for Spain, South America and Central America, Spanish for the U.S., and Swedish (University of Minnesota, n.d.).

The research regarding the assessment of immigrant groups has shown that the MMPI-2 has test generalizability and validity for different forensic applications, including the assessment of refugees, torture victims, and asylum seekers. The MMPI-2 has been utilized in the assessment of victims of torture (Pope & Garcia-Peltoniemi, 1991), with both English and accepted translations. There is a cross-cultural equivalence study of the MMPI-2 with Vietnamese refugees living in the U.S. (Dong & Church, 2003). This study demonstrated that some symptom patterns and cultural background are revealed in the test responses, while at the same time it showed that the MMPI-2 functioned in an equivalent and valid manner with this group. Research with the MMPI-2 in different cultures has shown that the test detects specific patterns or unusual symptom constellations that represent gender and culturally related expressions of distress, rather than the psychopathology traditionally attributed to scales (Cervantes, Salgado de Snyder, & Padilla, 1989; Saborio & Hass, 2012). The MMPI-2 has many adaptations and translations that permit its use across languages and cultures (Butcher, Mosch, Tsai, & Nezami, 2006), as well as with minority populations in the U.S. More information can be found in the book *Using the MMPI-2 in Forensic Assessment* (Butcher, Hass, Greene, & Nelson, 2015).

Personality Assessment Inventory

The Personality Assessment Inventory (PAI; Morey, 1991) is a 344-item multi-scale self-administered measure designed to provide information regarding diagnosis, treatment planning, and screening for psychopathology. It was developed for individuals' ages 18 through adulthood who read at least the fourth-grade level. The PAI contains 22 non-overlapping full scales, 4 validity scales, 11 clinical scales, 5 treatment consideration scales, and 2 interpersonal scales. The clinical scales are designed to measure: somatic complaints (SOM), anxiety (ANX), anxiety related disorders (ARD), depression (DEP), mania (MAN), paranoia (PAR), schizophrenia (SCZ), borderline personality features (BOR), antisocial features (ANT), drug problems (DRG), and alcohol problems (ALC). Each clinical scale contains three subscales, except for BOR, which contains four subscales.

The PAI is another generic test that has been researched for use cross-culturally and with culturally diverse individuals. The PAI is acceptable for individuals tested in a language different than English, with authorized translations available in Arabic, Brazilian Portuguese, Bulgarian, Chinese, Filipino, French Canadian, Greek, Icelandic, Korean, Norwegian, Polish, Serbian, Slovene, Swedish, Turkish, and Vietnamese (Psychological Assessment Resources, n.d.). Research has shown that the English- and Spanish-language validity scales perform similarly, and scores from the Negative Impression Management and the Positive Impression Management scales demonstrate the highest levels of equivalence and accuracy for the identification of simulators across language versions (Fernandez, Boccaccini, & Noland, 2008).

Morey and Meyer (2013) cite the PAI's advantages over other methods of forensic assessment including its low reading requirements, breadth of coverage and brevity, ease of interpretation, and ability to fit well with legal criteria. The PAI has also been used with immigrants in the U.S. and refugee populations. For instance, the PAI was studied with North Korean refugees showing clinically meaningful scores in several scales, demonstrating its ability to capture the traumatic experiences of the refugees (Jeon, Yu, Cho, & Eom, 2008; Yu & Jeon, 2008). In addition, the PAI has been found to be more reliable when differentiating *bona fide* PTSD from malingered PTSD as compared with the Detailed Assessment of Posttraumatic Stress (Wooley & Rogers, 2015). More examples of cross-cultural applications of the PAI can be found in the book *Clinical Applications of the Personality Assessment Inventory* (Blais, Baity & Hopwood, 2010).

Summary

We have presented an overview of the importance and potential power of psychological assessment methods with victims of trauma. Apart from simply reviewing the many useful methods of assessing psychological trauma, it is our hope that forensic assessors reading this book will see ways in which psychological testing can enhance their forensic practice by assisting in more accurate and evidence-based ways. The purpose of such measures can be conceptualized as bringing out the often horrific story of immigrant trauma victims in a clearer and more focused way, whether in written reports and testimony in IC. Working with the broken narrative of psychological trauma is complex and challenging, but ultimately highly rewarding. The forensic assessor can help the persecuted and traumatized immigrant survivor better describe their experiences, including deeply damaged views of themselves and their relationships with others. While becoming proficient in the application of psychological testing to forensic assessment in IC may appear daunting at first, there is a large and responsive professional assessment community to support this learning. We wish to personally extend an invitation for IC forensic assessors to embrace this challenge.

Chapter 10

Rorschach and Performance-Based Measures in Immigration Evaluations

The requirement for factual information obtained, in an objective manner, in forensic assessments makes the use of psychological testing with its empirical methods a natural fit with the requirements of the Immigration Court (IC). The purpose of this chapter is: (1) to provide an overview of Rorschach and other performance-based measures (PBMs) in forensic immigration practice; and (2) to discuss the particular value of these instruments in such evaluations within each forensic practice area. While this chapter discusses the special value of the Rorschach and other PBMs in forensic evaluations in immigration issues, it must be emphasized that all forensic psychological assessments must be conducted using a multi-method approach, including interviews, collateral information, and complementary psychological tests (see Erard & Evans, 2017; Erdberg, 2008).

It is also important to take into account the cautions noted by Pope and Garcia-Peltoniemi (1991) regarding the use of psychological tests in forensic assessment in IC, including issues of the test-taking situation being too evocative; of adequate norms, validation, and translation of tests; and of the IC respondent's educational level, reading capacity, and cultural background. Additionally, as with all forensic assessment, respondents must understand, and openly consent to, the use of these tests. With these cautions in mind, the Rorschach and other PBMs in such evaluations are especially valuable because of the broad international use of such instruments (see International Society for the Rorschach & Projective Measures at www.rorschach.com), as well as reduced requirements for reading capacity.

Why Performance-Based Measures?

Many, if not most, psychologists have been trained in psychological assessment to use the distinction of 'Objective' and 'Projective' tests. In the past, 'objective testing' was reserved for personality inventories such as the MMPI, PAI, and MCMI families of tests, where the client reveals underlying personality traits by responding to a series of predetermined questions. The 'projective' designation was usually reserved for instruments like the Rorschach and TAT, where individuals were seen as 'projecting' elements of their personality characteristics onto more or less ambiguous stimuli. The 'projective' designation of the Rorschach was not without its detractors, most notably John Exner, who vociferously argued that the Rorschach was not solely, or even mainly, a projective test. For example, Exner (1974) reminded us that a significant part of Hermann Rorschach's original research on schizophrenia was on Form Quality, i.e., the degree with which the client's percepts accurately fit objective reality.

While Exner's caution went unheeded for many years, recent advances in understanding the response processes in psychological testing has led to retiring 'objective' and' projective' as test descriptors. In their seminal article, Meyer and Kurtz (2006) persuasively argued that the science underlying psychological tests calls for reconceptualization. Like Exner, they contended 'object' and 'projective' carry a host of meanings, including some connotations that are very misleading when applied to personality assessment instruments and methods. For instance, the word 'objective' connotes greater precision, accuracy, and resistance to bias, even though objective tests are clearly influenced by the degree to which a person knows her/himself and to which a person wishes to reveal self-perception and inner experiences. For instance, the information we get from an 'objective' test about a person's psychotic experiences may have significant subjectivity, while a Form Quality score on the Rorschach may be a more objective reflection of the person's capacity for reality testing. In fact, Meyer and Kurtz (2006) reasoned that this distinction was so fraught with problems that the editorial policy of the *Journal of Personality Assessment* was changed so that this 'objective/projective' distinction is no longer to be used as classifying the nature of personality tests.

Based in large part on Bornstein's (2002) process-based conceptualization of personality assessment methods, the field of personality assessment has increasingly moved to the new distinction between *self-report* methods (e.g., MMPI, PAI, and MCMI) and *performance-based* methods (e.g., Rorschach, TAT, TEMAS, Roberts, and Adult Attachment Projective). This more current classification focuses on the *process* by which an individual responds to the particular assessment instrument and on the different kinds of information available as a result of these processes. In the case of *self-report* methods, the individual's process is one of self-attribution, i.e., introspection, retrospection, and self-presentation. When individuals read an item, say on the MMPI-2, they decide whether this item is salient to them, or not, based on thinking about themselves. As noted above, self-report measures are influenced by self-perceptual biases and self-presentation needs, which can affect accuracy of self-attribution. In the case of *performance-based* methods, the process is quite different in that it involves stimulus-based attribution with attention directed outward. The focus is on the task (not the self), to which the client provides meaning and structure and in turn is likely to be influenced by less self-conscious or implicit psychological processes.

As Mihura (2012) cogently argued, both self-report and performance-based methods are important in comprehensive, multi-method assessment. These methods can provide incremental validity for the same criterion variable (e.g., providing self-reported symptoms of psychosis on the MMPI-2 as opposed to directly assessing reality testing and thought disorder in psychosis on the Rorschach) as well as obtaining an overall picture for broader personality variables one is trying to assess. In the above example, the information from both the MMPI-2 and the Rorschach can be important in comprehending the difficulties of the client. With regard to such arguments, the old 'objective' vs. 'projective' dichotomy has given way to a new evidence-based and conceptually more powerful approach to understanding value of each method and how it can contribute to our understanding of persons.

In contrast to self-report measures, PBMs are usually less popular as they require more extensive training and take longer to administer, score, and interpret. Understanding the latent structure of the information available on PBMs may require some translation to more current ways of thinking. Additionally, the most widely known PBM, the Rorschach test, came under considerable criticism in the early 2000s (see Lilienfeld, Wood, & Garb, 2000). With this said, these criticisms have been largely rebutted with evidence that the Rorschach meets acceptable standards for clinical practice (Board of Trustees of the Society for Personality Assessment, 2005) and for admissibility in forensic settings (see McCann & Evans, 2007). Mihura, Meyer, Dumitrascu, and Bombel (2012) meta-analyses of the CS Rorschach variables further rebutted the prior criticism and gave rise to the R-PAS. As Evans (2017) noted, both the CS (with modifications) and the R-PAS (with cautions) more than meet the standards for admissibility noted by McCann and Evans (2007), making it an excellent method to use in forensic psychological assessment in IC matters.

In conclusion, the Rorschach and PBM personality tests have a unique and important role in psychological assessment, which can provide incremental validity as an important element in multi-method assessment in clinical and forensic settings. The requirement for intensive training and supervision can pay big dividends in terms of increased complexity of issues that can be assessed and serve as an alternative to the current psychiatric diagnostic approach, which, per the DSM-5 cautionary statement, may not be well-suited for forensic settings (American Psychiatric Association, 2013)

Rorschach Inkblot Method

Few psychological assessment instruments have as broad international usage as the Rorschach (Ritzler 2001; Viglione, 1999; Viglione & Meyer, 2007; Viglione & Hilsenroth, 2001) and have available a large cohort of international norms (Erdberg, 2005; Meyer, Erdberg & Shaffer 2007; Schaffer, Erdberg, & Meyer 2007). Current evidence-based Rorschach systems with strong international norms include the Exner Comprehensive System (CS) (Exner, 2003) and more recently the Rorschach Performance Assessment System (R-PAS) (Meyer, Viglione & Mihura, 2017; Meyer, Viglione, Mihura, Erard, & Erdberg, 2011). As stated above, the Rorschach has a wide acceptability and evidence base sufficient to be probative in immigration matters (see Meyer et al., 2017). The Rorschach has been identified as a valuable method in assessing psychological trauma (Kaser-Boyd & Evans, 2008) with an important trauma indicator called the Trauma Content Index (TSI: Armstrong & Lowenstein, 1990), which has been used to help identify victims of sexual abuse (Kamphuis, Kugeares, & Finn, 2000) and individuals with dissociative identity disorder (Brand, Armstrong, & Loewenstein, 2006).

Assessment of Torture and Rape and the Rorschach

The first caveat for psychological testing of torture victims is that the assessor must be mindful that the test-taking situation and the choice of psychological instrument may evoke overwhelmingly memories and feelings of the torture situation (Evans 2008; Pope & Garcia-Peltoniemi, 1991). Nowhere is this concern more relevant than with the use of the Rorschach. In their exploratory study using the Rorschach with Vietnam war veterans, van der Kolk and Ducey (1984, 1989) noted two distinct patterns of response – traumatic flooded presentations and traumatic avoidant presentations, reflecting biphasic response to trauma, in which intrusion and emotional flooding alternate with avoidance and psychic numbing (van der Kolk, 1994). Given its capacity to evoke powerful reactions, use of the Rorschach is precarious in the assessment of torture and other forms of extreme psychological trauma and should be approached with caution.

Evans (2008) wrote that his experience of assessing over 100 torture victims for IC led him to note a striking phenomenon. Instead of one element of the biphasic response dominating the experience of the torture victim as found in the van der Kolk and Ducey studies, he found that horrific and relentless intrusive experiences of the torture frequently overwhelm pervasive and extreme attempts at avoidance and numbing. This observation suggested that torture victims get little or no relief from their traumatic past, regardless of their attempts to interrupt the pain of recollection. In fact the inability to get relief from the horrific experience of torture is at the core of the torture experience. Torture methods are frequently so refined that there is no way to escape or mitigate suffering and lead to what Jay (1991) calls 'Terrible Knowledge.' For example, torture methods such as *falaka* or *falanga*, beating of the soles of the feet, disrupts torture victims' connection to the earth, literally making each step a terrifying reminder of their past persecution. Torture victims carry this unspeakable legacy with them and are literally tortured long after the actual event has ended.

This ongoing suffering for torture victims has important consequences for the use of the Rorschach in the assessment of torture in IC asylum cases. As Evans (2008) and Jacobs, Evans, and Patsilides (2001a, 2001b) stated, the use of the Rorschach with torture victims should be approached with restraint. The Rorschach was designed to be emotionally evocative and its images may easily overwhelm survivors of torture. For example, the darkness and color with its powerful pull for images of blood, damage, and despair on Card II may trigger disintegrative experiences for such individuals. Rorschach simply may be inappropriate for the assessment of torture victims, especially when the torture experience is recent; if the respondent was tortured at a young age; where rape, sexual humiliation, and torture were used; and when the types and variety of torture methods were especially brutal.

Opaas and Hartmann (2013) challenged Evans' (2008) caution about using the Rorschach with torture victims, finding in their study of 51 traumatized refugees from 15 different countries that the Rorschach was useful in confirming self-reported symptoms of traumatic re-experiencing and reduced quality of life. There was no indication in the article about how long after being tortured the refugees were assessed. They reported:

> Rorschach in a sense was 'easier' for the participants to respond to than the questionnaires. The Rorschach instruction was easily understood, the images were immediately evocative for many, and the participants could concentrate on finding words to express their own thoughts, instead of trying to understand more or less finely nuanced questions.
>
> (p. 468)

On the other hand, they noted that the Rorschach did indeed trigger painful memories and intrusive images in many of their participants. Further, a significant number of participants were unable to provide a complete protocol and the assessment was conducted in the context of a treatment setting (see Opaas, Hartmann, Wentzel-Larsen, & Varvin 2016 for treatment outcome follow-up) rather than during a forensic evaluation. As noted by both Pope and Garcia-Peltoniemi (1991) and Evans (2008), the setting of the evaluation, such as in the context of an IC legal proceeding, may activate more intensely the political nature of the torture setting and more fully stimulate the trauma response than a treatment setting.

Despite these cautions, the Rorschach remains a valuable assessment method in the forensic assessment of torture victims for IC. Ephraim (2002) wrote about his use of the Rorschach with survivors of torture and state violence, noting valuable contributions of the Rorschach in trauma assessment, especially evaluating cognitive disturbances associated with intrusive recollections, discerning avoidant and numbing defense patterns, deviations in identity and relatedness, and complications with self-regulation and dissociation in cases of co-occurring early trauma. Ephraim's cases included women who were not victims of *systematic* torture, but rather were victims of state violence. The Rorschach was valuable in their asylum application because it elucidated the psychological impact of their traumatic experiences to support their claim or was indicative of malingering or deception, addressing the critical issue of credibility in IC. One conclusion from this study is that Rorschach might also be considered, when the respondents' torture was not too recent and if their avoidant/numbing symptoms were prominent. He found the Rorschach especially useful when asylees and forensic examiners found it difficult to assess their experience through interview or more focused trauma-specific assessment methods. Also, as Tori (1989) found in his study of Mexican homosexuals, the Rorschach can be used to elucidate dysphoric mood, distorted perceptions, and significant coping difficulties with an increasingly dangerous social environment for members of particular scape-goated and persecuted groups of individuals seeking asylum.

To conclude, it is our strong belief that the Rorschach should be used with caution in the forensic assessment of asylum seekers, especially when recent political torture and rape is an issue before the IC. It has the potential for over-powering brittle defenses and for triggering painful re-experiencing of trauma-based emotions. Perhaps the Rorschach may be most useful when there is a question about whether the individual is malingering symptoms of trauma. Additionally, the Rorschach can be valuable for asylum seekers with more distant traumatic experiences of torture and trauma where avoidant/numbing symptoms of PTSD make it difficult for interview and self-report measures to document the impact of torture and rape.

Rorschach Assessment in Domestic Abuse and VAWA

The forensic psychological assessment of domestic abuse (spouse abuse and child abuse) is a related area of relevant forensic psychological expertise valu-able in the IC. Professional and scientific literature has emerged describing the psychology of women experiencing physical, sexual, and psychological abuse in their intimate relationships. (e.g., Dutton, 1992; Walker, 1979, 1994, 2009), as well as men (e.g., Bergman & Brismar, 1992; Cook, 2009; Smith & Loring, 1994). Warrier and Rose (2016) and Hass, Dutton, and Orloff (2000) have written about the special problems with domestic abuse for immigrants. Additionally, Donald Dutton (1995, 2007) developed valuable profiles of men who batter, which can be used to provide validation of women's descriptions of their reportedly abusive husbands. Immigration attorneys may find themselves in need of documenting spousal or child abuse as part of their client's petition for permanent residency under Subtitle G: Protections for Battered Immigrant Women and Children of the Violence Against Women Act of 1998 (VAWA). It is important to note that the abused spouse definition under this section of VAWA covers men as well as women.

Immigrant spouses and children of abusive U.S. citizens find themselves in a desperate situation in which they are under the virtual control and enslavement of the abusive spouse. In such situations, the abusive citizen will not support his or her immigrant spouse or child's application for permanent residency and often threatens to have the immigrant deported if she or he does not tolerate the citi-zen's abuse and comply with the citizen's wishes. In extreme cases of domestic violence, battered women and men report that they feel trapped and afraid of leaving because of the variety of severe threats by the batterer (Kaser-Boyd, 2004), including threats of having their reputations defamed in their home country to further enforce threats of divorce and deportation. An in-depth forensic psychological assessment can be crucial evidence in establishing the reported physical, sexual, or psychological abuse or extreme mental cruelty, as well as the credibility of the respondent, including why the immigrant may be slow to seek help and relief (Ahmad, Driver, McNally & Stewart, 2009).

Additionally, in suspension of deportation proceedings, psychological evidence of extreme hardship (see below) to the abused respondent also can be useful based on other relevant factors such as mental disorder and the need for treatment, medical problems, longevity in the U.S., family ties to other U.S. citizens and permanent residents, and cross-cultural factors, such as cultural reactions to divorce in the abused spouse's home country.

While there are psychological instruments that can be valuable in documenting the types and degree of domestic interpersonal violence (reviewed in Chapter 5, see Abusive Observation Behavior Checklist, Dutton, 1992; Conflict Tactics Scales, Strauss, 1979), they do not provide access to the inner experience of battered immigrant women and men. Battered immigrant spouses feel devalued, damaged, worthless, and ashamed, and the Rorschach reveals the inner reality of the battered spouse and helps corroborate her or his claims of abuse (Briere & Elliott, 1997; Kaser-Boyd, 1993, 2008).

Kaser-Boyd (1993) studied the Rorschachs of battered women who killed their battering spouses. She found battered women's Rorschach records divided between high lambda/constricted and low lambda/flooded styles consistent with van der Kolk's (1994) biphasic response of trauma victims (see also van der Kolk and Ducey, 1984, 1989). As would be expected, high lambda women exhibited Rorschach indicators of cognitive constriction, low internal resources for problem-solving, Ambient and passive problem-solving styles, poorly modulated affect, poor scanning for details in the environment, and eccentric reality testing. Women with low lambda records produced profiles that signified feelings of helplessness (m), morbid and aggressive images and images of entrapment, and clear signs of 'traumatic psychosis' (see Kaser-Boyd & Evans, 2008). These women's Rorschach protocols vividly demonstrated the inner experience of being battered.

Briere and Elliott (1997) also reviewed the use of the Rorschach in the psychological assessment of interpersonal victimization, finding similar distinct patterns including unusually extreme extratensive styles (Experience Balance [EB]), low human movement (M), and prominent Color responses with low form structure (CF and pure C > FC) reflective of posttraumatic intrusion. They noted Rorschach patterns consistent with avoidance and psychic numbing symptoms, including high lambdas and low affective ratios (Afr), while more extreme avoidance through dissociation can be found through elevated form dimension responses (FD) and introversive/pervasive introversive EB styles. Positive Hypervigilance Index (HVI) may reveal of traumatic hypervigilance in response to victimization, while experiences of helplessness and powerlessness may be evident in Rorschach variables of inanimate movement responses (m) and diffuse shading determinants. Not surprisingly, somatic anxiety (An, Sx, Bl) and damaged bodily concern (MOR and AG) are frequently found in victim protocols. Rorschach content revealing disorientation, perceptual distortion, or objects may be found in obscuring media such as fog or mist as well as indicators of cognitive confusion and even frank thought disorder, including confabulation may be found in victims' Rorschach protocols.

Additionally, severely battered women frequently exhibit intermittent dissociation and dissociative disorders (Coons, Cole, Pellow, & Milstein, 1990) and the Rorschach has proven to be an excellent assessment instrument of dissociative disorders (Armstrong, 2002; Brand, Armstrong, & Loewenstein, 2006; Scroppo, Weinberger, Drob, & Eagle, 1998). In particular, Brand et al. (2006) reported on a large Rorschach sample of 100 psychiatric in-patients who were severely dissociated and found clear signs of traumatic avoidance and traumatic intrusion in this population (for a detailed discussion, see Kaser-Boyd & Evans, 2008).

As mentioned earlier, the Rorschach can be valuable in assessing malingering and deception in trauma-based immigration evaluations where credibility is a central issue. Evans (2004) reported a case of a battered Pakistani woman seeking a hardship waiver where self-report psychological testing and interview data were equivocal. Her Rorschach indicated clear evidence of extreme psychological disturbance consistent with her description of a highly abusive childhood and subsequent battering by her U.S. spouse. As cautioned above, this woman became severely overwhelmed during the administration of the Rorschach and experienced a period of increased severe depression after the assessment. Under these circumstances, though, the benefits of receiving the extreme hardship waiver due to past domestic abuse outweighed the cost of her severe, but time-limited, distress in taking the Rorschach in order to provide invaluable support for her VAWA claim.

The Rorschach and Waivers of Extreme Hardship

As noted in Chapter 7, an extreme hardship waiver essentially allows the immigration judge discretion to suspend removal of an immigrant who otherwise would be deported for a violation of immigration law, because of the privation it would cause to qualifying spouse, children, or parents. The most obvious area of extreme psychological hardship involves a qualifying family member's mental disorder (such as depression or schizophrenia) and the impact of deportation on her or his condition, especially if appropriate treatment would not be available in the destination country. As part of assessing this hardship, the formal assessment of malingering and deception (see Rogers, 1997) can also help the IC with issues involving credibility of a claim of extreme psychological hardship (Evans, 2000; Frumkind & Friedland, 1995).

Another application of forensic psychology to extreme hardship waivers is the 'family impact statement,' establishing the impact of loss through deportation of a parent, child, or spouse on his or her family. While there is no psychological research on the impact of deportation on children, there is ample psychological literature that can illustrate the psychological impact of loss of a parent. Similarly, psychological assessment can also evaluate the U.S. citizen spouse or elderly parent for mental disorder caused or exacerbated by loss (Onrust & Cuijpers, 2006), for the impact of loss on health (Naef, Ward, Mahrer-Imhof, & Grande, 2013), and for vulnerability to suicide after profound and sudden loss (Stroebe & Stroebe, 1983). Finally, consistent with Horowitz's (1993) research on stress response syndromes, social disruption of the family arising from the deportation of a spouse or parent can also trigger powerful stress responses. More specifically, as has been noted (see Gotor & González-Juárez, 2004; Lee et al., 2015; Lin, 1986), the social disruption experienced by refugees commonly results in powerful emotional and behavioral manifestations of distress, including depression, anxiety, dissociation, and even reactive psychosis. The loss of a family member to deportation can activate a similar process.

Unlike the assessment of psychological trauma underlying its use in asylum and VAWA evaluations, the Rorschach serves a more general role in psychological testing in extreme psychological hardship evaluations. The Rorschach is especially useful in evaluating several areas specific to the kinds of distress experienced by families anticipating the loss of a family member through deportation. First, the Rorschach can be used to substantiate and support underlying processes in mental disorders. As Hake (1994) has noted, the presence of a pre-existing or coincident mental disorder is an important factor to consider for granting a waiver of extreme hardship. While the Rorschach is not designed to diagnose DSM (American Psychiatric Association, 2013) mental disorders (Exner, 2003), it can be highly useful in providing a fine-grained assessment of factors underlying mental disorder and its nexus to the psycholegal issue before the IC.

Second, when a wife or husband faces the sudden and irrevocable loss of her or his spouse (see Hays, Kasl, & Jacobs, 1994b), especially when there has been a past history of dysphoria (see Hays, Kasl, & Jacobs, 1994a), the Rorshach can also provide documentation of situational, though often severe, emotional distress underlying the common reactions of depression (e.g., D/AdjD; DEPI) and helplessness (e.g., m and FY). Additionally, acute reactive psychosis is also a known stress response to the social disruption experienced by family members (Horowitz, 1993), especially in response to the dislocation of a spouse and parent through deportation (Lin, 1986). The Rorschach is uniquely suited to assessing both the cognitive decompensation (e.g., PTI, including WSUM6) and intense emotional distress in acute reactive psychosis or its prodromal phase.

Third, the Rorschach can also be highly useful in gauging vulnerability and resiliency necessary to assess the legal question of 'extreme hardship beyond the normal stress of separation due to deportation.' The presumption in the IC is that individuals must show that the hardship due to the deportation of their spouse is extreme. The following case example is illustrative.

Mrs. S was a 34-year-old married woman with a four-year-old son, whose husband was placed in removal proceedings because of an aggravated felony committed 15 years prior. In spite of a childhood background of poverty, abuse, and neglect, she was a very competent mid-level manager for a telecommunications company and was a successful athlete in college. In spite of her seeming strengths, Mrs. S claimed that the loss of her husband would be devastating to her. A psychological evaluation was conducted to assess her claim of extreme psychological hardship. The results of her PAI were of marginal validity due to a defensive response style in which she denied psychological problems. Her Rorschach was interpretatively useful and documented her vulnerability to severe depression characterized by low self-esteem and a lack of emotional and interpersonal resources with which to handle stress. She currently experienced exceptionally high levels of situational stress as well as a chronic vulnerability to becoming upset, anxious, and disorganized. Mrs. S was highly susceptible to decompensation under stress, as demonstrated by her difficulty in thinking logically and coherently. She was withdrawn and isolated interpersonally and her social skills were limited, except in clearly structured situations. In summary, consistent with her history of tragic loss and emotional neglect, the psychological assessment revealed that Mrs. S was an emotionally vulnerable individual with high susceptibility to depression. It was clear that she had developed a very positive relationship with her husband, which provided considerable stability in her life in spite of her background. Based in part on the psychological assessment of extreme hardship to his wife, Mr. S was granted a waiver of deportation and a recent follow-up with their attorney indicated that Mrs. S continues to function adequately, though with the previously mentioned limitations.

This case illustrates how powerfully the Rorschach can bring alive the inner experience of individuals whose character defenses all but shut out inner suffering in their daily lives and on objective testing, which in turn speak directly to the issue of psychological vulnerability. As Hake and Banks (2005, p. 417) state, 'Exceptional cases may require a report from a forensic psychologist. In the rare cases, where there is no apparent outward hardship, but there is in fact very serious and unusual inward hardship.' In such circumstances, the Rorschach may provide critical information for fully documenting a claim of extreme psychological hardship as further demonstrated by Hopwood and Evans (2017).

The Rorschach in Assessment of Parole and Recidivism

Another role for forensic psychologists involves expert evaluation and testimony on IC issues involving the parole of individuals in indefinite detention and in suspension of mandatory deportation following an aggravated felony (see Chapter 8). Comprehensive psychological assessment can help document the presence of a mental disorder and establish credibility of the respondent. As Frumkind and Friedland (1995) point out, the psychologist expert can also consider the psychological impact of detention and imprisonment (see Haney & Zimbardo, 1998; Zimbardo, 1974). This assessment, combined with an assessment of potential dangerousness (see Monahan & Steadman, 1994; Webster, Douglas, Eaves, & Hart, 1997), can help establish whether or not continued confinement is in the best interest of the public. The use of such expert forensic mental health assessment and testimony was important in establishing the deleterious effects of incarceration in the landmark female genital mutilation case of Fauziya Kassindja (Kassindja & Miller, 1998).

To date, the most extensive research on the forensic use of the Rorschach has been the work of Gacono and his colleagues on antisocial and psychopathic personalities in criminal settings (see Gacono, Gacono, & Evans, 2008; Gacono & Meloy, 1994). Wood et al. (2010) challenged the scientific basis of Gacono and Meloy's work. In response, Cunliffe et al. (2013) cogently point out that Wood et al.'s critique is 'old wine in a new bottle' – i.e., using both Wood et al.'s lack of understanding of the Rorschach and conceptual and methodological problems in their meta-analysis that were addressed in earlier critiques of Wood et al.'s work (see Gacono & Evans, 2008).

The literature has been applied to forensic assessment of criminal matters in Immigration Court (Evans, 2000; Rosenberg & Evans, 2003), which in conjunction with the PCL-R (Hare, 2003) and risk assessment/recidivism risk assessment tools such as the Level of Service Inventory-Revised (LSI-R) (Andrews & Bonta, 1995) can assist in determinations of parole from indefinite detention and of waivers of deportation. Since risk/recidivism assessment tools have important limitations (see Zamble & Quinsey, 1997, for the problem static, 'tombstone' markers), the Rorschach allows for a thorough assessment of dynamic variables when assessing risk. Additionally, substantial forensic Rorschach reference group data (Gacono et al., 2008) allow for further empirical comparisons regarding the degree to which a particular individual is similar or dissimilar to known criminal populations. Such data are especially useful in assisting IC judges, because the presence of recidivistic criminals in IC has a much lower base rate than in Federal and state criminal courts.

The following case example is illustrative of how the Rorschach provided important information in assisting an IJ's determination of the rehabilitation and future recidivism risk of a 30-year-old legal permanent resident male placed in deportation proceedings for an aggravated felony committed nine years earlier after recent parole from USCIS detention.

Mr. W came to the U.S. from a Caribbean country at the age of 12 with his family. Within several years, he became involved with other adolescent antisocial peers and the predatory adults who supplied illegal drugs. He reported that his participation led to 14 arrests, both as a juvenile and as an adult, until he was convicted for possession with intent to distribute marijuana at the age of 18. He reported no legal or behavioral difficulties before coming to the U.S. and was never involved in stealing from others, vandalizing property, cruelty toward animals, or fire setting, nor was he enuretic after toilet training. After his last arrest, Mr. W determined to leave his life in drug culture, which he did by no longer associating with past street friends and by getting training and a job as an auto mechanic. Shortly afterward, he met his current wife and had a daughter with her. He became increasingly involved in raising his daughter and stepson, becoming the more nurturing of the two parents, and was noted for his reliability at work. A psychological evaluation was conducted to assess his claim of rehabilitation. His PCL-R score, while elevated due to his past arrests, was significantly lower than the average incarcerated felon, and his PAI was valid and showed situational anxiety, but otherwise indicated no psychopathology. The results of Mr. W's Rorschach indicated fewer psychological resources for coping with the demands of everyday living, as well as having an avoidant style and overly simplistic way of looking at the world to maintain a stable psychological equilibrium. His Rorschach showed good reality testing and sound judgment, indicating an ability to recognize and act on conventional expectations and modes of behavior and to engage in adaptive interpersonal behaviors. Most importantly, the results did not suggest that Mr. W had the aggressiveness, chronic excitement seeking and poor impulse control, externalization of responsibility, lack of remorse, and callous disregard for others found in chronic criminal offenders. Mr. W was granted a waiver of deportation by the IJ, in substantial part due to the results of his forensic assessment. The evaluation showed clear indications of rehabilitation and decreased future risk of criminality as well as the finding of extreme psychological hardship to his wife (who had a long history of depression) and to his children with whom he was deeply bonded. Follow-up with his attorney indicated that Mr. W. continues to do well at work and at home, including fathering another child with whom he is also very close.

This case illustrates how the Rorschach can provide important psychodynamic information in assessing recidivism risk in criminal immigration issues. As Rosenberg and Evans (2003) stated, such evaluations can help provide 'another chance,' or what Maruna (2001, p. 26) calls *desistence*, i.e., 'the long-term abstinence from crime by individuals who had previously engaged in a persistent pattern of criminal offending' or the process of 'making good.' Indeed, in such circumstances, the Rorschach may provide critical information for fully documenting a claim of rehabilitation and reduced recidivism risk. Such evaluations can assist in affording individuals judicial relief from harsh criminal immigration laws, when immigrants have rehabilitated well despite earlier legal problems.

Other Performance-Based Measures

While the focus of this chapter so far has been largely on the Rorschach because of the substantial literature supporting its use in a wide variety of forensic settings (see Erard & Evans 2017; Gacono & Evans 2008), other PBMs have the potential to make valuable contributions to forensic assessment in the IC. This section briefly reviews several PBMs with possible value in IC forensic assessment. Unfortunately, while their clinical utility is considerable, none of the instruments have a strong track record in forensic settings in general or IC in particular, and may not be seen as acceptable by forensic experts as suitable for court (see Lally 2003).[1] On the other hand, Archer and Wheeler (2013) suggest careful, evidence-based, and expert use of clinical psychological tests in forensic matters can eventually establish their probative value for the court with increased use. Deeply human descriptions derived from narrative PBMs, properly contextualized, can provide compelling evidence for the IC trier of fact beyond simple hearsay evidence derived solely from interviews. As stated in Chapter 1, the combination of clinical rich descriptive, as well as evidence-based, testimony may have special value. Naturally, following reputable multicultural guidelines such as recommended by Dana (2005) for the use of narrative PBMs establishes a more culturally based approach to psychological assessment (see Chapter 2).

It is also important to remember that the evidentiary standards and context within IC may allow for broader latitude regarding admissibility of evidence. For example, in an IC asylum hearing, IJs increasingly have enormous dockets (Jervis, Gomez, & Solis 2017) and are asked to make rapid decisions with limited evidence. Additionally, the legal standard for granting asylum has a relatively low bar (Anker, 2017), which suggests that research-based psychological evidence that rises above hearsay may be probative in these settings and welcomed by the IC.

Thematic Apperception Test (TAT)

The TAT (Murray, 1943) is perhaps the best-known narrative storytelling test and is one of the most highly researched projective tests (see Ryan, 1985), showing its capacity to measure durable personality traits and interpersonal proclivities. In terms of evidence-based clinical and forensic utility, it has been frequently challenged as having insufficient research showing sufficient validity to support its use. Because TAT studies show that the sets of stimulus cards used are so diverse, it is hard to establish generalization from one study to another or to clinical practice (Keiser & Prather, 1990). This appears to be due to the lack of consistency and specificity of materials and procedures. While it is tempting to dismiss the TAT in the forensic assessment in IC, there are a number of reasons to consider its judicious use.

Like other PBMs, the TAT use is much less restricted by educational level and reading capacity and can evoke rich descriptions of psychological themes and processes. Forensic psychological assessment applications using the TAT in the IC can include elucidating the inner damage to the self and relationships in trauma-based assessments such as torture-based asylum, T visa and VAWA matters as well as the fear of loss in spouses and children in extreme hardship cases. For example, Suárez-Orozco (1990) studied responses to political terror in Latin America by administering the TAT to newly arriving immigrants, finding preoccupation with themes of death, torture, and assassinations in the narratives. He related TAT responses to state-mandated terror to human psychological defense mechanisms of denial, rationalization, and internalization. Indeed, Esquivel, Oades-Sese, and Olitzky (2008) suggest the capacity for the TAT to tap underlying psychological themes in the context of social expectations as well as anticipation of future outcomes provides a highly personal narrative that can be more easily understood by others than say the Rorschach or the MMPI. Teglasi (2010) and Jenkins (2008) review the objective scoring methodology to provide more scientific rigor to TAT assessments. Indeed, time-efficient TAT scoring methods such as the SCORS-G (Global Rating Method: Hilsenroth, Stein, & Pinsker, 2007) and Cramer's (2006) Defense Mechanisms Manual are available to meld the narrative richness of the TAT with the research-based empirical sturdiness so valued in forensic contexts.

Tell-Me-A-Story (TEMAS)

An intriguing development in narrative PBMs relevant to forensic assessment in the IC is a method called Tell-Me-A-Story (TEMAS: Costantino, Malgady, & Rogler, 1988). An assessment measure designed for children and adolescents, it was originally normed on U.S. samples of Hispanic, African-American, and white groups. A standard set of 23 cards in chromatic color, with minority and non-minority versions, show ethnically diverse characters in culturally specific and relevant contexts. The stimulus cards are designed to stimulate specific responses and color is used to aid articulation and evocation of emotional states. TEMAS differs from the TAT by emphasizing personality functions arising from interpersonal relationship schemas rather than intrapsychic dynamics. The TEMAS cards are designed to evoke meaningful stories indicating conflict in contrast to the TAT use of less distinct stimuli. The TEMAS cards embody polarities of negative and positive emotions, cognitions, and interpersonal functions, as opposed to the TAT's valence toward negative emotions, depressive mood, and hostility. In general, the TEMAS stimulus cards are culturally relevant and gender-sensitive, have reduced ambiguity, and are scored on a variety of variables representing cognitive, affective, and self and interpersonal functioning.

Ritzler (2004) identified the TEMAS as a groundbreaking development in culturally sensitive projective testing. Costantino, Dana, and Malgady (2007) followed up on the publication of the TEMAS with a comprehensive book detailing the instrument and its cross-cultural validation with examples from Latin American, Caribbean, Italian, and Taiwanese studies. Flanagan, Costantino, Cardalda, and Costantino (2007) provided an in-depth description with case examples of the TEMAS and demonstrated its special place in multicultural assessment within the context of a multi-method assessment approach. Together these studies suggest TEMAS as a valuable and especially culturally relevant PBM for evaluating the children and adolescents for psychological difficulty and vulnerability, perhaps in the context of a comprehensive family impact study as part of IC forensic psychological assessment for extreme hardship.

Roberts-2

Like the TEMAS, the second edition of the Roberts Apperception Test for Children (Roberts-2; Roberts & Gruber, 2005) is a narrative storytelling PBM for children between the ages of 6 and 18. This PBM assesses both adaptive social and maladaptive or atypical social perception, including such concerns as anxiety, depression, rejection, and aggression, frequently within the context of parent and family relationships. This second edition was updated to include better age- and gender-specific normative data and includes Caucasian, African-American, and Hispanic versions of the test pictures, as well as gender-specific cards. Unlike the TAT, there are 16 cards that are always administered with a standard coding procedure that yields an age-based T-score for each of the 26 scales.

Within the context of forensic psychological assessment in the IC, the Roberts-2 can be especially valuable for a family impact study where extreme or exceptional hardship to a U.S. citizen child or adolescent is claimed in removal or deportation proceedings of an immigrant parent. The Roberts-2 can help establish valuable evidence that is probative to two major psycholegal issues in such IC proceedings: (1) assessing special psychological needs and vulnerabilities of the U.S. citizen child or adolescent; or (2) measuring adaptive functioning that demonstrates secure emotional bonding between the immigrant parent and U.S. citizen child. In the former case, the loss of a supportive parent by an emotionally disturbed and vulnerable child can worsen the child's already precarious psychological state. In the latter case, the impact of the child's loss of a secure relationship to the immigrant pattern can predispose the child to psychological difficulties later on.

Adult Attachment Projective Picture System (AAP)

The Adult Attachment Projective Picture System (AAP; George & West, 2012) is an exciting recent development in PBM. The AAP is a validated measure of adult attachment representation (i.e., the individual's internal working model status). The individual is presented with seven cards with projective attachment scenes in which the respondent tells a story to each card. Each card progressively increases activation of the individual's attachment system, with the latter cards pulling for relational trauma. The individual's stories are rigorously and reliably coded and the results designate one of the four standard Adult Attachment Interview classification groups (Autonomous, Dismissing, Preoccupied, Unresolved/Disorganized). Additionally, the AAP provides information about defensive processing patterns, attachment synchrony, and personal agency, especially in close intimate relationships. The AAP requires substantial training and certification by its developers (http://attachmentprojective.com/) in order to administer and code this PBM.

For forensic psychologists who go to the considerable effort to learn this powerful and promising instrument, the application to IC forensic assessment is considerable, especially in assessments of extreme hardship waivers. To illustrate, in one specialized area of extreme hardship waiver assessment, the J-1 visa waiver (see Chapter 7), determination of exceptional and highly unusual psychological hardship, beyond the ordinary hardship of separation, requires assessing hardship for the U.S. citizen under both of two prongs. The U.S. citizen must establish hardship if she or he travels to the spouse's foreign home country for a minimum of two years and, alternatively, if she or he remains in the U.S. while the citizen spouse returns to the foreign home country without the U.S. citizen. Demonstrating the alternate prong can frequently be a significant impediment, especially when the U.S. citizen is outwardly successful (see Hopwood & Evans, 2017). The AAP could become a valuable empirical measure to assess the psychological impact of separation of the immigrant spouse from the U.S. citizen.

Conclusion

This chapter explicates where and how the Rorschach and other PBMs can be used in IC and USCIS administrative proceedings to provide relevant, and often, critical information. The psycholegal issues in the IC are diverse and complex, but also highly rewarding for the forensic examiner who is willing to understand the legal issues involved and their nexus to psychological assessment. In this chapter, We have attempted to highlight how the Rorschach and selected other PBMs can be used in such evaluations in the context of relevant legal issues. It is our view that the Rorschach and other PBMs are especially well-suited for the appropriately trained assessor in forensic evaluation in the IC.

Note

1. It should be noted that Lally drew his conclusions on a survey of 64 forensic diplomates without assessing whether or not these psychologists actually ever used all the instruments they were judging.

Chapter 11

Report Writing and Expert Testimony

Immigration judges (IJs) and adjudicators are interested in evidence that the applicant has suffered or will suffer (for extreme hardship applications) emotional injuries, physical injuries, or both. However, technically only asylum requires a thorough forensic evaluation from a mental health or medical professional for Immigration Court. Forensic mental health evaluations regarding the mental or physical injuries of the applicant in immigration cases other than asylum are extremely helpful, but not required. Applicants may present other types of documentation that show evidence of the emotional or physical problems related to the grounds of their immigration petition. For instance, an applicant may present medical records from hospitals or clinics where they have been treated for injuries (either psychological or physical) related to the victimization they experienced. An applicant can also provide letters from physicians or mental health professionals who treated him or her. These letters are written specifically to describe the harm the applicant suffered as a victim of crime and the treatments received. These letters and documents often lack the level of detailed information that show the foundations for the professional opinions and may fail to make the link to criminal activity, deportation, or other immigration matters. More importantly, these documents will likely fail to make a comprehensive assessment of the applicant's credibility regarding the origin of their impairment. Given the high stakes for the applicant of immigration relief and the high level of rejected applications by immigration officials, it is becoming customary in many immigration courts (ICs) to present a forensic mental health evaluation to support the claims of the applicant in most immigration cases.

Of the different professionals providing documentation for immigration applicants, the forensic mental health expert is the most highly qualified when it comes to assessment of emotional harm and identification of its causes. Practitioners who provide therapeutic services to the applicant and render documentation for their client's legal matters are not forensic experts. Although they provide expert testimony, specifically mental status, diagnosis, progress, prognosis, and treatment, which may be relevant to the psycholegal issues, there are important limits to their contribution. Most importantly, their opinion is incidental to the treatment and their ongoing relationship with the applicant may compromise their objectivity. In addition, they may not have followed all the steps necessary to find and prove causality, reliability, and link those issues to the psycholegal concept.

Forensic mental health experts have been recognized in other areas of forensic practice for many years. Forensic mental health experts are trained to provide opinions and testimony about a person on psycholegal issues, particularly causation, which is essential in immigration cases. Forensic experts gather information and utilize techniques adequate to substantiate their findings (American Psychological Association, 2017, EPPCC Standards 2.04, 9.01), and only provide an opinion when they have sufficient foundation. They identify the potential threats to the credibility and validity of their opinions. They take many scientifically based steps to ensure that their decisions are unlikely to be speculative (American Psychological Association, 2013, Forensic Guidelines 4.02.02). Their training and ethical obligations are specifically designed to ensure that they inform the judicial and legal process, putting the needs of the law ahead of the examinee's when rendering their opinion. The document produced by this type of forensic mental health professional, the forensic mental health report, is what we will be discussing next.

While there are excellent authoritative books, book chapters, and articles about the writing of the forensic report (the reader will benefit from consulting de Ruiter & Kaser-Boyd, 2015; Griffith, Stankovic, & Baranoski, 2010; Otto, DeMier, & Boccaccini, 2014; Weiner, 2014a), they are focused on criminal or civil forensic practice. The lessons from this literature are very valuable, but for immigration cases there are specific issues unexplored by these writings. We next highlight relevant issues to consider when writing a report for immigration cases.

Report of a Forensic Mental Health Expert

A forensic report or affidavit documenting a mental health evaluation in immigration cases is not a 'letter' offering a diagnosis or an opinion. According to Griffith, Stankovic, and Baranoski (2010), because forensic reports are subjected to critical analysis, they should be 'acts of performance, requiring a degree of artistry and cogent argumentation' (p. 32). These authors further describe forensic examiners as transformers of the data into a narrative that makes situations and characters 'come to life and evoke emotions' (p. 33). In addition to artistic skills that help deliver a human story, there are scientific considerations, because the process of evaluation is also a research study, which documents factual knowledge about relevant psycholegal concerns. As in other areas of forensic psychology, the IC report has to include a number of issues of critical importance if we want the adjudicators to take it seriously and if we want to comply with our ethical and evidentiary obligations.

The legal requirements of an expert through the Federal Rules of Civil Procedure (2017) (Rule 26.a 2 – Disclosure of Expert Testimony) include: (1) a complete statement of opinions and reasoning; (2) the facts or data considered; (3) any exhibits that may be used during oral testimony if applicable (posters or audio-visual aids); (4) the expert witness qualifications; (5) a list of other cases in which, during the previous four years, the witness testified as an expert at trial or by deposition; and (6) a statement regarding compensation (para. 10). Although these factors vary by jurisdiction and also depend on the type of proceedings (i.e., criminal, civil, immigration), these are important issues that we need to include in the immigration report. These issues can be incorporated in the body of the report as illustrated below.

Outline of the Immigration Report

While the format and length of the report varies, there are a number of important elements that are considered essential to the report, such as (Otto, DeMier, & Boccaccini, 2014):

1. Identifying information: The title page of the report needs to identify clearly the examinee and the information of the examination, including the date(s) of the sessions, and the date of the report (de Ruiter & Kaser-Boyd, 2015).
2. Referral question: This information has to be stated early in the report because it defines its scope. In addition to the name, it is important to describe the title of the referral party and role in the immigration case.
3. Notification and informed consent: In this section, the examiner describes the notification and consent of the applicant and payer regarding the following issues: (a) the purpose of the assessment; (b) the nature of the examiner's role, including the fact that an evaluation is not the same as therapy; (c) the limits of confidentiality including who would be interviewed as a collateral source, who would obtain a copy of the report, and the extent to which this report may go to other professionals; (d) the compensation received for the evaluation, both tangible and intangible; (e) that you need to approach the evaluation with no particular result in mind; (f) that you will exercise independent professional judgment in all aspects of the evaluation; (g) that the payment of fees is not connected to the contents of any report or consultation or any particular finding or recommendation on the matter in question. This section of the report has been noted as lacking in many forensic reports (Heilbrun & Collins, 1995; Skeem, Golding, Cohn, & Berge, 1998), which is far from ideal.
4. Sources of information: This section includes documents reviewed, collateral interviews, and a subtitle of the procedures and methods of assessment utilized with the applicant. Here, the examiner also describes when and where the examinee was evaluated and how long each session was, and dates and length of time of collateral interviews and manner in which these interviews were performed.
5. Background information: This is the narrative story of the person derived from the collateral documents or interviews up to the point of the core issues

of the immigration case. It is important to include here previous traumatic history as well as previous mental health issues and treatment, including use of psychiatric medications. This is also the place where you can describe the examinee's present circumstances and challenges that he or she is facing.

6. Behavioral observations and mental status: This section helps the reader understand the state of mind of the examinee during the examination. It is important to note whether the client was aware and alert to participate in the evaluation, and whether his verbal and non-verbal behavior was conscious and voluntary. Basically, this section answers the questions regarding whether the client knew what he was doing and participated actively. The observations regarding how the applicant presented when relaying their account and when participating in assessment methods also go in this section. All these observations provide a foundation for the opinions that the examiner will proffer later on. It is appropriate here to also indicate the language utilized for the evaluation, if an interpreter was utilized, include her or his name and qualifications, and the cultural appropriateness of the tests or methods utilized.

In addition to these basic sections above, the following subheadings are recommended in order to create the document that is readily accessible to the IC judge or USCIS adjudicator.

7. Qualifications: In this section, you can briefly present the reasons why you are qualified to undertake this type of evaluation and the number of similar cases completed, as well as the number of similar cases in which you testified as an expert or were deposed. Because this section should be short, attaching your CV to the report is also recommended.

8. Credibility: Here, the examiner explains the reliability and validity of the information provided by the applicant and obtained through behavioral observations, correlation of the client's report and collateral data, reliability of data from the self-report and projective psychological tests, or other methods. It is in this section that the examiner can rule in or out the hypotheses regarding whether the examinee may be malingering, deceiving, or exaggerating, and the reasoning behind their opinion about the applicant's credibility. Problems with deviant response style do not automatically invalidate the psychological opinion as long as the psychological picture was still accurately revealed. There may be reasons why a respondent distorted his or her presentation and this could be explained. Because truthfulness and deception are not all-or-nothing concepts, the examiner may want to specify whether exaggeration, manipulation of facts, idealization, or other misrepresentation were apparent and what were the aspects in which facts appeared unrehearsed and genuine.

9. Specific case heading: Depending on the specific issue at hand, you may need to create an appropriate heading. For instance, for asylum, VAWA,

U visa, and T visa, the examiner may want to have a section describing thoroughly the relationship and experiences the applicant had with the perpetrator(s) of the criminal activity, including the applicant's detailed description of the abuse, and the applicant's report of the psychological difficulties in relation to the qualifying criminal activity. For example, this section can be labeled, 'Examinee's description of the …' (you can fill in the blanks with the appropriate issue, such as: domestic violence in the relationship with X/abuse experienced while working at X/experiences as a victim of trafficking/persecution and violence experience while living in their country of origin, etc.). For a case of extreme hardship or cancelation of removal, the section may be: Potential limitations and difficulties the applicant and family would endure if they have to reside in X country. This section includes the psycholegally specific information obtained through interviews and organized by the examiner, but presents the applicant's own words and perspective.

This section may have several other subheadings as the topic is explored from different perspectives. For instance, in a VAWA case those subheadings could be: (a) Relationship with the abuser, (b) Nature, severity and frequency of the abuse, (c) Examinee's experience of the abuse, and (d) Applicant's efforts to deal with the abuse. One of the best ways to organize the data and provide a focus is by using subheadings. This allows the reader to move from one topic to another, following a clear path of organization and building the details of the case to improve understanding. This requires some work from the examiner both during the interview and the report writing, since most applicants do not provide their stories in such an organized manner. It is important to put the name of the applicant in these subheadings and all over the report instead of using 'the examinee' or 'applicant' in order to personalize the report.

10. Collateral information: In this section, the examiner reports the information derived from interviews conducted with other relevant informants as well as relevant documents reviewed. This section is important because its provides sources of information that may corroborate the applicant's claims and inform the examiner's opinion. The importance of collateral information lies in the fact that it supplements the information obtained in the office through interview and psychological tests. Without collateral information, the basis of opinion derives solely from the applicant's self-report about social adjustment and functioning in the world, a practice which is perilously close to providing only hearsay information.

11. Results of assessment: Included here are the details of the information obtained from psychological tests and structured interviews, which provides empirical evidence of the applicant's claim regarding the psychological injury. Psychometric and clinical data should be placed in the individual context of the case and should not be reported directly from the test interpretation book or computerized interpretation to the report without first

matching it to the applicant's particular situation. Lewak and Hogan (2003) have emphasized that 'test integration, although more difficult, is more efficient and clinically useful. The integrative process involves examining discriminant and incremental data generated from a particular test and from different tests and combining them with history, clinical and feedback data' (p. 360). This means that, when a characteristic of the examinee is found in test data, behavioral observations of the examinee's behavior are noted to exemplify what it means.

This section of results from assessment measures may start or end with a diagnosis, if the examiner identified it and believes it is needed in the report, although as explained in Chapters 5 and 6, a diagnosis is not always necessary and may even by misleading. If a diagnosis is provided, then a detailed explanation about how the data findings meet the diagnostic criteria is necessary. When training on how to conduct immigration evaluations, this author (GAH) tends to emphasize that an asylum applicant's diagnosis, such as PTSD, is not like another person's PTSD. Like wine, each has notes and flavors of one or more factors that are unique to their situation and combined in an individual and special way. Indeed, as Galatzer-Levy and Bryant (2013) have pointed out, there are 636,120 ways to have PTSD, using the combinations of DSM-5 PTSD symptoms. It is sad to read reports that are filled with generalizations and statements so vague that could apply to anyone, or when the examiner only enumerates how the person meets diagnostic criteria, but the individuality and uniqueness of the person and her or his subjective experience of the trauma is lost. What is more important, rather than a diagnosis, is the answer to the psycholegal question using the functional data derived from the evaluation.

12. Literature review: This section is optional, but sometimes very helpful and characteristic of serious case analysis. This includes the review of the social science or country information relevant to the case, including proper citations showing that the sources are highly reliable. This section adds context to the applicant's allegations or provides a scientific background that is relevant to the issues that apply to the case. For instance, it can speak about the psychological consequences of a child when having to move to a foreign country taking into consideration the individual characteristics of the child of the deported applicant, or it can speak about the domestic violence literature or workplace abuse and exploitation.

13. Executive summary: A summary may be included at this point of the report when the report is long and a clear and concise foundation to the opinions needs to be established. The summary is the place where you can draw your inferences from the data already presented, making sure to differentiate facts from inference. According to Otto, DeMier, and Boccaccini (2014), 'inferences refer to the associations made between facts, especially with regards to causal relationships' (p. 37). Here, the examiner needs to show that she or he considered different hypotheses, why they were discarded, and how the

data considered support the expert's conclusion. The social science literature usually helps with this step of 'connecting the dots.'

14. Opinions: Here, you should state your final opinions clearly, concretely, and unambiguously. This means that the opinions section is where the examiner links the inferences to the psycholegal issue, after having laid the ground for the reader to follow the logic of the story and data provided earlier in the report. As an example, in a U visa case, the examiner notes the victim's behavioral description of the nature of the abuse in the workplace and her feelings about it (self-report facts). Then the examiner may review in collateral information documents that confirm that inspectors cited the place for violations in labor law and abuse of employees (documented facts). The examiner also found with assessment measures that the victim suffered from high levels of anxiety and depression and date them to the time when she took this job (more facts). The inference that goes in the summary would be that the abuse in the workplace is correlated to the high levels of psychological distress (which follows the implications of the facts). The opinion will be that the distress produced by abuse in the workplace fits the concept of substantial mental abuse.

The issue about whether the examiner should word clearly the ultimate opinion, such as 'the psychological injury described proves that the applicant suffered extreme cruelty,' has been debated. There are some judges that take issue when a mental health professional makes the type of legal decisions that are within the judge's purview, because after all, the trier of fact is the one who puts together the conclusions from the entire body of information. However, there are other judges who prefer to hear the concrete opinion of the expert in this matter as a proposal for consideration. Skeem, Golding, Cohn, and Berge (1998) even believe that providing an ultimate opinion is not even necessary when the examiner has provided clear reasoning that leads the reader to a conclusion of their own. Some forensic experts believe that opining on the ultimate issue is both an ethical risk and a leap from a mental health practitioner's area of expertise in most forensic evaluations (Borum & Grisso, 1996). Mental health examiners may want to consult with the attorney who hired them and who has greater familiarity with the local IC when deciding the wording of their opinions.

Basic Elements of the Report Writing Process

One of the most important aspects of the report is to organize it in a manner that makes the reader follow the examiner's line of thinking and presents the individuality of the examinee rather than a multitude of data or information. The writing of a report is for many examiners the act of organizing the thinking and pulling all the information together. In these cases, the report constitutes the best foundation for future testimony. However, a good report is more than that, as it makes the person and his or her story and plight come to light and allow the reader to feel related and empathic.

Weiner (2014a) emphasizes the need of 'being clear, relevant, informative and defensible' (p. 712). Clarity includes limited use of technical jargon, being transparent about all sources of information utilized and consulted, and explicitly answering the questions that are the focus of the evaluation. Relevance means presenting the information that bears directly on the issues of the case and the referral question. Being informative means that psychological data and impressions should be communicated in a way that the reader can recognize. We are being informative by making use of social science findings to make sense of the data from the evaluation. Being defensible means that the examiner recognizes the imperfect nature of the evaluation tools and avoids statements that could overstate the findings. In all cases, our findings 'correlate' to the psychological profile of a person having suffered the qualifying crime, but we cannot make direct causal inferences. In psychology, a causal determination can only be done through controlled experiments.

The Society for Personality Assessment (n.d.) developed an evaluation form to judge the quality of psychological reports presented by assessment psychologists as part of their proficiency certification. This form includes the most important elements that a proficient examiner should include in the report of a psychological evaluation. According to Hadas Pade (2015), SPA Proficiency Coordinator, one of the proficiency goals is to 'reduce poor- or low-quality services, often demonstrated by written reports which may be unhelpful or potentially harmful to the client' (p. 10). Although it was created for assessment psychologists, it is a description of competent standards that can apply to immigration reports written by any mental health expert and is described below (Society for Personality Assessment, n.d.). In immigration cases it makes more sense to replace recommendations with opinions.

1. Comprehensiveness
   a. Adequate and appropriate identifying information is presented.
   b. The referral source is clearly identified.
   c. A referral question or reason for the assessment is clearly stated.
   d. The history is adequate/relevant to the assessment question(s).
   e. Observations of the client's behavior and engagement in the assessment are presented.
   f. A summary section is included.
2. Integration
   a. The assessment includes at least three different assessment methods (e.g., self-report, performance-based, clinical interview).
   b. Cross-method interpretations are presented in an integrated manner.
   c. Conflicting findings are adequately addressed (if applicable).
3. Validity
   a. The validity of test findings and quality of data are discussed.

    b.   Test interpretations are consistent with the empirical literature and accepted clinical practice.

    c.   Assertions made from test results are consistent with the data collected.

    d.   Test interpretations are sensitive to issues of culture and diversity, including ethnicity, race, gender, age, sexual orientation, age, religion, ability, etc.

    e.   Diagnostic impressions and conclusions are reasonable based on the data presented.

4.   Client-centered

    a.   The referral question(s) is addressed adequately.

    b.   Overall, individual test results are presented in a way that is clearly and specifically about the individual being evaluated (e.g., not directly copied from computer reports).

    c.   Overall, the report is 'person-focused' rather than 'test-focused.'

    d.   Recommendations flow directly and clearly from the data, including the test findings, client's clinical presentation, referral question, and history.

    e.   Recommendations are clear, specific to the person, and reasonable.

5.   Overall writing

    a.   Test scores and response examples are appropriately used (if applicable).

    b.   The report is clear, coherent, and generally jargon-free.

    c.   Overall, the report is well written, organized, and mostly free from grammatical errors.

Given these important aspects that need to be included, it is not surprising that these reports are longer than some specific-issue criminal reports (i.e., competency to stand trial), which stand at an average of 3.9 pages (Heilbrun & Collins, 1995). Outside the forensic criminal field, custody reports are on average 21 pages and within a range of 4–80 pages (Bow & Quinnell, 1998). The best advice is provided by de Ruiter and Kaser-Boyd (2015), who advocate for meticulous editing, stating 'forensic reports should be as brief as possible but as long as needed' (p. 245).

Affidavits

Affidavits are summary reports and include many but not all the sections of the immigration report in a different, more legalistic format based on numbering the paragraphs. According to Otto, DeMier, and Boccaccini (2014) it includes: identification of the examiner and qualifications, data sources, and expert opinions. They also refer to the case proceedings. The characteristic of affidavits is that, because they are not presented in court and cross-examined, they are made under oath. Usually, the examiner takes the report to be notarized or otherwise affirmed by another person having such authority.

Feedback Session

We are not obligated to discuss the report with the examinee (American Psychological Association, 2013, Forensic Guidelines, 10.05). We are advised to 'take reasonable steps' (p. 16) and if not possible to explain it to the examinee. However, it is good practice to try, as often as possible, to provide a feedback session with the petitioner and the referral attorney after the report has been written. The petitioner should have an opportunity to review the data and make sure that the story has been captured accurately. They may have feedback that enriches the description of the psychological picture you are explaining, Further, because often applicants may have limited familiarity with psychological and psychotherapeutic processes, they may need guidance regarding how to manage their anxiety when intimate issues are revealed in immigration hearings or where to seek out services to deal with the psychological disturbances found.

The attorney who referred the case is also an important source of input in terms of the legal sufficiency of the expert's report language. They have an eye for wording that may raise unwarranted issues or may point to clarifications that are needed when the examiner used obscure or brief language. However, extreme care must be exercised to allow neither the petitioner nor the referral attorney compromise the objectivity and independent opinion of the examiner.

Expert Testimony

Mental health experts practicing in the immigration field possess specialized knowledge that assist decision-makers in immigration cases to understand the evidence put forth by the respondent and his or her legal representative. Forensic assessors may be called to the IC as an expert witness in either of two different instances: (1) by evaluating the respondent or his or her relatives and providing a report and testimony stating their expert opinion regarding their claims; or (2) by providing an expert opinion that, while they did not personally conduct the evaluation of the petitioner, they have expert knowledge that is relevant to the case. The more probative expert opinion is when the examiner personally conducted the evaluation of the respondent (or his or her relatives for extreme hardship cases) and used evidence-based instruments to obtain psychological data. In fact, using psychological tests provides a solid and valid foundation for testimony (Lally, 2003). Of course, perfect cases do not exist and our approach needs to adjust to reality while staying as close as possible to best practices and minimizing bias.

A mental health assessment may be introduced in either an affirmative or defensive process in an immigration case. An affirmative process occurs when the applicant voluntarily applies for immigration relief. A defensive process occurs when an individual has been placed in deportation proceedings. The hearing in the defensive process is adversarial and places the burden of the defense on the respondent (De Jesus-Rentas, Boehnlein, & Sparr, 2010). Consequently, the forensic report submitted by mental health examiners supporting immigration relief is likely to be highly scrutinized. Sometimes, the adjudicators may request clarifications or further information from the mental health examiner, and in cases such as asylum and cancelation of removal, the expert needs to testify and be cross-examined by both the USCIS attorney and the IC judge.

The testimony of a mental health expert needs to be guided by the Federal Rules of Evidence (Vaisman-Tzachor, 2012), though IC judges exercise broader discretion in considering evidence than do other Federal judges. The following issues are at the core of the credibility of a mental health expert opinion in Immigration Court: (1) there must be a reasonable degree of psychological certainty based on the scientific method, including testability and acceptance in the field (Melton et al., 2007); and (2) the psychological tests utilized need to be reliable, commercially available, relevant to the legal issue, applicable to the population, administered in a standardized fashion, and used for the purpose for which it was developed (American Psychological Association, 2002).

It is critical to select sources of information that withstand scrutiny regarding their relevance, validity, and reliability (Grisso, 2003). Clearly, much can be said about the need to utilize assessment instruments that provide valid information through reliable methods, whether they are interviews or tests. There are instruments that lack empirical support and are not reliable methods to assess the applicants. For instance, projective drawings have very little scientific value in a forensic evaluation (Lally, 2003), although in the clinical field they may be helpful. The information derived from such instruments is vulnerable to being inadequate for IC purpose and their use suggests examiner bias regarding its interpretation.

Mental health examiners testifying in IC should prepare in the same way as do experts who testify in civil or criminal courts. The report should be the starting point of preparation for the examiner who needs to testify consistently regarding the report findings as the basis for both direct and cross-examination. Experts who are most successful think of themselves as educators, as opposed to defensively trying to win their case. Prepare for testimony as you would prepare to give a lecture on the case to a curious and skeptical audience. You want to have up-to-date knowledge within your focus of practice, your instruments, your data, and the process of assessment. Kwartner and Bocaccini (2007) have named the following factors as critical for good testimony:

1. Credibility: The expert should appear to be knowledgeable, well informed, confident in their education, and poised when presenting in order to project trustworthiness and likeability.
2. Clarity: The use of non-technical jargon makes a big difference to the judge's perception of the expert's mastery of the subject, and make the arguments more persuasive.
3. Clinical knowledge: The presentation of dry facts, tests results and graphs is less well received by judges than a clinical explanation of the case (see research by Krauss & Sales, 2001).

4. Certainty: Tentativeness is an undesirable attitude in the expert and it chips away at the trust in the expert's knowledge. An expert is expected to state the limits of their opinions, and not overstate conclusions but be reasonably persuasive.

By performing the evaluation to the best possible standards and maintaining integrity from the outset to the end of the case, the mental health examiner should find satisfaction in the humane and professional aspects of the role instead of investing a great deal of pride in the outcome of the case. While experts should learn from every case to do even better next time, they also should try not to equate success with performance. Judges' and adjudicators' opinions rely on a number of complex factors that go beyond the expert opinion. Recognizing this fact helps the expert find satisfaction in their job and develop resiliency to stay in the field.

Bibliography

Aber, L., Bennett, N. G., Conley, D. C., & Li, J. (1997). The effects of poverty on child health and development. *Annual Review of Public Health, 18*, 463–483.

Achenbach, T. M., & Rescorla, L. A. (2000). *Manual for the ASEBA preschool forms & profiles.* Burlington, VT: ASEBA.

Achenbach, T. M., & Rescorla, L. (2001). *ASEBA school-age forms & profiles.* Burlington, VT: ASEBA.

Achenbach, T. M., & Rescorla, L. A. (2007). *Multicultural understanding of child and adolescent psychopathology: Implications for mental health assessment.* New York: Guilford Press.

Achenbach, T. M., & Rescorla, L. A. (2010). *Multicultural supplement to the manual for the ASEBA preschool forms & profiles.* Burlington, VT: University of Vermont, Research Center for Children, Youth, & Families.

Ahmad, F., Driver, N., McNally, M. J., & Stewart, D. E. (2009). 'Why doesn't she seek help for partner abuse?' An exploratory study with South Asian immigrant women. *Social Science & Medicine, 69*(4), 613–622.

Ainsworth, M. D. S., Blehar, M. C., Waters, E., & Wall, S. (1978). *Patterns of attachment: A psychological study of the strange situation.* Oxford: Lawrence Erlbaum Association.

Alegria, M., Atkins, M., Farmer, E., Slaton, E., & Stelk, W. (2010). One size does not fit all: Taking diversity, culture and context seriously. *Administration and Policy in Mental Health and Mental Health Services Research, 37*(1–2), 48–60.

Aleinikoff, T., Martin, D., Motomura, H., & Fullerton, M. (2011). *Immigration and citizenship: Process and policy.* St. Paul, MN: West Academic Press.

Allen, B., Cisneros, E. M., & Tellez, A. (2015). The children left behind: The impact of parental deportation on mental health. *Journal of Child and Family Studies, 24*(2), 386–392.

Allodi, F. A. (1991). Assessment and treatment of torture victims: A critical review. *Journal of Nervous & Mental Disease, 179*(1), 4–11.

Amato, P. R. (1991). Parental absence during childhood and depression in later life. *The Sociological Quarterly, 32*(4), 543–556.

Amato, P. R., & Keith, B. (1991) Parental divorce and the well-being of children: A meta-analysis. *Psychological Bulletin, 110*, 26–46.

American Bar Association. (2015). *Representing detained immigration respondents of diminished capacity: Ethical challenges and best practices.* Washington, DC: Author.

American Psychiatric Association (2000). *Diagnostic and statistical manual of mental disorders* (4th ed., rev.). Washington, DC: American Psychiatric Press.

American Psychiatric Association (2013). *Diagnostic and statistical manual of mental disorders* (5th ed.). Washington, DC: American Psychiatric Press.

American Psychological Association. (1996). *Report of the APA presidential task force on violence and the family.* Washington, DC: Author.

American Psychological Association. (2002). *APA ethical principles of psychologists and code of conduct.* Washington, DC: Author.

American Psychological Association. (2003). Guidelines on multicultural education, training, research, practice, and organizational change for psychologists. *American Psychologist, 58*(5), 377–402.

American Psychological Association. (2010). 2010 Amendments to the 2002 'Ethical principles of psychologists and code of conduct'. *American Psychologist, 65*(5), 493–493.

American Psychological Association (2012a). *Crossroads: The psychology of immigration in the new century. Report of the Presidential Task Force on Immigration.* Washington, DC: Author.

American Psychological Association. (2012b). Guidelines for psychological practice with lesbian, gay, and bisexual clients. *American Psychologist, 67*(1), 10–42.

American Psychological Association. (2013). Specialty guidelines for forensic psychology. *American Psychologist, 68,* 7–19.

American Psychological Association. (2017). Ethical principles of psychologists and code of conduct. Retrieved from www.apa.org/ethics/code.

Ammar, N. H., Orloff, L., Dutton, M. A., & Hass, G. A. (2004, September). Children of battered immigrant women: An assessment of the cumulative effects of violence, access to services and immigrant status. Paper presented at the *Meeting of International Family Violence Conference*, San Diego, CA (pp. 19–25).

Ammar, N. H., Orloff, L., Dutton, M. A., & Hass, G. (2005). Calls to police and police response: A case study from the Latina immigrant women in the U.S. *Journal of International Police Science and Management, 7*(4), 230–244.

Ammar, N., Orloff, L. E., Dutton, M. A., & Hass, G. A. (2012). Battered immigrant women in the United States and protection orders: An exploratory research. *Criminal Justice Review, 37*(3), 337–359.

Amnesty International. (2015). *Amnesty International report 2014/2015: The state of the world's human rights.* London: Author.

Andrews, D. A., & Bonta, J. (1995). *The level of service inventory – revised manual.* North Tonawanda, NY: Multi-Health Systems.

Anker, D. E. (2016) *Law of asylum in the United States.* Eagan, MN: Thomson West.

Anker, D. (2017). *Law of asylum in the United States,* (2017 ed.). Eagan, MN: Thomson West Academic.

Arbisi, P. A., Kaler, M. E., Kehle-Forbes, S. M., Erbes, C. R., Polusny, M. A., & Thuras, P. (2012). The predictive validity of the PTSD checklist in a nonclinical sample of combat-exposed national guard troops. *Psychological Assessment, 24*(4), 1034–1040.

Archer, R. P., & Wheeler, E. M. (Eds.). (2013). *Forensic uses of clinical assessment instruments.* New York: Routledge.

Armstrong, J. G. (1991). The psychological organization of multiple personality disordered patients as revealed in psychological testing. *Psychiatric Clinics of North America, 14,* 533–546.

Armstrong, J. G. (2002). Deciphering the broken narrative of trauma: Signs of traumatic dissociation on the Rorschach. *Rorschachiana, 25*(1), 11–27.

Armstrong, J. G., & Lowenstein, R. (1990). Characteristics of patients with multiple personality and dissociative disorders on psychological testing. *Journal of Nervous and Mental Disease, 174,* 448–454.

Baldas, T. (2017, April 22). *Genital mutilation victims break their silence: This is demonic.* New York, NY: Free Press.

Balgopal, P. R. (Ed.). (2000). *Social work practice with immigrants and refugees.* New York, NY: Columbia University Press.

Basoglu, M. (Ed.). (1992). *Torture and its consequences: Current treatment approaches.* Cambridge: Cambridge University Press.

Bauer, M., & Ramírez, M. (2010). *Injustice on our plates: Immigrant women in the U.S. food industry.* Montgomery, AL: The Southern Poverty Law Center.

BBC News (2017, April 22). Lebanon rape law: Wedding dresses hang in Beirut sea front protest. Retrieved from www.bbc.com/news/world-middle-east.

Beare, M. E. (1999). Illegal migration: Personal tragedies, social problems, or national security threats? *Illegal Immigration and Commercial Sex, 11,* 30.

Beck, A. T., Epstein, N., Brown, G., & Steer, R. A. (1988). An inventory for measuring clinical anxiety: Psychometric properties. *Journal of Consulting and Clinical Psychology.* 56: 893–897.

Beck, A. T., Ward, C. H., Mendelson, M., Mock, J., & Erbaugh, J. (1961). An inventory for measuring depression. *Archives of General Psychiatry,* 4 (6), 561–71.

Bengston, B., & Baldwin, C. (1993). The international student: Female circumcision issues. *Journal of Multicultural Counseling and Development, 21*(3), 168–173.

Bergman, B. K., & Brismar, B. G. (1992). Do not forget the battered male! A comparative study of family and non-family violence victims. *Scandinavian Journal of Social Medicine, 20,* 179–183.

Bernstein, E., & Putnam, F. (1986). Development, reliability, and validity of a dissociation scale. *Journal of Nervous and Mental Disease, 174,* 727–734.

Blais, M. A., Baity, M. R., & Hopwood, C. J. (Eds.). (2010). *Clinical applications of the Personality Assessment Inventory.* New York: Routledge.

Blake, D. D., Weathers, F. W., Nagy, L. M., Kaloupek, D., Gusman, F. D., Charney, D. S., & Keane, T. M. (1995). The development of a clinician-administered PTSD scale. *Journal of Traumatic Stress, 8*(1), 75–90.

Blanchard, E. B., Jones-Alexander, J., Buckley, T. C., & Forneris, C. A. (1996). Psychometric properties of the PTSD checklist (PCL). *Behavioral Research & Therapy, 34,* 669–673.

Bliese, P. D., Wright, K. M., Adler, A. B., Cabrera, O., Castrol, C. A., & Hoge, C. W. (2008). Validating the primary care posttraumatic stress disorder screen and the posttraumatic stress disorder checklist with soldiers returning from combat. *Journal of Consulting and Clinical Psychology, 76,* 272–281.

Board of Immigration Appeals (2011). *Matter of M-A-M-25 I&N* Dec. 474.

Board of Trustees of the Society for Personality Assessment. (2005). The status of the Rorschach in clinical and forensic practice: An official statement by the Board of Trustees of the Society for Personality Assessment. *Journal of Personality Assessment, 85*(2), 219–237.

Boer, D. P., Hart, S. D., Kropp, P. R., & Webster, C. D. (1997). *Manual for the Sexual Violence Risk-20.* Vancouver, BC: British Columbia Institute Against Family Violence.

Bornstein, R. F. (2002). A process dissociation approach to objective–projective test score interrelationships. *Journal of Personality Assessment, 78*(1), 47–68.

Bornstein, R. F. (2006a). Toward a process-based framework for classifying personality tests: Comment on Meyer and Kurtz. *Journal of Personality Assessment, 89*(2), 202–207.

Bornstein, R. F. (2006b). Rorschach assessment of dependent personality disorder. In S. K. Huprich (Ed.), *Rorschach assessment to the personality disorders: The LEA series in personality and clinical psychology.* (pp. 289–310). Mahwah, NJ: Lawrence Erlbaum Associates.

Borum, R., & Grisso, T. (1996). Establishing standards for criminal forensic reports: An empirical analysis. *Bulletin of the American Academy of Psychiatric Law, 24*(3), 297–317.

Bourg, S., Connor, E. J., & Landis, E. E. (1995). The impact of expertise and sufficient information on psychologists' ability to detect malingering. *Behavioral Sciences & the Law, 13*(4), 505–515.

Bow J. N., & Quinnell, F. A. (2001). Psychologists' current practices and procedures in child custody evaluations: five years after American Psychological Association guidelines. *Professional Psychology, 32*, 261–268.

Bowlby, J. (2008). *A secure base: Parent–child attachment and healthy human development.* New York, NY: Basic Books.

Brabeck, K., & Xu, Q. (2010). The impact of detention and deportation on Latino immigrant children and families: A quantitative exploration. *Hispanic Journal of Behavioral Sciences, 32*(3), 341–361.

Brabender, V. M., & Mihura, J. L. (Eds.). (2016). *Handbook of gender and sexuality in psychological assessment.* New York, NY: Routledge.

Brand, B. L (2016, November 18). *I don't trust you but you are my last hope: Assessing and treating complex trauma.* Speech presented at the DCPA Center for Learning & Professional Development in the Chicago School of Professional Psychology, Washington, DC.

Brand, B. L., Armstrong, J. G., & Loewenstein, R. J. (2006). Psychological assessment of patients with dissociative identity disorder. *Psychiatric Clinics of North America, 29*, 145–168.

Breiding, M. J., Black, M. C., & Ryan, G. W. (2008). Chronic disease and health risk behaviors associated with intimate partner violence: 18 U.S. states/territories, 2005. *Annals of Epidemiology, 18*(7), 538–544.

Breslau, N., Kessler, R. C., Chilcoat, H. D., Schultz, L. R., Davis, G. C., & Andreski, P. (1998). Trauma and posttraumatic stress disorder in the community: The 1996 Detroit area survey of trauma. *Archives of General Psychiatry, 55*(7), 626–632.

Briere, J. (1995). *Trauma symptom inventory professional manual.* Odessa, FL: Psychological Assessment Resources.

Briere, J. (2001). *Detailed assessment of posttraumatic stress (DAPS).* Odessa, FL: Psychological Assessment Resources.

Briere, J. (2004). *Psychological assessment of adult posttraumatic states: Phenomenology, diagnosis, and measurement* (2nd ed.). Washington, DC: American Psychological Association.

Briere, J. (2010). *Trauma symptom inventory: Second edition (TSI-2),* Odessa, FL: Psychological Assessment Resources.

Briere, J., & Elliott, D. M. (1997). Psychological assessment of interpersonal victimization effects in adults and children. *Psychotherapy: Theory, Research, Practice, Training, 34*(4), 353–364.

Briere, J., & Scott, C. (2014). *Principles of trauma therapy: A guide to symptoms, evaluation, and treatment, 2nd edition, DSM-5 update*. Thousand Oaks, CA: Sage.

Bronfenbrenner, K. (2009, May 20). *No holds barred: The intensification of employer opposition to organizing* (Briefing Paper No. 235). Washington, DC: Economic Policy Institute. Retrieved from www.epi.org/publication/bp235/.

Bronfenbrenner, U. (1977). Toward an experimental ecology of human development. *American Psychologist, 37*(7), 513–531.

Brooks-Gunn, J., & Duncan, G. J. (1997). The effects of poverty on children. *Future of Children, 7,* 55–57.

Brown, L. S. (2008). *Cultural competence in trauma therapy: Beyond the flashback.* Washington, DC: American Psychological Association.

Browne, A. (1987). *When battered women kill.* New York, NY: Free Press.

Bryer, J. B., Nelson, B. A., Miller, J. B., & Krol, B. A. (1987). Childhood sexual and physical abuse as factors in adult psychiatric illness. *American Journal of Psychiatry, 144,* 1426–1430.

Bureau of Labor Statistics, US Department of Labor (2017) *Agricultural workers, occupational outlook handbook* (13th ed.). Retrieved from www.bls.gov/ooh/farming-fishing-and-forestry/agricultural-workers.htm.

Butcher, J. N. (1996). *International adaptations of the MMPI-2: Research and clinical applications.* Minneapolis, MN: University of Minnesota Press.

Butcher, J. N. (2010). Personality assessment without borders: Adaptation of the MMPI-2 across cultures. *Journal of Personality Assessment, 83,* 90–104.

Butcher, J. N., & Perry, J. N. (2008). *Personality assessment in treatment planning: Use of the MMPI-2 and BTPI.* New York: Oxford University Press.

Butcher, J. N., Dahlstrom, W. G., Graham, J. R., Tellegen, A., & Kaemmer, B. (1989). *Minnesota Multiphasic Personality Inventory 2 (MMPI-2): Manual for administration and scoring.* Minneapolis, MN: University of Minnesota Press.

Butcher, J. N., Hass, G. A., Greene, R. L., & Nelson, L. (2015). *Using the MMPI-2 in forensic assessment.* Washington, DC: American Psychological Association.

Butcher, J. N., Mosch, S. C., Tsai, J., & Nezami, E. (2006). *Cross-cultural applications of the MMPI-2.* Washington, DC: American Psychological Association.

Buys, C. G. (2013). Right to counsel for immigrants: Franco-Gonzalez v. Holder. *The Globe, 51*(1), 5–6.

Campbell, J. C. (1992). 'If I can't have you, no one can': Power and control in homicide of female partners. In J. Radford & D. E. H. Russell (Eds.), *Femicide: The politics of woman killing* (pp. 99–113). New York, NY: Wayne.

Campbell, J. C., Webster, D. W., & Glass, N. (2009). The danger assessment: Validation of a lethality risk assessment instrument for intimate partner femicide. *Journal of Interpersonal Violence, 24*(4), 653–674.

Canales, E. J., Kan, L. Y., & Varela, J. G. (2017). Forensic assessment with Hispanic and limited English-proficient Hispanic evaluees: A survey of practice. *Professional Psychology: Research and Practice, 48*(2), 122–130.

Capital Area Immigrant's Rights Coalition. (2013, January). *Practice manual for pro bono attorneys representing detainees with mental disabilities in the immigration detention and removal system* (2nd ed.). S. Dekovich & L. McGrail (Eds.). Retrieved from www.caircoalition.org.

Carll, E., Gard, B., Salton, W. (Speakers), & APA Refugee Mental Health Resource Network Webinar. (Producer). (2017, May). *Working with interpreters with refugee populations in healthcare settings and for asylum evaluations* [Video]. Available form www.apatraumadivision.org.

Carlson, E. B. (1997). *Trauma assessments: A clinician's guide.* New York, NY: Guilford Press.

Carlson, E. B., & Putnam, F. W. (1993). An update on the dissociative experience scale. *Dissociation 6*(1), 16–27.

Carlson, E. B., Smith, S. R., Palmieri, P. A., Dalenberg, C. J., Ruzek, J. I., Kimerling, R., … & Spain, D. A. (2011). Development and validation of a brief self-report measure of trauma exposure: The trauma history screen. *Psychological Assessment, 23*, 463–477. Retrieved from www.ptsd.va.gov/professional/assessment/te-measures/ths.asp.

Carnelley, K. B., Wortman, C. B., & Kessler, R. C. (1999). The impact of widowhood on depression: Findings from a prospective survey. *Psychological Medicine, 29*, 1111–1123.

Cassidy, J., & Shaver, P. R. (Eds.). (2008). *Handbook of attachment: Theory, research, and clinical applications* (2nd ed.). New York: Guilford Press.

Cavazos-Rehg, P. A., Zayas, L. H., & Spitznagel, E. L. (2007). Legal status, emotional well-being and subjective health status of Latino immigrants. *Journal of the National Medical Association, 99*, 1126.

Center for Reproductive Rights. (n.d.). *Female genital mutilation (FGM): Legal prohibitions worldwide* [Fact sheet]. Retrieved from www.reproductiverights.org/document/female-genital-mutilation-fgm-legal-prohibitions-worldwide.

Cerel, J., Fristad, M. A., Verducci, J., Weller, R. A., & Weller, E. B. (2006). Childhood bereavement: Psychopathology in the 2 years postparental death. *Journal of the American Academy of Child & Adolescent Psychiatry, 45*(6), 681–690.

Cervantes, J. M., Mejía, O. L., & Guerrero Mena, A. (2010). Serial migration and the assessment of extreme and unusual psychological hardship with undocumented Latina/o families. *Hispanic Journal of Behavioral Sciences, 32*(2), 275–291.

Cervantes, R. C., Salgado de Snyder, V. N., & Padilla, A. M. (1989). Posttraumatic stress in immigrants from Central America and Mexico. *Hospital & Community Psychiatry, 40*, 615–619.

Cho, E. H., Hass, G. A., & Saucedo, L. (2015). A new understanding of substantial abuse: Evaluating harm in U visa petitions for immigrant victims of workplace crime. *Georgetown Immigration Law Journal, 29* (1), 5–43.

Code of Federal Regulations of the United States of America (C.F.R). (2015). Retrieved from www.govinfo.gov/help/cfr.

Colls, C. G., & Marks, A. K. (2012). *The immigrant paradox in children and adolescents: Is becoming American a developmental risk?* Washington, DC: American Psychological Association.

Committee on the Ethical Guidelines for Forensic Psychologists. (1991). Specialty guidelines for forensic psychologists. *Law and Human Behavior, 15*, 655–665.

Compton, K. M., & Chechile, D. (1998). Female genital mutilation. In E. J. Kramer, S. L. Ivy, & Y. W. Ying (Eds.), *Immigrant women's health: Problems and solutions* (pp. 194–395). New York, NY: Jossey Bass.

Conroy, M. A. & Kwartner, P. P. (2006). Malingering. *Applied Psychology in Criminal Justice, 2* (3), 29–48.

Cook, P. W. (2009). *Abused men: The hidden side of domestic violence.* Westport, CT: Praeger.

Coons, P. M., Cole, C., Pellow, T. A., & Milstein, V. (1990). Symptoms of posttraumatic stress and dissociation in women victims of abuse. In R. P. Kluft (Ed.), *Incest-related syndromes of adult psychopathology.* (pp. 205–225). Washington, DC: American Psychiatric Association.

Cooper, B. (2002). A new approach to protection and law enforcement under the victims of trafficking and violence protection act. *Emory Law Journal, 51*(3), 1041–1058.

Costantino, G., Dana, R. H., & Malgady, R. G. (2007). *TEMAS (tell-me-a-story) assessment in multicultural societies.* Mahwah, NJ: Lawrence Erlbaum Associates.

Costantino, G., Malgady, R. G., & Rogler, L. H. (1988). *TEMAS: (tell-me-a-story).* Los Angeles, CA: Western Psychological Services.

Courtois, C. A., & Ford, J. D. (2009). *Treating complex traumatic stress disorders: An evidence-based guide.* New York, NY: Guilford Press.

Craig, L. A., Browne, K. D., & Beech, A. R. (2008). *Assessing risk in sex offenders: A practitioner's guide.* Chichester: John Wiley & Sons.

Cramer, P. (2006). *Protecting the Self: Defense mechanisms in action.* New York, NY: Guilford Press.

Cunliffe, T. B., Gacono, C. B., Meloy, R., Smith, J. M., Taylor, E. E., & Landry, D. (2013). Psychopathy and the Rorschach: A response to Wood et al. (2010). *Archives of Assessment Psychology, 2*(1), 1–31.

Dana, R. H. (2005). *Multicultural assessment: Principles, applications, and examples.* Mahwah, NJ: Lawrence Erlbaum Associates.

Davis, D., & Follette, W. C. (2001). Foibles of witness memory for traumatic/high profile events. *Journal of Air Law and Commerce, 66*(4), 1421.

Dawes, S. E., Palmer, B. W., & Jeste, D. V. (2008). Adjudicative competence. *Current Opinion in Psychiatry, 21*(5), 490–494.

De Jesús-Rentas, G., Boehnlein, J., & Sparr, L. (2010). Central American victims of gang violence as asylum seekers: The role of the forensic expert. *Journal of the American Academy of Psychiatry and Law, 38*(4), 490–498.

de Ruiter, C., & Kaser-Boyd, N. (2015). *Forensic psychological assessment in practice: Case studies.* New York, NY: Taylor & Francis.

de Vries, B., Davis, C. G., Wortman, C. B., & Lehman, D. R. (1997). Long-term psychological and somatic consequences of later life parental bereavement. *Omega: Journal of Death & Dying, 35*, 97–117.

Department of Homeland Security New classification for victims of criminal activity; eligibility for 'U' nonimmigrant status; interim Rule, 72 Federal Register. § 179 (Proposed Sep. 17, 2007) (to be codified at 8 C.F.R. pt. 103, 212, 214, 248, 274a and 299).

Department of Homeland Security. (2015). *U and T Visa Law Enforcement Resource Guide for Federal, State, Local, Tribal and Territorial Law Enforcement, Prosecutors, Judges, and Other Government Agencies.* Retrieved from http://niwaplibrary.wcl. American.edu/pubs/dhs-updated-u-certification-resource-guide-2015.

Dignam, Q. (1992). The burden and the proof: Torture and testimony in the determination of refugee status in Australia. *International Journal of Refugee Law, 4*, 343–363.

Doezema, J. (2000). Loose women or lost women? The re-emergence of the myth of white slavery in contemporary discourses of trafficking in women. *Gender Issues, 18*(1), 23–50.

Domestic Abuse Intervention Program. (n.d.) Power and control wheel [Poster]. Retrieved from www.theduluthmodel.org/wheels.

Dong, Y-L. T., & Church, A. T. (2003). Cross-cultural equivalence and validity of the Vietnamese MMPI-2: Assessing psychological adjustment of Vietnamese refugees. *Psychological Assessment, 15*(3), 370–377.

Douglas, K. S., Hart, S. D., Webster, C. D., & Belfrage, H. (2013). *HCR-20V3: Assessing risk of violence: user guide.* Burnaby: Mental Health, Law, and Policy Institute, Simon Fraser University.

Dross, P. (2000). *Survivors of politically motivated torture: A large, growing, and invisible population of crime victims.* Washington, DC: Office of Justice Programs, U.S. Department of Justice.

Dusky v. United States, No. 504 (April 18, 1960).

Dutton, D. G. (1995). *The batterer: A psychological profile.* New York, NY: Basic Books.

Dutton, D. G. (2007). The *abusive personality: Violence and control in intimate relationships* (2nd ed.). New York, NY: Guilford Press.

Dutton, M. A. (1992). *Empowering and healing the battered woman: A model for assessment and intervention.* New York, NY: Springer.

Dutton, M. A. (2000). *Empowering and healing the battered woman.* New York, NY: Springer.

Dutton, M. A. (2015). *IPV threat appraisal scale and fear scale* [Measurement instrument]. Retrieved from http://niwaplibrary.wcl.American.edu/pubs/traum-temp-ipvappraisalfearsc.

Dutton, M. A., & Goodman, L. A. (2005). Coercion in intimate partner violence: Towards a new conceptualization. *Sex Roles, 52*(11–12), 743–756.

Dutton, M. A., & Hass, G. A. (2004). Use of expert testimony concerning battering and its effects on immigrant women. In *Domestic violence and immigration: Applying the immigration provisions of the Violence Against Women Act: A training manual for attorneys and advocates.* Washington, DC: American Bar Association.

Dutton, M. A., Orloff, L. E., & Hass, G. (2000). Characteristics of help-seeking behaviors: Resources and service needs of battered immigrant Latinas: Legal and policy implications. *Georgetown Journal on Poverty, Law & Policy, VII* (2), 245–305.

Dutton, M. A., Szabo, K., Molina, R., Fletcher, M. A., Lorduy, M. V., Yang, E., & Orloff, L. (2013). Trauma informed structured interview questionnaires for immigration cases (SIQI). The National Immigrant Women's Advocacy Project. Retrieved from: http://library.niwap.org/wp-content/uploads/2015/TRAUM-Tool-InterviewQuestions SIQI-7.10.17.pdf.

Einarsen, S., Hoel, H., Zapf, D., & Cooper, C. L. (Eds.). (2011). *Bullying and harassment in the workplace: Developments in theory, research and practice* (2nd ed.). London: CRC Press.

Elhai, J. D., Frueh, B. C., Gold, P. B., Gold, S. N., & Hamner, M. B. (2008). Clinical presentations of posttraumatic stress disorder across trauma populations: A comparison of MMPI-2 profiles of combat veterans and adult survivors of child sexual abuse. *Journal of Nervous & Mental Disease, 88*, 708–713.

Ephraim, D. (2002). Rorschach trauma assessment of survivors of torture and state violence [Assessment instrument]. In A. Andronikof (Ed.), *Rorschachiana XXV: Yearbook of the International Rorschach Society.* (pp. 58–76). Ashland, OH: Hogrefe & Huber.

Erard, R. E., & Evans, F. B. (Eds.). (2017). *The Rorschach in multimethod forensic assessment conceptual foundations and practical applications.* New York, NY: Routledge.

Erdberg, P. (2005, July). Intercoder agreement as a measure of ambiguity of coding guidelines. Paper presented at the *XVIII International Congress of Rorschach and Projective Methods*, Barcelona, Spain.

Erdberg, P. S. (2008). Multimethod assessment as a forensic standard. In C. B. Gacono, F. B. Evans (Eds.) & N. Kaser-Boyd, L. A. Gacono (Collaborators), *The handbook of forensic Rorschach assessment* (pp. 561–566). New York: Routledge.

Erdberg, P., & Schaffer, T. W. (1999). International symposium on Rorschach nonpatient data: Findings from around the world. Paper presented at the *International Congress of Rorschach and Projective Methods*, Amsterdam, the Netherlands.

Esquivel, G. B., Oades-Sese, G. V., & Olitzky, S. L. (2008). Multicultural issues in projective assessment. In L. A. Suzuki & J. G. Ponterotto (Eds.), *Handbook of multicultural assessment: Clinical, psychological, and educational applications* (pp. 346–374). San Francisco, CA: Jossey Bass.

Evans, F. B., III. (2000). Forensic psychology and immigration court: An introduction. In R. Auberbach (Ed.) *Handbook of immigration and nationality law* (Vol. 2, pp. 446–458). Washington, DC: American Immigration Lawyers Association.

Evans, F. B. (2002). *Evans evaluation of difficulties interview (EEDI)*. Asheville, NC: Author.

Evans, F. B., III. (2004). Family violence, immigration law, and the Rorschach. *Yearbook of the International Rorschach Society, 26*(1), 147–157.

Evans, F. B., III. (2005). Trauma, torture, and transformation in the forensic assessor. *Journal of Personality Assessment, 84*(1), 25–28.

Evans, F. B. (2008). *The Rorschach and immigration evaluations*. In C. B. Gacono & F. B. Evans III (Eds.), *The LEA series in personality and clinical psychology: The handbook of forensic Rorschach assessment* (pp. 489–504). New York, NY: Routledge.

Evans, F. B. (2012). Assessment in psychological trauma: Methods and intervention. In L. L. Levers (ed.). *Trauma counseling: Theories and interventions* (pp. 471–492). New York, NY: Springer.

Evans, F. B. (2016). What torture survivors teach assessors about being more fully human. *Journal of Personality Assessment, 98*(6), 590–593.

Evans, N., & Levinson, S. C. (2009). The myth of language universals: Language diversity and its importance for cognitive science. *Behavioral and Brain Sciences, 32*(5), 429–492.

Exner, J. E, Jr. (2003). *The Rorschach: A comprehensive system, basic foundations* (4th ed.). New York, NY: John Wiley & Sons.

Exner, J. E., Jr. (1974). *The Rorschach: A comprehensive system* (Vol. 1). *Basic foundations*. New York, NY: John Wiley & Sons.

Federal Rules of Civil Procedure (2017). Rule 26: Duty to disclose; General provisions governing discovery. Retrieved from www.federalrulesofcivilprocedure.org/frcp/title-v-disclosures-and-discovery/rule-26-duty-to-disclose-general-provisions-governing-discovery.

Fernandez, K., Boccaccini, M., & Noland, R. (2008). Detecting over- and underreporting of psychopathology with the Spanish-language personality assessment inventory: findings from a simulation study with bilingual speakers. *Psychological Assessment, 20*(2), 189–194.

Filone, S., & DeMatteo, D. (2017). Assessing 'credible fear': A psychometric examination of the trauma symptom inventory-2 in the context of immigration court evaluations. *Psychological Assessment, 29*(6), 701–709.

Finn, S. E. (2007). *In our clients' shoes: Theory and techniques of therapeutic assessment*. Mahwah, NJ: Lawrence Erlbaum Associates.

Finn, S. E., & Tonsager, M. E. (2002). How therapeutic assessment became humanistic. *The Humanistic Psychologist, 30* (1–2), 10–22.

First, M. B., Williams, J. B. W., Karg, R. S., & Spitzer, R. L. (2015). *Structured clinical interview for DSM-5 disorders, clinician version (SCID-5-CV)*. Arlington, VA: American Psychiatric Association.

Fitzgerald, L. F., Drasgow, F., Hulin, C. L., Gelfand, M. J., & Magley, V. J. (1997). Antecedents and consequences of sexual harassment in organizations: A test of an integrated model. *Journal of Applied Psychology, 82*(4), 578.

Fitzgerald, L. F., Swan, S., & Fischer, K. (1995). Why didn't she just report him? The psychological and legal implications of women's responses to sexual harassment. *Journal of Social Issues, 51*(1), 117–122.

Fitzpatrick, M., & Orloff, L. E. (2016). Abused, abandoned, or neglected: Legal options for immigrant women and girls. *Penn State Journal of Law and International Affairs, 4*(2), 614–685.

Flanagan, R., Costantino, G., Cardalda, E., & Costantino, E. (2007). TEMAS: A multicultural test and its place in an assessment battery. *Handbook of Multicultural Assessment: Clinical, Psychological, and Educational Applications*, 323–345.

Foa, E. B. (1995). *Posttraumatic stress diagnostic scale (PDS) manual*. Minneapolis, MN: Pearson Assessments.

Foa, E. B., & Rothbaum, B. O. (1998). *The trauma of rape: Cognitive-behavioral therapy for PTSD*. New York, NY: Guilford Press.

Foa, E. B., & Tolin, D. F. (2000). Comparison of the PTSD symptom scale-interview version and the clinician administered PTSD scale. *Journal of Traumatic Stress, 13*, 181–191.

Foa, E. B., Riggs, D. S., Dancu, C. V., & Rothbaum, B. O. (1993). Reliability and validity of a brief instrument for assessing post-traumatic stress disorder. *Journal of Traumatic Stress, 6*, 459–473.

Foner, N. (2002). Second generation transnationalism, then and now. In P. Levitt & M. Waters. (Eds.), *The changing face of home: The transnational lives of the second generation* (pp. 242–252). New York, NY: Russell Sage Foundation.

Fontes, L. A. (2017, March). Translating trauma: Foreign language interpreting in therapy. *Psychology Today*. Retrieved from www.psychologytoday.com/blog/invisible-chains/201703/translating-trauma-foreign-language-interpreting-in-therapy.

Fontes, L. A., & McCloskey, K. A. (2011). Cultural issues in violence against women. In C. M. Renzetti, J. L. Edleson, & R. K. Bergen (Eds.), *Sourcebook on violence against women* (2nd ed., pp. 151–168). Thousand Oaks, CA: Sage.

Freire, P. (2005). *Pedagogy of the oppressed*. New York, NY: Continuum.

Freire, P., & Macedo, D. (1995). A dialogue: Culture, language, and race. *Harvard Educational Review. 65*(3), 377–403.

Freire, P., & Macedo, D. P. (1987). *Literacy: Reading the word & the world*. Westport, CT: Bergin & Garvey.

Frueh, B. C., Elhai, J. D., Gold, P. B., Monnier, J., Magruder, K. M., Keane, T. M., & Arana, G. W. (2003). Disability compensation seeking among veterans evaluated for posttraumatic stress disorder. *Psychiatric Services, 54*(1), 84–91.

Frumkind, I. B., & Friedland, J. (1995). Forensic evaluations in immigration cases: Evolving issues. *Behavioral Sciences and the Law, 13*, 477–489.

Fujimoto, J. J. (2000, June 16) Discussant on a paper by F. B. Evans III, forensic assessment and testimony in immigration court on the panel 'Practice Before the Immigration

Court'. Paper presented at the *Annual Meeting of the American Immigration Lawyers Association*, Chicago, IL.

Fuligni, A. (2001). A comparative longitudinal approach to acculturation among children from immigrant families. *Harvard Educational Review, 71*(3), 566–578.

Gacono, C. B., & Evans, F. B., III. (Eds.). (2008). The LEA series in personality and clinical psychology. In N. Kaser-Boyd, & L. A. Gacono (Collaborators), *The handbook of forensic Rorschach assessment.* New York, NY: Routledge.

Gacono, C., & Meloy, R. (1994). *The Rorschach assessment of aggressive and psychopathic personalities.* Hillsdale, NJ: Lawrence Erlbaum Associates.

Gacono, C. B., Evans, F. B., III., & Viglione, D. J. (2002). The Rorschach in forensic practice. *Journal of Forensic Psychology Practice, 2,* 33–54.

Gacono, C. B., Loving, J. L., Evans, F. B., III., & Jumes, M. T. (2002). The psychopathy checklist-revised: PCL-R testimony and forensic practice. *Journal of Forensic Psychology Practice, 2,* 11–32.

Gacono, C. B., Evans, F. B., III., & Viglione, D. J. (2008). Essential issues in Rorschach testimony. In C. B. Gacono & F. B. Evans III (Eds.), N. Kaser-Boyd, & L. A. Gacono (Collaborators), *The LEA series in personality and clinical psychology: The handbook of forensic Rorschach assessment.* New York, NY: Routledge.

Gacono, C., Gacono, L., & Evans, F. B., III. (2008). Conduct disorder, antisocial personality disorder, psychopathy & the Rorschach. In C. B. Gacono & F. B. Evans III (Eds.), *Handbook of forensic Rorschach psychology.* Mahwah, NJ: Lawrence Erlbaum Associates.

Galatzer-Levy, I. R., & Bryant, R. A. (2013). 636,120 ways to have posttraumatic stress disorder. *Perspectives on Psychological Science, 8,* 651–662.

Ganley, A. (1989). Integrating feminist and social learning analysis of aggression: Creating multiple models for intervention with men who battered. In P. Caesar & L. Hamberger (Eds.), *Treating men who batter: Theory, practice and programs* (pp. 196–235). New York City, NY: Springer.

Garb, H. N. (1998). *Studying the clinician: Judgment research and psychological assessment.* Washington, DC: American Psychological Association.

Garcia v. Audubon Communities Mgmt., L.L.C., No. 08-cv-01291-HGB-KWR (E.D. La. 2008).

Gardiner, S., & Mohan, G. (2001, March 21). Smuggled for sex: The sex slaves from Mexico. *Newsday*, A.05.

Gass, G. Z., & Nichols, W. C. (1988). Gaslighting: A marital syndrome. *Journal of Contemporary Family Therapy, 10*(1), 3–16.

George, C., & West, M. L. (2012). *The adult attachment projective picture system: Attachment theory and assessment in adults.* New York, NY: Guilford Press.

Getachew, E. (2004). Psychological consequences of female genital mutilation: Clinical implications. (Unpublished clinical research project). Argosy University, Washington DC

Giorgi, G., Ando, M., Arenas, A., Shoss, M. K., & Leon-Perez, J. M. (2013). Exploring personal and organizational determinants of workplace bullying and its prevalence in a Japanese sample. *Psychology of Violence, 3*(2), 185–197.

Gjersing, L., Caplehorn, J. R. M., & Clausen, T. (2010). Cross-cultural adaptation of research instruments: Language, setting, time and statistical considerations. *BMC Medical Research Methodology, 10,* 13.

Gorst-Unsworth, C., Van Velsen, C., & Turner, S. W. (1993). Prospective pilot study of survivors of torture and organized violence: Examining the existential dilemma. *Journal of Nervous and Mental Disease, 181*(4), 263–264.

Gotor, L., & González-Juárez, C. (2004). Psychiatric hospitalization and continuity of care in immigrants treated in Madrid (Spain). *Social Psychiatry and Psychiatric Epidemiology*, *39*(7), 560–568.

Graham, B., Herlihy, J., & Brewin, C. R. (2014). Overgeneral memory in asylum seekers and refugees. *Journal of Behavior Therapy and Experimental Psychiatry*, *45*(3), 375–380.

Grandey, A. A., Kern, J. H., & Frone, M. R. (2007). Verbal abuse from outsiders vs. insiders: Comparing frequency, impact on emotional exhaustion, and the role of emotional labor. *Journal of Occupational Health Psychology*, *12*(1), 63–79.

Gray, M. J., Litz, B. T., Hsu, J. L., & Lombardo, T. W. (2004). The psychometric properties of the Life Events Checklist. *Assessment, 11*, 330–341.

Gray-Little, B. (2002). The assessment of psychopathology in racial and ethnic minorities. In J. Butcher (Ed.), *Clinical personality assessment: Practical approaches* (pp. 171–189). New York: Oxford.

Greenberg, S. A. (2003). Personal injury examinations in torts for emotional distress. In A. M. Goldstein (Ed.), *Handbook of psychology: Forensic psychology* (Vol. 11, pp. 233–257). Hoboken, NJ: John Wiley.

Greenberg, S. A., & Shuman, D. W. (1997). Irreconcilable conflict between therapeutic and forensic roles. *Professional Psychology: Research & Practice, 28*, 50–57.

Greenberg, S. A., Otto, R. K., & Long, A. C. (2003). The utility of psychological testing in assessing emotional damages in personal injury litigation. *Assessment, 10*(4), 411–419.

Greene, R. L. (2000). *The MMPI-2: An interpretive manual* (2nd ed.). Needham Heights, MA: Allyn & Bacon.

Greenwood, R. M. (2012). Standing at the crossroads of identity: An intersectional approach to women's social identities and political consciousness. In S. Wiley, G. Philogène, & T. A. Revenson (Eds.), *Social categories in everyday experience*: Decade of behaviour (1st ed.; pp. 103–129). Washington, DC: American Psychological Association.

Griffith, E. E. H. (1998). Ethics in forensic psychiatry: A cultural response to Stone and Appelbaum. *Journal of the American Academy of Psychiatry and the Law, 26*, 171–184.

Griffith, E. E. H., Stankovic, A., & Baranoski, M. (2010). Conceptualizing the forensic psychiatry report as performative narrative. *The Journal of the American Academy of Psychiatry and the Law, 38*(1), 32–42.

Grisso, T. (2003). *Evaluating competencies: Forensic assessments and instruments* (2nd ed.). New York, NY: Kluwer Academic/Plenum Publishers.

Guttfreund, D. G. (1990). Effects of language usage on the emotional experience of Spanish-English and English-Spanish bilinguals. *Journal of Consulting and Clinical Psychology, 58*(5), 604–607.

Hagen, M. A. (1997). *Whores of the court: The fraud of psychiatric testimony and the rape of American justice*. New York: HarperCollins.

Hake, B. A. (1994). Hardship waivers for J-1 physicians. *Immigration Briefings, 94*(2), 1–71.

Hake, B. A., & Banks, D. L. (2005). The Hake hardship scale: A quantitative system for assessment of hardship in immigration cases based on a statistical analysis of AAO decisions. *Bender's Immigration Bulletin, 10*, 403–420.

Halperin, R. (2011). Sex trafficking of minors as a human rights issue. *Journal of Applied Research on Children: Informing Policy for Children at Risk, 2*(1), 1–4.

Hambleton, R. K. (2005). Issues, designs, and technical guidelines for adapting tests into multiple languages and cultures. In R. K. Hambleton, P. F. Merenda, & C. D. Spielberger (Eds.), *Adapting educational and psychological tests for cross-cultural assessment* (pp. 3–38). Mahwah, NJ: Lawrence Erlbaum.

Haney, C., & Zimbardo, P. (1998). The past and future of U.S. prison policy: Twenty-five years after the Stanford prison experiment. *American Psychologist, 53*, 709–727.

Hare, R. D. (1993). *Without conscience: The disturbing world of the psychopaths among us.* New York, NY: Guilford Press.

Hare, R. D. (1998). The Hare PCL-R: Some issues concerning its use and misuse. *Legal and Criminological Psychology, 3*, 101–122.

Hare, R. D. (2003). *Hare psychopathy checklist – revised manual* (2nd ed.). North Tonawanda, New York: Multi-Health Systems.

Hare, R. D., Clark, D., Grann, M., & Thornton, D. (2000) Psychopathy and the predictive validity of the PCL-R: An international perspective. *Behavioral Sciences and the Law, 18*, 623–645.

Harris, G. T., Rice, M. E., & Cormier, C. A. (1993). Violent recidivism of mentally disordered offenders: The development of a statistical prediction instrument. *Criminal Justice and Behavior, 20*, 315–335.

Hart, S. D., Cox, D. N., & Hare, R. D. (1995) *Manual for the psychopathy checklist: Screening version (PCL: SV).* Toronto: Multi-Health Systems.

Hartsough, T. (2002). Asylum for trafficked women: Escape strategies beyond the T visa. *Hastings Women's Law Journal, 13*(1), 77–116.

Hass, G. A., Ammar, N., & Orloff, L. E. (2006). *Battered immigrants and U.S. citizen spouses..* Retrieved from www.mincavaumn.edu/cgi-bin/documents.

Hass, G. A., Dutton, M. A., & Orloff, L. E. (2000). Lifetime prevalence of domestic violence against Latina immigrants: Legal and policy implications. *International Review of Victimology, 7*(1–3), 93–113.

Hays, J. C., Kasl, S., & Jacobs, S. (1994a). Past personal history of dysphoria, social support, and psychological distress following conjugal bereavement. *Journal of the American Geriatrics Society, 42*, 712–718.

Hays, J. C., Kasl, S. V., & Jacobs, S. C. (1994b). The course of psychological distress following threatened and actual conjugal bereavement. *Psychological Medicine, 24*, 917–927.

Hays, P. (2008). *Addressing cultural complexities in practice* (2nd ed.). Washington, DC: American Psychological Association.

Heeren, M., Mueller, J., Ehlert, U., Schnyder, U., Copiery, N., & Maier, T. (2012). Mental health of asylum seekers: A cross-sectional study of psychiatric disorders. *BioMed Central Psychiatry, 12*(1), 114–122.

Heilbrun, K., & Collins, S. (1995). Evaluations of trial competency and mental state at time of offense: Report characteristics. *Professional Psychology: Research and Practice, 26*, 61–67.

Heller, P. (2009). Challenges facing LGBT asylum-seekers: The role of social work in correcting oppressive immigration processes. *Journal of Gay & Lesbian Social Services, 21*(2–3), 294–308.

Herlihy, J., & Turner, S. W. (2007). Asylum claims and memory of trauma: Sharing our knowledge. *British Journal of Psychiatry, 191*, 3–4.

Herlihy, J., Jobson, L., & Turner, S. (2012). Just tell us what happened to you: Autobiographical memory and seeking asylum. *Applied Cognitive Psychology, 26*, 661–676.

Herlihy, J., Scragg, P., & Turner, S. (2002). Discrepancies in autobiographical memories: Implications for the assessment of asylum seekers – repeated interviews study. *British Medical Journal, 324*(7333), 324–327.

Herman, J. (1992a). *Trauma and recovery*. New York: Basic Books.

Herman, J. L. (1992b). *Trauma and recovery: The aftermath of violence from domestic abuse to political terror*. New York, NY: Basic Books.

Herman, J. L. (1992c). Complex PTSD: A syndrome in survivors of prolonged and repeated trauma. *Journal of Traumatic Stress, 5*, 377–391.

Herman, J. L. (1997) *Trauma and recovery* (rev. ed.). New York, NY: Basic Books.

Herman, J. L. (2011). Shattered shame states and their repair. In J. Yellin & K. White (Eds.), *Shattered states* (pp. 157–170). London: Karnac Books.

Herman J. L., Perry, J. C., & van der Kolk, B. A. (1989). Childhood trauma in borderline personality disorder. *American Journal of Psychiatry, 146*, 490–495.

Hilsenroth, M., Stein, M., & Pinsker, J. (2007). Social cognition and object relations scale: Global rating method (SCORS-G) (Unpublished manuscript). The Derner Institute of Advanced Psychological Studies, Adelphi University, Garden City, NY.

Hilton, N. Z., Harris, G. T., & Rice, M. E., (2010). *Risk assessment for domestically violent men: Tools for criminal justice, offender intervention, and victim services*. Washington, DC: American Psychological Association.

Hopwood, C., & Evans, F. B. (2017). Integrating the personality assessment inventory and Rorschach inkblot method in forensic assessment. In R. E. Erard & F. B. Evans (Eds.), *The Rorschach in multimethod forensic assessment: Conceptual foundations and practical applications* (pp. 131–159). New York, NY: Routledge.

Horowitz, M. J. (1993). Stress–response syndromes: A review of posttraumatic stress and adjustment disorders. In J. P. Wilson & B. Raphael (Eds.). *International handbook of traumatic stress syndromes* (pp. 49–60). New York, NY: Plenum Press.

Human Rights Watch. (2007). Forced apart: Families separated and immigrants harmed by United States deportation policy [Report]. *Human Rights Watch, 19*(3G). Retrieved from www.hrw.org/report.

Human Rights Watch (2013, July). *Egypt: Epidemic of sexual violence*. Retrieved from www.hrw.org/news/2013/07/03/egypt-epidemic-sexual-violence.

Human Rights Watch. (2017). Anti-LGBT violence in Chechnya: When filing 'official complaints' is not an option. Retrieved from: www.hrw.org/news/2017/04/04/anti-lgbt-violence-chechnya.

Huminuik, K. (2017). Special competencies for psychological assessment of torture survivors. *Transcultural Psychiatry, 54*(2), 239–259.

Immigration and Nationality Act of 1990, 8 U.S.C. § 1101(a) (27J).

Institute for Work and Health. (2011). At work. *Ethnicity & Health, 15*(6), 601–619.

International Center for Research on Women. (2016). Taking action to address child marriage: The role of different sectors [Fact sheet]. Retrieved from www.girlsnotbrides.org/wp-content/uploads/2016/03/1.-Overview-Addressing-child-marriage-role-of-diff-sectors.pdf.

International Women's Health Coalition (n.d.). The facts on child marriage [Fact sheet]. Retrieved from: https://iwhc.org/resources/facts-child-marriage.

Jacobs, U. (2008). Documenting the neurobiology of psychological torture: Conceptual and neuropsychological observations. In A. E. Ojeda (Ed.), *The trauma of psychological torture* (pp. 163–72). Westport, CT: Praeger.

Jacobs, U., Evans, F. B., & Patsilides, B. (2001a). Forensic psychology and documentation of torture (Pt. 1). *Torture, 11*(3), 85–89.

Jacobs, U., Evans, F. B., & Patsilides, B. (2001b). Forensic psychology and documentation of torture (Pt. 2). *Torture, 11*(4), 100–102.

Jay, J. (1991). Terrible knowledge. *Family therapy networker, 15*, 18–29.

Jenkins, S. R. (ed.). (2008). *A handbook of clinical scoring systems for thematic apperceptive techniques.* Mahwah, NJ: Lawrence Erlbaum Associates.

Jeon, W., Yu, S., Cho, Y., & Eom, J. (2008). Traumatic experiences and mental health of North Korea refugees in South Korea. *Psychiatry Investigation,* 5(4): 213–220. Retrieved from: www.ncbi.nlm.nih.gov/pmc/articles/PMC2796004/.

Jervis, R., Gomez, A., & Solis, G. (2017, April 17) Trump's new rules could swamp already backlogged immigration courts. *USA Today.* Retrieved from www.usatoday.com.

Jesus-Rentas, G., Boehnlein, J., & Sparr, L. (2010). Central American victims of gang violence as asylum seekers: The role of the forensic expert. *Journal of the American Academy of Psychiatry and the Law, 38*, 490–498.

Johnson, K. R., Aldana, R. E., Hing, B. O., Leticia, S., & Trucios-Haynes, E. (2015). *Understanding immigration law* (2nd ed.). Danvers, MA: LexisNexis.

Kaffman, M., & Elizur, E. (1984). Children's bereavement reactions following death of the father. *International Journal of Family Therapy, 6*, 259–283.

Kamphuis, J. H., Kugeares, S. L., & Finn, S. E. (2000). Rorschach correlates of sexual abuse: Trauma content and aggression indexes. *Journal of Personality Assessment, 75*(2), 212–224.

Kandel, W., & Parrado, E. A. (2005). Restructuring of the U.S. meat processing industry and new Hispanic migrant destinations. *Population Development. and Review, 31*(3) 447–471.

Kapoor, S. (2000). *Domestic violence against women and girls.* Florence: United Nations Children's Fund.

Kaser-Boyd, N. (1993). Rorschachs of women who commit homicide. *Journal of Personality Assessment, 60*, 458–470.

Kaser-Boyd, N. (2004). Battered woman syndrome: Clinical features, evaluation, and expert testimony. In B. J. Cling (Ed.). *Sexualized violence against women and children: A psychology and law perspective.* (pp. 41–70). New York, NY: Guilford Press.

Kaser-Boyd, N. (2008). Battered woman syndrome: Assessment-based expert testimony. In C. B. Gacono & F. B. Evans (Eds.), *Handbook of forensic Rorschach psychology.* Matwah, NJ: Lawrence Erlbaum Associates.

Kaser-Boyd, N., & Evans, F. B. (2008). Rorschach assessment of psychological trauma. In C. B. Gacono & F. B. Evans (with N. Kaser-Boyd & L. A. Gacono) (Eds.), *Handbook of forensic Rorschach psychology* (pp. 255–277). New York, NY: Routledge.

Kassindja, F., & Miller, L. M. (1998). *Do they hear you when you cry.* New York, NY: Delta.

Keane, T. M., Caddell, J. M., & Taylor, K. L. (1988). Mississippi scale for combat-related posttraumatic stress disorder: Three studies in reliability and validity. *Journal of Consulting and Clinical Psychology, 56*, 85–90.

Keane, T. M., Malloy, P. F., & Fairbank, K. A. (1984). Empirical development of an MMPI subscale for the assessment of combat-related posttraumatic stress disorder. *Journal of Consulting & Clinical Psychology,* 51, 888–891.

Keane, T., Fairbank, J., Caddell, J., Zimering, R., Taylor, K., & Mora, C. (1989). Clinical evaluation of a measure to assess combat exposure. *Psychological Assessment, 1*, 53–55.

Keiser, R. E., & Prather, E. N. (1990). What is the TAT? A review of ten years of research. *Journal of Personality Assessment, 55*(3–4), 800–803.

Kesselbrenner, D., & Rosenberg, L. D. (2016). *Immigration law and crimes* (2nd ed.). New York, NY: Clark Boardman Callaghan.

Kessler, R. C., Sonnega, A., Bromet, E., Hughes, M., & Nelson, C. B. (1995). Posttraumatic stress disorder in the national comorbidity survey. *Archives General Psychiatry. 52*, 1048–1060.

Kim, H. Y. (2007). Do I really understand? Cultural concerns in determining diminished competency. *Elder Law Journal, 15*, 265.

Kissane, M., Szymanski, L., Upthegrove, R., & Katona, C. (2014). Complex posttraumatic stress disorder in traumatised asylum seekers: A pilot study. *European Journal of Psychiatry, 28*(3), 137–144.

Knapp, S., & VandeCreek, L. (2001). Ethical issues in personality A assessment in forensic psychology. *Journal of Personality Assessment, 77*(2), 242–254.

Korngold, C., Ochoa, K., Inlender, T., McNiel, D., & Binder, R. (2015). Mental health and immigrant detainees in the United States: Competency and self-representation. *Journal of the American Academy of Psychiatry and Law, 43*(3), 277–281.

Kowalski, D. M. (2015, September 25). Immigrant with mental disabilities may reopen deportation cases: Franco Gonzalez v. Holder. *LexisNexis Legal Newsroom Immigration Law*. Retrieved from www.lexisnexis.com/legalnewsroom.

Krauss, D. A., & Sales, B. D. (2001). The effects of clinical and scientific expert testimony on juror decision making in capital sentencing. *Psychology, Public Policy, and Law, 7*(2), 267–310.

Krug, E. G., Dahlberg, L. L., Mercy, J. A., Zwi, A. B., & Lozano, R. (Eds.). (2002). *World report on violence and health: Violence by intimate partners*. Geneva: World Health Organization.

Kubiszyn, T., Meyer, G. J., Finn, S. E., Eyde, L. D., Kay, G. G., Moreland, K. L., Dies, R. R., & Eisman, E. J. (2000). Empirical support for psychological assessment in clinical health care settings. *Professional Psychology: Research and Practice, 31*(2), 119–130.

Kwartner, P. P., & Boccaccini, M. T. (2007). Testifying in court: Evidence-based recommendations for expert witness testimony. In R. Jackson (Ed.). *Learning forensic assessment* (pp. 565–588). New York, NY: Routledge.

Lally, S. J. (2003). What tests are acceptable for use in forensic evaluations? A survey of experts. *Professional Psychology: Research and Practice, 34*(5), 491–498.

Lax, R. F. (2000). Socially sanctioned violence against women: Female genital mutilation in its most brutal form. *Clinical Social Work Journal, 28*(4), 403–412.

Lee, M. C., Friedmann, E., Kverno, K., Newhouse, R., Zhang, D., & Thomas, S. (2015). Psychological distress among Chinese immigrants to the USA. *International Journal of Culture and Mental Health, 8*(2), 150–161.

Lehman, D. R., Lang, E. L., Wortman, C. B., & Sorenson, S. B. (1989). Long-term effects of sudden bereavement: Marital and parent/child relationships and children's reactions. *Journal of Family Psychology, 2*, 344–367.

Lewak, R. W., & Hogan, R. S. (2003). Integrating and applying assessment information: Decision making, patient feedback, and consultation. In L. E. Beutler & G. Groth-Marnat (Eds.), *Integrative assessment of adult personality* (2nd ed.; pp. 356–399). New York, NY: Guilford Press.

Li, G. (1995). The interaction effect of bereavement and sex on the risk of suicide in the elderly: An historical cohort study. *Social Science & Medicine, 40*, 825–828.

Lightfoot-Klein, H. (1989). *Secret wounds*. Bloomington, IN: Authorhouse.

Lilienfeld, S. O., Wood, J. M., & Garb, H. N. (2000). The scientific status of projective techniques. *Psychological Science in the Public Interest*, *1*(2), 27–66.

Lin, K. (1986). Psychopathology and social disruption in refugees. In C. L. Williams & J. Westermeyer (Eds.). *Refugee mental health in resettlement countries* (pp. 61–73). Washington, DC: Hemisphere.

Lockhart, L. L., & Mitchell, J. (2010). Cultural competency and intersectionality: Emerging frameworks and practical approaches. In L. L. Lockhart & F. S. Davis (Eds.), *Domestic violence: Intersectionality and culturally competent practice* (pp. 1–28). New York, NY: Columbia University Press.

Long, M. E., Elhai, J. D., Schweinle, A., Gray, M. J., Grubaugh, A. L., & Frueh, B. C. (2008). Differences in posttraumatic stress disorder diagnostic rates and symptom severity between Criterion A1 and non-Criterion A1 stressors. *Journal of Anxiety Disorders*, *22*(7), 1255–1263.

Lopez, M. H., & Taylor, P. T. (2010). *Latinos and the 2010 Census: The foreign born are more positive*. Washington, DC: Pew Hispanic Center.

Lustig, S. L. (2007). Psychiatric evaluations of asylum seekers: It's both ethical practice and advocacy, and that's ok! [Letters to the editor]. *Psychiatry*, *4*(6), 17–18.

Lustig, S. L. (2008). Symptoms of trauma among political asylum applicants: Don't be fooled. *Hastings International and Comparative Law Review*, *31*, 725–734.

Lustig, S. L., Kureshi, S., Delucchi, K. L., Iacopino, V., & Morse, S. C. (2008). Asylum grant rates following medical evaluations of maltreatment among political asylum applicants in the United States. *Journal of Immigrant and Minority Health*, *10*(1), 7–15.

Lyons, J. A., & Wheeler-Cox, T. (1989). MMPI, MMPI-2 and PTSD: Overview of scores, scales and profiles. *Journal of Traumatic Stress*, *2*, 175–183.

Maciejewski, P. K., Prigerson, H. G., & Mazure, C. M. (2001). Sex differences in event-related risk for major depression. *Psychological Medicine*, *31*, 593–604.

MacKinnon, C. A. (1989). *Toward a feminist theory of the state*. Cambridge, MA: Harvard University Press.

Mairi Nunag Tanedo et al. v. Universal Placement Int'l., No. 13-56750 (9th Cir. 2015).

Marcos, L. (1988). Understanding ethnicity in psychotherapy with Hispanic patients. *The American Journal of Psychoanalysis*, *48*(1), 35–42.

Marouf, E. F. (2014). Incompetent but deportable: The case for a right to mental competence in removal proceedings. *Hastings Law Journal*, *65*, 929–998.

Marsella, A. J., & Yamada, A. M. (2010). Culture and psychopathology: Foundations, issues, directions. *Journal of Pacific Rim Psychology*, *4*, 103–115.

Martikainen, P., & Valkonen, T. (1996). Mortality after the death of a spouse: Rates and causes of death in a large Finnish cohort. *American Journal of Public Health*, *86*, 1087–1093.

Maruna, S. (2001). *Making good: How ex-convicts reform and rebuild their lives*. Washington, DC: American Psychological Association.

Marvin, R., Cooper, G., Hoffman, K., & Powell, B. (2002). The circle of security project: Attachment-based intervention with caregiver–pre-school child dyads. *Attachment & Human Development*, *4*(1), 107–124.

Maselko, J., & Kubzansky, L. D. (2006). Gender differences in religious practices, spiritual experiences and health: Results from the US general social survey. *Social Science and Medicine*, *62*(11), 2848–2860.

Matter of E-F-H-L, 26 I&N Dec. 319, 322 (BIA 2014).

Matter of Fefe, 20 I&N Dec 116, 118 (BIA 1989).

McCann, J., & Evans, F. B., III. (2007). Admissibility of the Rorschach: An update. In C. B. Gacono & F. B. Evans (with N. Kaser-Boyd & L. A. Gacono) (Eds.), *The Handbook of forensic Rorschach psychology* (pp. 55–78). New York, NY: Routledge.

McConaughy, S. H. (2013). *Clinical interviews for children and adolescents: Assessment to intervention* (2nd ed.). New York, NY: Guilford Press.

McConaughy, S. H., & Achenbach, T. M. (1996). Contributions of a child interview to multimethod assessment of children with EBD and LD. *School Psychology Review, 25*(1), 24–39.

McConaughy, S. H., & Achenbach, T. M. (2001). *Manual for the semistructured clinical interview for children and adolescents* (2nd ed.). Burlington, VT: ASEBA.

McGoldrick, M., Giordano, J., & Garcia-Preto, N. (Eds.). (2005). *Ethnicity and family therapy* (3rd ed.). New York, NY: Guilford Press.

Meek, C. L. (1990). Evaluation and assessment of post-traumatic and other stress-related disorders. In C. L. Meek (Ed.), *Post-traumatic stress disorder: Assessment, differential diagnosis, and forensic evaluation* (pp. 9–61). Sarasota, FL: Professional Resource Exchange.

Melton, G. B., Petrila, J., Poythress, N. G., Slobogin, C. (with Lyons, P. M., Jr., & Otto, R. K.). (2007). *Psychological evaluations for the courts: A handbook for mental health professionals and lawyers* (3rd ed.). New York: Guilford Press.

Messman-Moore, T. L., & Long, P. J. (2003). The role of childhood sexual abuse sequelae in sexual revictimization: An empirical review and theoretical reformulation. *Clinical Psychology Review, 23*(4), 537–571.

Meyer, G. J. (1996). The Rorschach and MMPI: Toward a more scientifically differentiated understanding of cross-method assessment. *Journal of Personality Assessment, 67*(3), 558–578.

Meyer, G. J. (1997). On the integration of personality assessment methods: The Rorschach and MMPI. *Journal of Personality Assessment, 68*(2), 297–330.

Meyer, G. J., & Kurtz, J. E. (2006). Advancing personality assessment terminology: Time to retire 'objective' and 'projective' as personality test descriptors. *Journal of Personality Assessment, 87*(3), 223–225.

Meyer, G. J., Finn, S. E., Eyde, L. D., Kay, G. G., Moreland, K. L., Dies, R. R., ..., & Reed, G. M. (2001). Psychological testing and psychological assessment: A review of evidence and issues. *American Psychologist, 56*(2), 128–165.

Meyer, G. J., Erdberg, P., & Shaffer, T. W. (2007). Toward international normative reference data for the comprehensive system. *Journal of Personality Assessment, 89*(S1), S201–S216.

Meyer, G. J., Viglione, D. J., Mihura, J. L, Erard, R. E., & Erdberg, P. (2011). *Rorschach performance assessment system: Administration, coding, interpretation, and technical manual*. Toledo, OH: Rorschach Performance Assessment System, LLC.

Meyer, G., Viglione, D., & Mihura, J. (2017). Psychometric foundations of the Rorschach performance assessment system (R-PAS). In R. E. Erard & F. B. Evans (Eds.), *The Rorschach in multimethod forensic assessment* (pp. 23–91). New York: Routledge.

Mihura, J. L. (2012). The necessity of multiple test methods in conducting assessments: The role of the Rorschach and self-report. *Psychological Injury and Law, 5*(2), 97–106.

Mihura, J. L., Meyer, G. J., Dumitrascu, N., & Bombel, G. (2012). The validity of individual Rorschach variables: Systematic reviews and meta-analyses of the comprehensive system. *Psychological Bulletin, 139*, 548–605.

Mikulincer, M., & Shaver, P. R. (2015). Attachment-related contributions to the study of psychopathology. In P. Luyten, L. C. Mayes, P. Fonagy, M. Target, & S. J. Blatt (Eds.), *Handbook of psychodynamic approaches to psychopathology* (pp. 27–46). New York, NY: Guilford Press.

Miller, G. A. (1956). The magical number seven, plus or minus two: Some limits on our capacity for processing information. *Psychological Review, 63*, 81–97.

Miller, H. A. (2005). The Miller forensic assessment of symptoms test (M-FAST): Test generalizability and utility across race, literacy, and clinical opinion. *Criminal Justice and Behavior, 32*(6), 591–611.

Millon, T. (1977). *Millon multiaxial clinical inventory manual.* Minneapolis, MN: National Computer Systems.

Millon, T., Millon, C., & Davis, R. (2003). *MCMI-III corrections report user guide.* San Antonio, TX: Pearson.

Mollica, R. F., Caspi-Yavin, Y., Bollini, P., Truong, T., Tor, S., & Lavelle, J. (1992). The Harvard trauma questionnaire: Validating a cross-cultural instrument for measuring torture, trauma, and posttraumatic stress disorder in Indochinese refugees. *Journal of Nervous and Mental Disease. 180*, 111–116.

Mollica, R. F., Wyshak, G., & Lavelle, J. (1987). The psychosocial impact of war trauma and torture among southeast Asian refugees. *American Journal of Psychiatry, 144*, 1567–1572.

Monahan, J., & Steadman, H. J. (Eds.). (1994). *Violence and mental disorder: Developments in risk assessment.* Chicago, IL: University of Chicago Press.

Morey, L. C. (1991). *Personality Assessment Inventory: Professional manual.* Odessa, FL: Psychological Assessment Resources.

Morey, L. C. (1996). *An interpretive guide to the personality assessment inventory (PAI).* Odessa, FL: Psychological Assessment Resources.

Morey, L. C. (2003). *Essentials of PAI assessment.* Hoboken, NJ: John Wiley & Sons.

Morey, L. C. (2007). *Personality assessment inventory: Professional manual.* Lutz, FL: Psychological Assessment Resources.

Morey, L. C., & Meyer, J. K. (2013). Forensic assessment with the Personality Assessment Inventory. In R. P. Archer & E. M. A. Wheeler (Eds.), *Forensic uses of clinical assessment instruments* (pp. 140–174). New York: Routledge.

Morgan, C. A. (2007). Psychiatric evaluations of asylum seekers: Is it ethical practice or advocacy? *Psychiatry (Edgemont), 4*(4), 26–33.

Murray, H. A. (1943). *Thematic apperception test manual.* Cambridge, MA: Harvard University Press.

Musalo, K. (1998) Ruminations on Re: Kasinga: the decision's legacy. *Southern California Review of Law and Women's Studies, 7*, 357–371.

Musalo, K., & Rice, M. (2008). The implementation of the one-year bar to asylum. *Hastings International and Comparative Law Review, 31*, 693–724.

Musalo, K., Meffert, S. M., & Abdo, A. O. (2010). The role of mental health professionals in political asylum processing. *Journal of the American Academy of Psychiatry & the Law, 38*, 479–489.

Naef, R., Ward, R., Mahrer-Imhof, R., & Grande, G. (2013). Characteristics of the bereavement experience of older persons after spousal loss: An integrative review. *International Journal of Nursing Studies, 50*(8), 1108–1121.

National Action Alliance for Suicide Prevention. (2012). The 2012 national strategy for suicide prevention: Groups with increased suicide risk [Fact sheet].

National Immigration Women's Advocacy Project. (2015). *Comparing forms of immigration relief for immigrant victims of crime.* Washington, DC: Author. Retrieved from http://niwaplibrary.wcl.American.edu/pubs/imm-relief-forms-comparison.

National Immigration Women's Advocacy Project. (n.d.) Human trafficking 101 [Information sheet]. Retrieved from http://library.niwap.org/wp-content/uploads/bc-infosheet-human-trafficking-101-english.pdf.

Nelson, K. E. (2002). Sex trafficking and forced prostitution: Comprehensive new legal approaches. *Houston Journal of International Law, 24,* 551–557.

New York Times (April 21, 2017). They starve you. They shock you. Inside the anti-gay pogrom in Chechnya. Retrieved from: www.nytimes.com/2017/04/21/world/europe/chechnya-russia-attacks-gays.html.

Nickerson, A., Cloitre, M., Bryant, R. A., Schnyder, U., Morina, N., & Schick, M. (2016). The factor structure of complex posttraumatic stress disorder in traumatized refugees. *European Journal of Psychotraumatology, 7*(1), 33253.

O'Neill Richard, A. (2000). *International trafficking in women to the United States: A contemporary manifestation of slavery and organized crime.* Washington, DC: Center for the Study of Intelligence. Retrieved from www.cia.gov.

Occupational Safety and Health Act of 1970, 29 U.S.C. § 654, et seq. (2004).

Office for Victims of Crime. (n.d.). Human trafficking. Retrieved from https://ovc.ncjrs.gov/humantrafficking/publicawareness.html.

Office on Violence Against Women. (2017, January 6) What is human trafficking? Retrieved from www.justice.gov/humantrafficking/what-is-human-trafficking.

Okawa, J. B. (2008). Considerations for the cross-cultural evaluation of refugees and asylum seekers. In L. A. Suzuki & J. G. Ponterotto (Eds.), *Handbook of multicultural assessment: Clinical, psychological, and educational applications* (pp. 165–194). San Francisco, CA: Jossey-Bass.

Onrust, S. A., & Cuijpers, P. (2006). Mood and anxiety disorders in widowhood: A systematic review. *Aging & Mental Health, 10*(4), 327–334.

Opaas, M., & Hartmann, E. (2013). Rorschach assessment of traumatized refugees: An exploratory factor analysis. *Journal of Personality Assessment, 95,* 457–470.

Opaas, M., Hartmann, E., Wentzel-Larsen, T., & Varvin, S. (2016). Relationship of pre-treatment Rorschach factors to symptoms, quality of life, and real-life functioning in a 3-year follow-up of traumatized refugee patients. *Journal of Personality Assessment, 98,* 247–260.

Orloff, L. E. (2014). VAWA confidentiality: History, purpose, DHS, implementation and violations of VAWA confidentiality protections. Retrieved from: http://library.niwap.org/wp-content/uploads/2015/pdf/CONF-VAWA-Man-Ch3-Confidentiality-9.25.14.pdf.

Orloff, L. E., & Feldman, P. E. (2011, November 29). *National survey on types of criminal activities experienced by U visa recipients.* Washington, DC: NIWAP, American University, Washington College of Law. Retrieved from http://library.niwap.org.

Orloff, L., Dutton, M. A., Hass, G. A., & Ammar, N. (2003). Battered immigrant women's willingness to call for help and police response. *UCLA Women's Law Journal, 13*(1), 43–100.

Orloff, L. E., Roberts, B., & Gliter, S. (2013). *Battering or extreme cruelty: Drawing samples from civil protection orders and family law cases.* Washington, DC: National Immigrant Women's Advocacy Project, American University, and Washington College of Law. Retrieved from http://niwaplibrary.wcl.American.edu/pubs/extreme-cruelty-examples-protection-order.

Otto, R. K., & Douglas, K. S. (Eds.). (2010). *Handbook of violence risk assessment.* New York: Routledge.

Otto, R. K., DeMier, R. L., & Bocaccini, M. T. (2014). *Forensic reports and testimony: A guide to effective communication for psychologists and psychiatrists.* Hoboken, NJ: John Wiley & Sons.

Ozer, E. G., Best, S. R., Lipsey, T. L., & Weiss, D. S. (2003). Predictors of posttraumatic stress disorder and symptoms in adults: A meta-analysis. *Psychological Bulletin, 129,* 52–73.

Pade, H. (2015). An update on the Proficiency in Personality Assessment. *SPA Exchange, 27*(2).

Palic, S., Zerach, G., Shevlin, M., Zeligman, Z., Elklit, A., & Solomon, Z. (2016). Evidence of complex posttraumatic stress disorder (CPTSD) across populations with prolonged trauma of varying interpersonal intensity and ages of exposure. *Psychiatry Research, 246,* 692–699.

Pearson (n.d.). Products MMPI-2. Retrieved from www.pearsonclinical.com/psychology/products/100000743/minnesota-multiphasic-personality-inventory2.

Pelcovitz, D., van der Kolk, B. A., Roth, S., Mandel, F., Kaplan, S., & Resick, P. (1997). Development of a criteria set and a structured interview for the disorders of extreme stress (SIDES). *Journal of Traumatic Stress, 10,* 3–16.

Phenix, A., & Hoberman, H. M. (Eds.). (2016). *Sexual offending: Predisposing antecedents assessments and management.* New York, NY: Springer.

Phinney, J. S., Horenczyk, G., Liebkind, K., & Vedder, P. (2001) Ethnic identity, immigration, and well-being: An interactional perspective. *Journal of Social Issues, 57,* 493–510.

Pope, K. S. (2013). Psychological assessment of torture survivors: Essential steps, avoidable errors, and helpful resources. *International Journal of Law and Psychiatry, 35*(5–6), 418–426.

Pope, K. S., & Garcia-Peltoniemi, R. E. (1991). Responding to victims of torture: Clinical issues, professional responsibilities, and useful resources. *Professional Psychology: Research and Practice, 22,* 269–276.

Pope, K. S., & Vasquez, M. J. T. (2016). *Ethics in psychotherapy and counseling: A practical guide.* Hoboken, NJ: John Wiley & Sons.

Porter, S., & Yuille, J. C. (1996). The language of deceit: An investigation of the verbal clues to deception in the interrogation context. *Law and Human Behavior, 20,* 443–458.

Psychological Assessment Resources (PAR). (n.d.). Permissions. Retrieved from: www.parinc.com/Resources/Permissions-and-licensing#99085-personality-assessment-inventory-paispan-classreg-tmregspan.

Pumariega, A. J., Rothe, E., & Pumariega, J. B. (2005). Mental health of immigrants and refugees. *Community Mental Health Journal, 41*(5), 581–597.

Putnam, F. W. (1989). *Diagnosis and treatment of multiple personality disorder: Foundations of modern psychiatry.* New York, NY: Guilford Press.

Putnam, F. W. (1997). *Dissociation in children and adolescents: A developmental perspective.* New York: Guilford Press.

Quandt, S. A., Grzywacs, J. G., Marin, A., Carrillo, L., Coates, M. L., Burke, B., & Arcury, T. A. (2006). Illnesses and injuries reported by Latino poultry workers in western North Carolina. *American Journal of Industry Medicine, 49,* 343–344.

Quinsey, V. L., Harris, G. T., Rice, M. E., & Cormier, C. A. (1998) *Violent offenders: Appraising and managing risk.* Washington, DC: American Psychological Association.

Ragins, B. R., & Cornwell, J. M. (2001). Pink triangles: Antecedents and consequences of perceived workplace discrimination against gay and lesbian employees. *Journal of Applied Psychology, 86,* 1244.

Raymond, J. G., & Hughes, D. M. (2001). Sex trafficking of women in the United States: International and domestic trends (Research report 187774). Retrieved from: www. ncjrs.gov/pdffiles1/nij/grants/187774.pdf.

Reid, P. T., Lewis, L. J., & Wyche, K. F. (2014). An intersectional framework for a multicultural analysis of gender. In F. T. L. Leong, L. Comas-Díaz, G. C. Nagayama Hall, V. C. McLoyd, & J. E. Trimble (Eds.), *APA handbook of multicultural psychology, Vol. 1. Theory and research* (pp. 379–394). Washington, DC: APA.

Resick, P. A., Bovin, M. J., Calloway, A. L., Dick, A. M., King, M. W., Mitchell, K. S., ..., & Wolf, E. J. (2012). A critical evaluation of the complex PTSD literature: Implications for DSM-5. *Journal of Traumatic Stress, 25*(3), 241–251.

Resnick, P. J. (1997). Malingering of posttraumatic disorders. In R. Rogers (Ed.), *Clinical assessment of malingering and deception* (2nd ed.; pp. 130–152). New York, NY: Guilford Press.

Resnick, P. J. (2003). Guidelines for the evaluation of malingering in PTSD. In R. I. Simon (Ed.), *Posttraumatic stress disorder in litigation: Guidelines for forensic assessment* (2nd ed.; pp. 117–134). Washington, DC: American Psychiatric Association Publishing.

Rettenberger, M., Boer, D. P., & Eher, R. (2011) The predictive accuracy of risk factors in the Sexual Violence Risk-20 (Svr-20). *Criminal Justice and Behavior, 38,* 1009–1027.

Risen, J. (2014). *Pay any price: Greed, power, and endless war.* New York, NY: Houghton Mifflin Harcourt.

Ritzler, B. A. (2001). Multicultural usage of the Rorschach. In L. A., Suzuki, J. G. Ponterotto, & P. J. Meller (Eds.), *Handbook of multicultural assessment: Clinical, psychological, and educational applications* (2nd ed.; pp. 237–252). San Francisco, CA: Jossey-Bass.

Ritzler, B. (2004). Cultural applications of the Rorschach, apperception tests, and figure drawings. In M. J. Hilsenroth & D. L. Segal (Eds.), *Comprehensive handbook of psychological assessment, Vol. 2. Personality assessment* (pp. 573–585). Hoboken, NJ: John Wiley & Sons.

Roberts, G. E., & Gruber, C. (2005). *Roberts apperception test for children: 2 (Roberts-2).* Los Angeles, CA: Western Psychological Services.

Robinson, J. S., & Larson, C. (2010). Are traumatic events necessary to elicit symptoms of posttraumatic stress? *Psychological Trauma, 2,* 71–76.

Rogers, H., Fox, S., & Herlihy, J. (2014). The importance of looking credible: The impact of the behavioural sequelae of post-traumatic stress disorder on the credibility of asylum seekers, *Psychology, Crime & Law, 21*(2), 139–155.

Rogers, R. (Ed.). (1997). *Clinical assessment of malingering and deception* (2nd ed.). New York, NY: Guilford.

Rogers, R. (2001). *Handbook of diagnostic and structured interviewing.* New York, NY: Guilford Press.

Rogers, R. (Ed.). (2008). *Clinical assessment of malingering and deception* (3rd ed.). New York, NY: Guilford Press.

Rogers, R., Flores, J., Ustad, K., & Sewell, K. W. (1995). Initial validation of the Personality Assessment Inventory-Spanish Version with clients from Mexican American communities. *Journal of Personality Assessment, 60,* 554–560.

Rogers, R., Sewell, K. W., & Gillard, N. D. (2010). *Structured interview of reported symptoms-2 professional manual*. Lutz, FL: Psychological Assessment Resources.

Rojas-Flores, L., Clements, M. L., Hwang Koo, J., & London, J. (2017). Trauma and psychological distress in Latino citizen children following parental detention and deportation. *Psychological Trauma: Theory, Research, Practice, and Policy, 9*(3), 352–361.

Romo, R. (2015, November). Human trafficking survivor: I was raped 43,200 times. *CNN Freedom Project*. Retrieved from www.cnn.com.

Root, M. P. P. (1992). Reconstructing the impact of trauma on personality. In L. S. Brown & M. Ballou (Eds.), *Personality and psychopathology: Feminist reappraisals* (pp. 229–265). New York, NY: Guilford Press.

Root, M. P. P. (2002). Methodological issues in multiracial research. In G. Nagayama Hall and S. Okazaki (Eds.), *Asian American Psychology: Scientific innovations for the 21st Century* (pp. 171–193). Thousand Oaks, CA: Sage Publications.

Rosen, G. M. (2006). DSM's cautionary guideline to rule out malingering can protect the PTSD data base. *Journal of Anxiety Disorder, 20*, 530–535.

Rosenberg, L. D. (2006). Doing the right thing in immigration law practice. *ASISTA Technical Assistance for Immigrant Survivors Newsletter*.

Rosenberg, L. D. (2012). Doing the right thing in immigration law practice. Retrieved from www.asistahelp.org/documents/resources/Doing_the_Right_Thing_in_Immigratio_ED353B1876004.pdf.

Rosenberg, L. D., & Evans, F. B (2003). Another chance: Forensic psychological assessment of recidivism and dangerousness in immigration adjudications. *Bender's Immigration Bulletin. 8*(9), 768–779.

Roth, S., Newman, E., Pelcovitz, D., van der Kolk, B., & Mandel, F. S. (1997). Complex PTSD in victims exposed to sexual and physical abuse: Results from the DSM-IV field trial for posttraumatic stress disorder. *Journal of Traumatic Stress, 10*, 539–555.

Ryan, R. M. (1985). *Thematic apperception test*. In D. J. Keyser & R. C. Sweetland (Eds.), *Test critiques* (Vol. 2, pp. 799–814). Kansas City, MO: Test Corporation of America.

Sabet, R. F., Marques, D. S., Schaefer, A., Suarez, L., Becker Herbst, R., Swanson, A., ..., & Aldarondo, E. (2016, October 1). Toward an understanding of unaccompanied immigrant minors in the U.S. Poster presentation at the meeting of National Latina/o Psychological Association, Orlando, Fl.

Saborío, C., & Hass, G. (2012, March). The psychological functioning of sexually assaulted women through the MMPI-2 and restructured clinical scales. Paper presented at the *Society of Personality Assessment Conference*, Chicago, IL.

Sadoff, R. L. (2011). Ethical issues in forensic psychiatry in the United States. In R. L. Sadoff (Ed.), *Ethical issues in forensic psychiatry: Minimizing harm* (pp. 3–26). Hoboken, NJ: Wiley.

Sadruddin, H., Walter, N., & Hidalgo, J. (2005). Human trafficking in the United States: Expanding victim protection beyond prosecution witnesses. *Stanford Law & Policy Review, 16*, 379–412.

Sales, P. P. (2016). *Psychological torture: Definition, evaluation and measurement*. New York, NY: Routledge.

Salton, W. (2017, May 17). Working with interpreters with refugee populations in healthcare settings and for asylum evaluations. American Psychological Association Division 56 webinar.

Saltzburg, S. A., Martin, M. M., & Capra, D. J. (2011). *Federal rules of evidence*. Washington, DC: Lexis-Nexis Group.

Saltzman, L. E., Fanslow, J. L., McMahon, P. M., & Shelley, G. A. (1999). Intimate partner violence surveillance: Uniform definitions and recommended data elements (Version 1.0). Atlanta, GA: Centers for Disease Control and Prevention, National Center for Injury Prevention and Control.

Scaros, C. E. (2007). *Learning about immigration law* (3rd ed.). Independence, KY: Cengage.

Schaffer, T. W., Erdberg, P., & Meyer, G. J. (2007). Introduction to the JPA special supplement on international reference samples for the Rorschach comprehensive system. *Journal of Personality Assessment, 89*(S1), S2–S6.

Schock, K., Böttche, M., Rosner, R., Wenk-Ansohn, M., & Knaevelsrud, C. (2016). Impact of new traumatic or stressful life events on pre-existing PTSD in traumatized refugees: Results of a longitudinal study. *European Journal of Psychotraumatology, 7*, Article ID 32106.

Scroppo, J. C., Weinberger, J. L., Drob, S. L., & Eagle, P. (1998). Identifying dissociative identity disorder: A self-report and projective study. *Journal of Abnormal Psychology, 107*, 272–284.

Sellbom, A. A., & Bagby, R. M. (2008). The utility and comparative incremental validity of the MMPI-2 and trauma symptom inventory validity scales in the detection of feigned PTSD. *Psychological Assessment, 20*, 317–326.

Shannon, S. (1999). Prostitution and the mafia: The involvement of organized crime in the global economy. In P. Williams (Ed.), *Illegal immigration and commercial sex: The new slave trade* (pp. 119–144). London: Frank Cass.

Shmueli-Goetz, Y., Target, M., Fonagy, P., & Datta, A. (2008). The child attachment interview: A psychometric study of reliability and discriminant validity. *Developmental Psychology, 44*, 939–956.

Shor, I., & Freire, P. (1987). *A pedagogy for liberation: Dialogues on transforming education.* Westport, CT: Greenwood.

Sidahmed, A. S. (2001). Problems in contemporary applications of Islamic criminal sanctions: The penalty for adultery in relation to women. *British Journal of Middle Eastern Studies, 28*, 187–204.

Silver, M. S. (2015). *Handbook of mitigation in criminal and immigration forensics: Humanizing the client towards a better legal outcome* (5th Ed.). New York, NY: Mark Silver.

Simon, G. F., & Charles, D. F. (Eds.). (2017). Ethnologue languages of the world (20th ed.). Dallas, TX: SIL International. Retrieved from www.ethnologue.com.

Simon, R. I. (Ed.). (2008). *Posttraumatic stress disorder in litigation: Guidelines for forensic assessment.* Washington, DC: American Psychiatric.

Skeem, J., Golding, S., Cohn, N., & Berge, G. (1998). Logic and reliability of evaluations of competence to stand trial. *Law and Human Behavior, 22*, 519–547.

Skinner, H. A., Steinhauer, D., & Santa-Barbara, J. (1995). *Family assessment measure version III* [Assessment instrument]. Cheektowaga, NY: Multi-Health Systems.

Smith, B. L. (1990). The origins of interpretation in the countertransference. *Psychoanalytic Psychology, 7*(Suppl.), 89–104.

Smith, B. L. (2005). The observer observed: Discussion of articles by Evans, Finn, Handler, and Lerner. *Journal of Personality Assessment, 84*, 33–36.

Smith, B. L. & Evans, F. B. (2017) Collaborative/therapeutic assessment in multimethod forensic evaluations. In Erard, R. & Evans, F. B. (Eds.), *The Rorschach in multimethod forensic assessment.* (pp 291–315). New York: Routledge.

Smith, R., & Loring, M. T. (1994). The trauma of emotionally abused men. *Journal of Psychology, 31*(3/4), 1–4.

Snyder, D. K. (1997). *Marital satisfaction inventory, revised (MSI-R).* Torrance, CA: Western Psychological Services.

Society for Personality Assessment. (n.d.). Proficiency application. Retrieved from http://personality.org/about/proficiency-application.

Society for Personality Assessment (2006). Standards for education and training in psychological assessment: Position of the society for personality assessment. *Journal of Personality Assessment, 87*(3), 355–357.

Solomon, Z., Mikulincer, M., & Avitzur, E. (1988). Coping, locus of control, social support, and combat related posttraumatic stress disorder: A prospective study. *Journal of Personality and Social Psychology, 55*(2), 279–285.

Sossin, K. M., Bromberg, Y., & Haddad, D. (2014). Loss of a parent during childhood and adolescence. In P. Cohen, K. M. Sossin, & R. Ruth (Eds.), *Healing after parent loss in childhood and adolescence: Therapeutic interventions and theoretical considerations* (pp. 1–27). Lanham, MD: Rowman & Littlefield.

Southwick, S. M., Rasmusson, A., Barron, J., & Arnsten, A. (2005). Neurobiological and neurocognitive alterations in PTSD: A focus on norepinephrine, serotonin, and the hypothalamic–pituitary–adrenal axis. In J. J. Vasterling & C. R. Brewin (Eds.), *Neuropsychology of PTSD: Biological, cognitive, and clinical perspectives* (pp. 27–58). New York: Guilford Press.

Spanier, G. B. (1976). Measuring dyadic adjustment: New scales for assessing the quality of marriage and similar dyads. *Journal of Marriage and the Family, 38,* 15–28.

Spitzer, R. L., Williams, J. W., Gibbon, M., & First, M. B. (1990). *Structured Clinical Interview for DSM-lll-R: Patient edition (SCID-P).* Washington, DC: American Psychiatric Press.

Stark, A. E. B. (1996). Posttraumatic stress disorder in refugee women: How to address PTSD in women who apply for political asylum under grounds of gender-specific persecution. *Georgetown Immigration Law Journal, 11*(3), 167–197.

Stark, E. (2007). *Coercive control: How men entrap women in personal life.* New York: Oxford.

Stark, E. (2011). *Re-presenting battered women: Coercive control and the defense of liberty* [PDF]. Lecture presented for the meeting of Second International Conference on Violence Against Women: Complex Realities and New Issues in a Changing World. Quebec, Canada. Lecture retrieved from www.stopvaw.org.

Steinberg, M. (1994). *Structured clinical interview for DSM-IV dissociative disorders-revised.* Washington, DC: American Psychiatric Press.

Steinberg, M., & Schnall, M. (2001). *The stranger in the mirror: Dissociation – the hidden epidemic.* New York: HarperCollins.

Steinhaus, M., Gregowski, A., Stevanovic Fenn, N., & Petroni, S. (2016). *She cannot just sit around waiting to turn twenty: Understanding why child marriage persists in Kenya and Zambia.* Washington, DC: International Center for Research on Women.

Stephenson, M. (2000). Development and validation of the Stephenson Multigroup Acculturation Scale (SMAS). *Psychological Assessment, 12*(1), 77–88.

Stokes v. INS, No. 74-1022 (S.D.N.Y. Nov. 10, 1976).

Strauss, M. (1979). Measuring intrafamily conflict and violence: The conflict tactics scales. *Journal of Marriage and the Family, 41,* 75–88.

Stroebe, M. S., & Stroebe, W. (1983). Who suffers more? Sex differences in health risks of the widowed. *Psychological Bulletin, 93*(2), 279–301.

Suárez-Orozco, C., & Carhill, A. (2008). Afterword: New directions in research with immigrant families and their children. In H. Yoshikawa & N. Way. (Eds.), *New direction for child and adolescent development* (pp. 87–104). Hoboken, NJ: John Wiley & Sons.

Suárez-Orozco, M. M. (1990). Speaking of the unspeakable: Toward a psychosocial understanding of responses to terror. *Ethos, 18*(3), 353–383.

Sussman, D. (2005). What is wrong with torture? *Philosophy and Public Affairs, 33*(1), 1–33.

Sullivan, H. S. (1953). *The interpersonal theory of psychiatry.* New York, NY: Norton.

Sullivan, H. S. (1954). *The psychiatric interview.* New York, NY: Norton.

Target, M., Fonagy, P., & Shmueli-Goetz, Y. (2003). Attachment representations in school-age children: The development of the child attachment interview (CAI). *Journal of Child Psychotherapy, 29*, 171–186.

Teglasi, H. (2010). *Essentials of TAT and other storytelling assessments* (2nd ed.). New York, NY: John Wiley and Sons.

Tiefenbrun, S. (2002a). The saga of Susannah: A U.S. remedy for sex trafficking in women – the Victims of Trafficking and Violence Protection Act of 2000, 2002. *Utah Law Review, 1*, 107–175.

Tiefenbrun, S. W. (2002b). Sex sells but drugs don't talk: Trafficking of women sex workers and an economic solution. *Thomas Jefferson Law Review, 24*, 161–170.

Tjaden, P., & Thoennes, N. (2000). *Full report of the prevalence, incidence, and consequences of violence against women: Findings from the national violence against women survey.* Washington, DC: National Institute of Justice and the Centers for Disease Control and Prevention.

Tolman, R. (1999). The validation of the Psychological Maltreatment of Women Inventory. *Violence and Victims, 14*, 25–37.

Tori, C. D. (1989). Homosexuality and illegal residency status in relation to substance abuse and personality traits among Mexican nationals. *Journal of Clinical Psychology, 45*, 814–821.

Tribe, R., & Sanders, M. (2003). Training issues for interpreters. In R. Tribe & H. Raval (Eds.), *Working with interpreters in mental health* (pp. 54–68). New York, NY: Brunner-Routledge.

United Nations (2013). *Elimination and prevention of all forms of violence against women and girls.* Commission on the Status of Women: Agreed Conclusions. UN Entity for Gender Equality and Empowerment of Women. Retrieved from www.un.org/womenwatch/daw/csw/csw57/CSW57_Agreed_Conclusions_(CSW_report_excerpt).pdf.

United Nations Children's Fund. (2013). *Ending child marriage: Progress and prospects.* Retrieved from www.unicef.org/media/files/Child_Marriage_Report_7_17_LR.pdf.

United Nations Children's Fund. (2014). *Hidden in plain sight: A statistical analysis of violence against children.* New York, NY: UNICEF.

United Nations Children's Fund. (2016). *Female genital mutilation/cutting: Global concern.* New York, NY: UNICEF.

United Nations Economic and Social Council. (2002). *Integration of the human rights of women and the gender perspective: Cultural practices in the family that are violent toward women.* New York: United Nations.

United Nations General Assembly (1951, July 28). Convention relating to the status of refugees. United Nations, Treaty Series (Vol. 189), p. 137. Retrieved from www.refworld.org/docid/3be01b964.html.

United Nations General Assembly. (1967, January 31). Protocol relating to the status of refugees. United Nations, Treaty Series (Vol. 606), p. 267. Retrieved from www.refworld.org/docid/3ae6b3ae4.html.

United Nations General Assembly. (1984). Convention against torture and other cruel, inhuman or degrading treatment or punishment. United Nations, Treaty Series (Vol. 1465), pp. 85–98. Retrieved from www.refworld.org/docid/3ae6b3a94.html.

United Nations High Commissioner for Refugees. (2017). Refugees. Retrieved from www.unhcr.org/refugees.html.

United Nations Human Rights Council. (2011, July 14). Human rights, sexual orientation and gender identity: Resolution adapted by Human Rights Council. A Human Rights Council Res. 17/19. Retrieved from www.refworld.org/docid/512f0bd22.html.

United Nations Human Rights Office of the High Commissioner. (2012). *Born free and equal: Sexual orientation and gender identity in international human rights law.* New York, NY: Author.

United Nations Human Rights Office of the High Commissioner. (n.d.). *The core international human right instruments and their monitoring bodies.* Geneva: Author. Retrieved from www.ohchr.org/EN/ProfessionalInterest/Pages/CoreInstruments. aspx.

United Nations Office of the High Commissioner for Human Rights. (2004). *Manual on the effective investigation and documentation of torture and other cruel, inhuman or degrading treatment or punishment ('Istanbul protocol').* Geneva: United Nations.

United Nations Regional information Centre, & the Office of the United Nations High Commissioner for Human Rights. (2015). *Universal declaration of human rights.* Herndon, VA: United Nation.

United States Citizenship and Immigration Service. (1998). *What factors are considered in evaluating extreme hardship?* Retrieved from www.uscis.gov/ilink/docView/FR/HTML/FR/0-0-0-1/0-0-0-42380/0-0-0-44857/0-0-0-47481/0-0-0-47683.html.

United States Citizenship and Immigration Services. (2007a). *Federal Register, 72* (73). Retrieved from www.gpo.gov/fdsys/pkg/FR-2007-04-17/html/E7-7228.htm.

United States Citizenship and Immigration Services. (2007b). Questions for CIS re: U visas. Washington, DC: ASISTA. Retrieved from www.asistahelp.org/documents/resources.

United States Citizenship and Immigration Services. (2017). *Policy manual citizenship and naturalization guidance: Exceptions and accommodations.* Washington, DC: Author. Retrieved from www.uscis.gov/us-citizenship/citizenship-through-naturalization/exceptions-accommodations.

United States Citizenship and Immigration Services. (n.d.). *Policy manual.* Retrieved from www.uscis.gov/policymanual/HTML/PolicyManual-Volume12-PartF.html.

United States Customs and Border Protection. (2015, January 15). Human trafficking. Retrieved from www.cbp.gov/border-security/human-trafficking.

United States Department of State. (2016). *Country reports on human rights practices, bureau of democracy, human rights and labor.* Retrieved from www.state.gov/j/drl/rls/hrrpt/humanrightsreport/index.htm#fndtn-panel1-1.

United States Department of State (2017). *Trafficking in persons report.* Washington, DC: Author. Retrieved from: www.state.gov/j/tip.

United States Immigration and Nationality Act of 1952 Pub. L. N. 101(a) § 42.

United States Refugee Act of 1980, Pub. L. No. 96-212 § 94 Stat. 102.

University of Minnesota (n.d.). Permissions. Retrieved from: www.upress.umn.edu/test-division/translations-permissions/permissions.

USCIS. (2016, December 14). Immigrants part J: special immigrant juveniles. In *USCIS policy manual* (Vol. 6). Retrieved from http://library.niwap.org/wp-content/uploads/USCIS-Policy-Manual-Vol-6-7-Part-J-SIJS-Full-Dec-14-2016.pdf.

Vaisman-Tzachor, R. (2012). Psychological evaluations on federal immigration courts: Fifteen years in the making – lessons learned. *The Forensic Examiner, 21*(2), 42–53.

van der Kolk, B. A. (1987). *Psychological trauma.* Washington, DC: American Psychiatric Press.

van der Kolk, B. A. (1994). The body keeps score: Memory and the evolving psychobiology of posttraumatic stress. *Harvard Review of Psychiatry, 1*, 235–265.

van der Kolk, B. A. (1998). Trauma and memory. *Psychiatry and Clinical Neurosciences, 52*(S1), S52–S64.

van der Kolk, B. A., & Ducey, C. (1984). Clinical implications of the Rorschach in posttraumatic stress disorder. In B. A. van der Kolk (Ed.), *Post-traumatic stress disorder: Psychological and biological sequelae* (pp. 29–42). Washington, DC: American Psychiatric Press.

van der Kolk, B. A., & Ducey, C. (1989). The psychological processing of traumatic experience: Rorschach patterns in PTSD. *Journal of Traumatic Stress, 2*, 259–274.

van der Kolk, B. A., & McFarlane, A. C. (1996). The black hole of trauma. In B. A. van der Kolk, A. C. McFarlane, & L. Weisaeth (Eds.), *Traumatic stress* (pp. 3–23). New York, NY: Guilford Press.

van der Kolk, B. A., McFarlane, A., & Weisaeth, L. (Eds.). (1996). *Traumatic stress.* New York: Guilford.

van der Kolk, B. A., Roth, S., Pelcovitz, D., Sunday, S., & Spinazzola, J. (2005). Disorders of extreme stress: The empirical foundation of a complex adaptation to trauma. *Journal of Traumatic Stress, 18*(5), 389–399.

van der Kolk, B., & Pelcovitz, D. (1999). Clinical applications of the structured interview for disorders of extreme stress (SIDES). *National Center for PTSD Clinical Quarterly, 8*, 1–4.

Vanderpool, D. (2016). Professional liability for forensic activities: Liability without a treatment relationship. *Innovations Clinical Neuroscience, 13*(7–8), 41–44.

Vega, W. A., & Amaro, H. (1994). Latino outlook: Good health, uncertain prognosis. *Annual Review of Public Health, 15*(1), 39–67.

Viglione, D. J. (1999). A review of recent research addressing the utility of the Rorschach. *Psychological Assessment, 11*(3), 251–265.

Viglione, D. J., & Hilsenroth, M. J. (2001). The Rorschach: Facts, fictions, and future. *Psychological Assessment, 13*(4), 452–471.

Viglione, D. J., & Meyer, G. J. (2007). Scientific status of the Rorschach. In C. B. Gacono, & E. B. Evans (Eds.), *Handbook of forensic Rorschach psychology.* Mahway, NJ: Lawrence Erlbaum Association.

Violence Against Women Act (1994). Title IV of the Violent Crime Control and Law Enforcement Act of 1994, Pub. L. No. 103-322, § 108 Stat. 2151.

Violence Against Women Act. (1994). Pub. L. No. 103-322, § 108 Stat. 1796 (1994).

Violence Against Women Act of 2000, Pub. L. No. 106-386, § 7101, 114 Stat. 464 (2000).

Violence Against Women Act of 2005, Pub. L. No. 109-162, § 119 Stat. 2960.

Waldinger, R., & Lichter, M. I. (2003). *How the other half works: Immigration and the social organization of labor.* Berkeley, CA: University of California Press.

Walker, L. E. A. (1979). *The battered woman.* New York, NY: Harper & Row.

Walker, L. E. A. (1994). *Abused women and survivor therapy: A practical guide for the psychotherapist.* Washington, DC: American Psychological Association.

Walker, L. E. A. (2000). *Abused women and survivor therapy.* Washington, DC: American Psychological Association.

Walker, L. E. A. (2009). *The battered woman syndrome* (3rd ed.). New York, NY: Springer.

Wallerstein, J. S., & Kelly, J. B. (1980). *Surviving the breakup: How children and parents cope with divorce.* New York, NY: Basic Books.

Walters, G. D. (2003). Predicting institutional adjustment and recidivism with the psychopathy checklist factor scores: A meta-analysis. *Law and Human Behavior, 27*(5), 541–558.

Warrier, S., & Rose, J. (2016). Women, gender-based violence, and immigration. In F. Chang-Muy & E. P. Congress (Eds.), *Social work with immigrants and refugees: Legal issues, clinical skills, and advocacy* (pp. 237–256). New York, NY: Springer.

Warrier, S., Dagdagan, M., Marin, L., & Schmitter, M. (2005). *Culture handbook.* San Francisco, CA: Family Violence Prevention Fund.

Weathers, F. W., Litz, B., Herman, D., Huska, J., & Keane, T. (1993, October). *The PTSD checklist (PCL): Reliability, validity, and diagnostic utility.* Paper presented at the Annual Convention of the International Society for Traumatic Stress Studies, San Antonio, TX.

Weathers, F. W., Ruscio, A. M., & Keane, T. M. (1999). Psychometric properties of nine scoring rules for the clinician-administered PTSD scale (CAPS). *Psychological Assessment, 11*, 124–133.

Weathers, F. W., Keane, T. M., & Davidson, J. R. T. (2001). Clinician-administered PTSD scale: A review of the first ten years of research. *Depression and Anxiety 13*, 132–156.

Weathers, F. W., Blake, D. D., Schnurr, P. P., Kaloupek, D. G., Marx, B. P., & Keane, T. M. (2013). *The Clinician-administered PTSD scale for DSM-5 (CAPS-5).* Interview available from the National Center for PTSD at www.ptsd.va.gov.

Webster, C. D., Douglas, K. S., Eaves, D., & Hart, S. D. (1997). *HCR-20: Assessing risk for violence (Version 2).* Burnaby, British Columbia: Mental Health, Law, and Policy Institute, Simon Fraser University.

Weigert, E. (1970). *The courage to love. Selected papers of Edith Weigert M.D.* Oxford: Yale University Press.

Weil, J. H. (October, 2016). Immigration evaluations. American Academy of Forensic Psychology Workshop. Alexandria, Virginia.

Weiner, I. B. (2014a). Writing forensic reports. In R. K. Otto, & I. B. Weiner (Eds.), *The handbook of forensic psychology* (4th ed.; pp. 711–733). Hoboken, NJ: John Wiley & Sons.

Weiner, I. B. (2014b). *Principles of Rorschach interpretation* (2nd ed.). Oxford: Routledge.

Weiner, I. B., & Otto, R. K. (Eds.). (2014). *The handbook of forensic psychology* (4th ed.). Hoboken, NJ: John Wiley & Sons.

Weisath, L. (1989). A study of behavioral responses to an industrial disaster. *Acta Psychiatrica Scandinavica, 355*, 13–71.

Weiss, R. A., & Rosenfeld, B. (2012). Navigating cross-cultural issues in forensic assessment: Recommendations for practice. *Professional Psychology: Research and Practice, 43*, 234–240.

Weissbrodt, D., & Danielson, L. (2011). *Immigration law and procedure: In a nutshell* (6th ed.). St. Paul, MN: West Academic.

Whitehorn, J., Ayonrinde, O., & Maingay, S. (2002). Female genital mutilation: Cultural and psychological implications. *Sexual and Relationship Therapy, 17*(2), 161–170.

William Wilberforce Trafficking Victims Protection Reauthorization Act of 2008, H.R. 731, 110d Cong (2008).

Wilson, J. P., & Keane, T. M. (2004). *Assessing psychological trauma and PTSD* (2nd ed.). New York, NY: Guilford Press.

Wilson, J. P., & Walker, A. J. (2000). Toward an MMPI trauma profile. *Journal of Traumatic Stress, 3*, 151–168.

Wilson, M., & Daly, M. (1993). Spousal homicide risk and estrangement. *Violence and Victims, 8*(1), 3–16.

Wisco, B. E., Marx, B. P., Wolf, E. J., Miller, M. W., Southwick, S. M., & Pietrzak, R. H. (2014). Posttraumatic stress disorder in the US veteran population: Results from the national health and resilience in veterans study. *Journal of Clinical Psychiatry, 75*(12), 1338–1346.

Wolchik, S. A., & Karoly, P. (1988). *Children of divorce: Empirical perspectives on adjustment.* New York: Gardner Press.

Wood, J. M., Lilienfeld, S. O., Nezworski, M. T., Garb, H. N., Allen, K. H., & Wildermuth, J. L. (2010). Validity of Rorschach inkblot scores for discriminating psychopaths from nonpsychopaths in forensic populations: A meta-analysis. *Psychological Assessment, 22*(2), 336–349.

Wooley, C. N., & Rogers, R. (2015). The effectiveness of the Personality Assessment Inventory with feigned PTSD: An initial investigation of Resnick's model of malingering. *Assessment, 22* (4), 449–458.

World Health Organization (1992). *The ICD-10 classification of mental and behavioral disorders.* Retrieved from www.icd10data.com/ICD10CM/Codes/F01-F99/F40-F48/F43-/F43.1.

Yu, S. E., & Jeon, W. T. (2008). Mental health of North Korean refugees in protective facilities in China. *Psychiatry Investigation, 5*(2), 70–77.

Zamble, E., & Quinsey, V. (1997). *The criminal recidivism process.* Cambridge: Cambridge University Press.

Zimbardo, P. G. (1974). The psychological power and pathology of imprisonment. *Catalog of Selected Documents in Psychology, 3*, 45.

Zimmer, W. K. (2013). *Approaching the bench from inside the immigration court.* Bloomington, IN: AuthorHouse.

Index

Page numbers in *italics* denote tables, those in **bold** denote figures.